HEADSTART IN HISTORY

POWER AND THE PEOPLE 1066–1485

SERIES EDITOR: ROSEMARY REES

JUDITH KIDD

LINDA RICHARDS

Heinemann Educational Publishers
Halley Court, Jordan Hill, Oxford, OX2 8EJ
Part of Harcourt Education
Heinemann is the registered trademark of Harcourt Education Ltd

First published 2002
10-digit ISBN: 0 435323 02 4
13-digit ISBN: 978 0 435323 02 8
06
10 9 8 7 6 5 4

Produced by Gecko Ltd, Bicester, Oxon

Illustrated by Brett Breckon, John Storey and Geoff Ward

Original illustrations © Heinemann Educational Publishers 2002

Cover design by Hicksdesign

Picture research by Frances Topp

Printed and bound in the United Kingdom by Bath Colourbooks

Photographic acknowledgements
The authors and publisher would like to thank the following for permission to reproduce photographs:

Aerofilms: 163A, 246A, 246B; AKG: 21B, 38C, 155D, 157A, 164C, 170A, 203A, 206E, 224C, 229F, 231A, 235A, 235B, 238A; AKG/British Library: 177A, 190A; AKG/Jean-Louis Nou: 196A; Ancient Art and Architecture: 11B; Art Archive: 43 (top), 45A, 149E, 176F; .../Bibliotheque Nationale, Paris: 83B; .../British Library: 42 (all), 88A, 91B, 180A, 209A; .../Musee Thomas Dobree, Nantes: 85C; Bridgeman Art Library: 69C, 102A, 110G, 144H, 148B, 212A, 220D, 225A; .../Birmingham Museums and Art Gallery: 116A; .../British Museum: 43 (centre); .../Corpus Christi College, Cambridge: 112J; .../Lambeth Palace Library: 204A; .../Victoria and Albert Museum: 141A; .../Westminster Abbey: 105B; British Library: 57D, 99F, 138B, 228D; British Museum: 11A; Cambridge University: 167A; Corbis/Eric Crichton: 174E; Corpus Christi College, Cambridge: 93A; Mary Evans Picture Library: 43 (bottom); Michael Holford: 23A, 65A, 142C, 164B, 196B; National Museums and Galleries of Wales: 66B; National Portrait Gallery: 117B, 117C, 119D; P.J. Gates: 244H; Ronald Grant Archive: 48B; Scotland in Focus: 72A; Sonia Halliday: 161A, 187B; Stockscotland/Iain Sarjeant: 74C; Tony Bates and the Vicar of Parochial Church Council of Bere Regis: 122H

Cover photograph: © British Library. Picture is a manuscript illustration of pilgrims on horseback.

Written source acknowledgements
The author and publisher gratefully acknowledge the following publications from which written sources in the book are drawn. In some sentences the wording or sentence structure has been simplified:

M. Ashley, *British monarchs: the complete genealogy, gazetteer and biographical encyclopaedia of the kings and queens of Britain* (Robinson, 1998): 120F
R.J. Cootes, *The Middle Ages* (Longman, 1972): 33C
H.W.C. Davies, *England under the Normans and Angevins* (Methuen, 1905): 62
John Gillingham, *The Wars of the Roses: peace and conflict in fifteenth-century England* (Weidenfeld and Nicolson, 1981): 120G
Geraldine McCaughrean, *The Canterbury Tales (retold)* (Oxford University Press, 1984): 167B
A.A. Milne, *Now We Are Six* (E.P. Dutton & Co, 1927): 49C
T. Douglas Murray, *Jeanne D'Arc: Maid of Orleans and Deliverer of France* (William Heinemann, 1903): 86E
L. du Garde Peach, *King John and the Magna Carta* (Wills and Hepworth, 1969): 49D, 56B
L. du Garde Peach, *Richard the Lionheart* (Wills and Hepworth, 1965): 55A, 57C
Sharon K. Penman, *Falls the Shadow* (Penguin, 1989): 100H, 101I
A.J. Pollard, *The Wars of the Roses* (Macmillan Educational, 1988): 120E
A.L. Poole, *From Domesday to Magna Carta* (Oxford University Press, 1962): 62

Tel: 01865 888058 www.heinemann.co.uk

Contents

England before 1066

History always remembers the winners, and it is usually written by the winners. The Normans were very good winners and we know a lot about them, so who were they?

The Normans are seen as a 'good thing'. Sellars and Yeatman wrote a book with the title, *1066 and All That*. Although this is a 'spoof' history book, the jokes and comments are firmly rooted in real people and real events in the past. In this book, they highlighted what they saw as all the really important things in history, and very few of them seem to have happened before 1066. The Normans were seen as the basis for future English success, and success is hard to criticise.

The Normans came from Normandy, the northern part of modern France. What was the attraction? What was England like in 1066? We need to find out why the Normans wanted to invade England.

Medieval life – the highs and lows of life before the Normans

Between half a million and 1 million people lived in England in the early tenth century. For how long did people live, and what were their lives like?

At Raunds in Northamptonshire, there is an Anglo-Saxon cemetery. By investigating the bones of those buried in the cemetery, archaeologists have discovered that the average life expectancy at birth was 21 years (life expectancy is the length of life you are expected to live).

- One sixth of all children died before reaching the age of two.

- One third of all children died before reaching their sixth birthday.

- If you survived to the age of 12 your chances of a long life were better.

- A few individuals reached the age of 60 or more.

- The age of 12 seems to have been widely recognised as the age of maturity; the laws of Æthelstan decreed that any man over 12 years old could be killed if found guilty of theft.

- Poor hygiene and nutrition were probably the most common causes of death. Females were most at risk.

- Men were much more likely to reach their late thirties than women.

The structure of society

Anglo-Saxon society was rigidly hierarchical, with a small aristocracy living off the labour of a great many peasants. A hierarchy is a ladder structure, where the most important person is at the top, and least powerful people are at the bottom. At the top was the king and his ealdormen (called jarls or earls by the Danes and eleventh-century Anglo-Saxons). Then came the thegns, or landholders, who later became knights or lords of the manor. Next there were various grades of agricultural workers, and finally a large slave class, possibly up to one quarter of the population.

The hierarchical nature of Anglo-Saxon society.

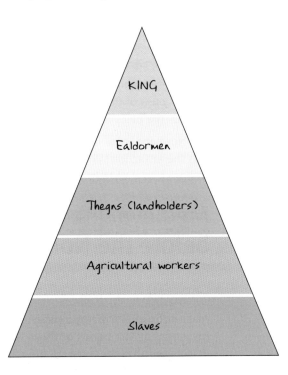

KING

Ealdormen

Thegns (landholders)

Agricultural workers

Slaves

Agriculture was the most important part of the Anglo-Saxon economy but, in southern and eastern England, towns began to emerge. London and York acted as centres of royal and ecclesiastical (Church) administration, as well as of trade and industry. A special class of trading ports, or wics, such as Hamwic (Southampton) and Ipswich, played an important role in foreign trade.

Question time

1   Why do you think children might have died at a very young age?

2   Why do you think women were most at risk from death because of poor hygiene and nutrition? Can you think of a link with children?

3   From the diagram above, who had the most power and who had the least power?

4   If the slaves worked on the land as well as the agricultural workers, what does that tell you about the main source of wealth in Anglo-Saxon England?

Life in the countryside

Most of the Anglo-Saxon population lived in the countryside, where mixed farming took place. Farms had some fields for crops and some fields for animals (for products such as wool, feathers, eggs and milk). After they had been kept for a number of years, the slaughtered animals would provide other resources such as bone, sinew and skin (hide). Most animals, too, provided fresh meat for eating.

Look back at the pyramid on page 6. You will see that thegns were the landowners. Most people worked directly for a thegn who would in return, allow them a home and some land to grow their own food. Slaves did not have any personal freedom. They were not allowed to travel away from the village, and they had to do everything their lord asked of them. There would be good years when crops were plenty, and bad years when famine and disease were the order of the day. There were laws which governed people's behaviour, but most of them would favour the landowner. Life was hard for the slaves.

Agricultural prosperity

In Anglo-Saxon England, there was a large increase in the area of land that was farmed. In the late ninth and tenth centuries, shorter and milder winters, combined with longer and warmer summers, allowed the cultivation of land in areas such as the Peak District and the Yorkshire Dales, which had not been used before. The heavy plough was used to cultivate this land, and the forests around places such as York were cut down to provide new fertile land for farming. Some historians argue that the great open fields which increased food production started about 200 years before the Norman conquest of 1066.

All of this agricultural prosperity made England a tempting place for potential invaders. Four main cereals were grown: wheat, rye, barley and oats. Wheat and rye were used for bread; oats were used for animal fodder as well as for porridge; barley was used for brewing and for cooking. Remember there were no potatoes, rice or pasta to fill up on. In addition, a wide range of fruit and nuts were grown, including apples, blackberries, raspberries, hazelnuts and walnuts. In London, some people ate rare and expensive figs and grapes. This tells us that there was enough wealth at the time to buy such luxuries. These were very rare and expensive.

The wool industry

Sheep farming was England's major industry during this period, with sheep being kept mainly as a source of wool. English cloth was prized throughout Europe and was a valuable export. Again, this source of wealth would be attractive to an invader. Cloth was sold at fairs and markets, and there were traders who travelled to sell their wares.

Question time

1 Why was agriculture such an important part of the Anglo-Saxon economy?

2 Think about the kind of work that most people did in Anglo-Saxon England. Why do you think that all of the four cereals were used in some way for food? What would be the most important food?

3 What would be the main difference between the food which was available to the Anglo-Saxons and the food which you have today?

4 Explain what a conqueror would gain by invading England and taking over all the land.

Towns and markets

Although England had a strong agricultural economy, there was also a developing town life. Towns and markets were growing, and prosperity was increasing. However, only about 10 per cent of the population lived in towns, because most people needed to work on the land to provide enough food to feed the population. Nevertheless, the Domesday Book (see page 37) records about 100 towns with a population of more than 1000, with larger towns such as Lincoln and Norwich having over 5000 inhabitants.

Many of these towns had started life as Saxon wics or camps, such as Hamwic (Southampton) and Eoforwic (York). These sites were originally founded and supported by the kings so that trade could be protected. The kings made money from the wics by taxing any trade which took place. The towns were planned, with a system of streets on which traders' properties were carefully sited. Archaeological finds in London and York show us that, even when Viking raids disrupted trading, the merchants just moved to a more secure part of the town and carried on trading.

Map showing the location of Southampton, York, London and Ipswich and their associated rivers.

The burghs

Viking raids became more and more disruptive, and so the Anglo-Saxons developed burghs. A burgh was a defended area created to withstand Viking raids. King Alfred (849–99) created a network of burghs, so that no part of his kingdom of Wessex was more than 32 km (20 miles) from a burgh. The enclosed area of a burgh meant that trade could be protected and encouraged, and in this way trade expanded under the Saxon kings.

As we have seen, trade and business happened in towns. The markets sold the produce of the countryside, but most people in towns still had enough land to keep a few animals and grow some basic food for themselves. Most houses, even in towns, had a grinding stone, which townspeople used to grind their own grain to make their bread. Archaeological evidence of tooth wear suggests that the bread must have been very coarse because teeth are well worn from eating bread with un-ground grains in it! Traders in the towns had more chance of becoming wealthier than farmers in the countryside because they were less dependent on the weather. However, travel for traders was a very risky business: journeys between towns took a long time, and any merchant was in danger of being attacked and robbed.

Life in towns was easier than in the countryside in some ways, but there was the ever-present danger of disease as the number of people living in the towns increased, and the sanitation got worse. Rubbish pits and latrine pits were dug in the back gardens to get rid of rubbish and human waste. The Romans were the last rulers who had been concerned about the need for sewers in towns and, although York and other cities built and developed by the Romans still had their water supply channelled through Roman pipes, nobody had bothered to repair them or keep them in good order. Roman knowledge about disease had also been lost, and the smells that accompanied human life were simply seen as a natural part of everyday life rather than a warning that cramped living conditions and poor sanitation meant that towns were ideal breeding grounds for disease.

The economy

The medieval trading economy developed partly because merchants began using coins, or money, based on silver. Each burgh had a mint which made money and had the royal authority to produce coins with royal heads on. By the eleventh century, coins were in general use. Some coins found in London and York have been cut in half and into quarters, showing that the coins were even used for giving change. Money was also used for paying rents on land at this time. Before this, all rents were paid 'in kind', i.e. the landlord would receive a part of the tenant's produce in payment. The difficulty here was that the produce would often decay before the landlord had used it.

Question time

1   Town life based on trade was easier in some ways than an agricultural life, but it still had its problems. Using the information given above, write an account of the life of a trader in Anglo-Saxon York. Do not forget to write about the bad side as well as the good side. Think about the smells and the disease.

2   Why do you think coins had royal heads stamped on them?

3   Why do you think landlords would prefer to have money rather than goods?

4   Why do you think anyone would want to invade England in 1066 and take control of the towns and markets?

England as a target for invaders

Wealth

England in 1066 was a wealthy country. It had abundant natural resources and had always been seen as a tempting target for invaders. The Romans, the Anglo-Saxons and the Vikings all invaded and then stayed to take advantage of the benefits of the fertile land and mineral resources. Whoever had been in control, the main wealth-creating system of agriculture had continued to exist. The wool trade was a great attraction for any would-be conqueror, and the royal burghs and towns, with their potential for royal taxes, were also seen as something worth fighting for. William of Poitiers, the Duke of Normandy's biographer, wrote that England was 'many times richer than Normandy in wealth and military strength'.

The most successful leaders in any period of history have learnt that financial benefits are a good reason for invading a county. Not only would the ruler benefit, but also being wealthy would put the ruler in a position to gain followers who wished to benefit from newly acquired riches.

Evidence that England was a place of wealth can be seen from some of the buildings of this period. As England became more stable after the invasions of the Anglo-Saxons and Scandinavians, larger buildings and palaces were constructed. While much of the evidence for this wealth has been lost because most of the buildings were wooden, at places such as Cheddar, North Elmham and Waltham Abbey archaeological excavations have revealed large wooden buildings. Other evidence of increasing wealth can be found in the beautiful jewellery, pottery and illuminated (illustrated) manuscripts that have been found by archaeologists. All of these provide evidence that not only was there a desire for beautiful objects, there was also the wealth to create it.

A gold buckle found at Sutton Hoo in Suffolk, an Anglo-Saxon burial site.

Religion

SOURCE B

St Lawrence Church, Bradford-on-Avon, built c. 700.

There were other reasons why Anglo-Saxon England was a worthy prize for a conqueror. England had a strong Christian background, and a high standing because of its reputation as a religious nation. The Synod of Whitby in 664 confirmed that England's Christianity was Roman Christianity, and English religious festivals followed those of the church in Rome. The existence of Saxon churches points to a wealthy society which valued religion enough to invest a lot of money in stone buildings. Most buildings at this time were wooden because building in stone was expensive; having stone churches shows the value and importance placed on religion. The Wessex kings under Alfred forced the Danish Vikings to convert to Christianity, thus linking royalty and the Christian Church.

In England a network of minster churches had grown up during the seventh and eighth centuries and covered the country. These ranged from major town buildings such as in York or Cirencester, to smaller churches in rural sites such as St Gregory's minster at Kirkdale near Helmsley in North Yorkshire.

In addition, rural parishes and parish churches expanded rapidly in the tenth and eleventh centuries. The construction of new churches is thought to have taken place in around 1000. By the time of the Domesday Book (see page 37) there were over 2600 local churches and maybe several thousand more which have not survived to the present time. This boom in church building was partly a response to the desire of new landholders to show their high position or status. New churches were usually built next to or near new manors that were being built at the time; Wharram Percy in North Yorkshire is a good example of this kind of building. Many of the new landlords were Scandinavian, and wanted to show that they belonged to the community.

Church building was not just restricted to the countryside, it was also happening in towns. All of this activity showed the wealth of the country. It also showed that incomers to England could be included in society and was therefore a place worth visiting or invading. The Scandinavian invaders of Alfred's reign settled in the Danelaw area and adopted many of the ways of life in England. The Danelaw area occupied northern and eastern England (about half the total area of the country). In this area Danish law and customs were practised.

Danish influences

Alfred's descendants were not quite as successful with the next wave of Viking invaders. The later Anglo-Saxon kings, such as Æthelred, tried to pay off the Danes with Danegeld (money). Nonetheless this protection money only bought a temporary peace and soon England faced large armies bent on political conquest. For several decades during the early eleventh century England was ruled by the Danish king, Cnute. There is a story that he demonstrated the limits of his power to his nobles by showing them that even he couldn't stop the tide coming in. However, by 1066 England was a country with its own sense of nationality and language. The Danelaw had been absorbed into England, but English customs of law and social organisation under lords began to be used throughout the kingdom.

Question time

1   What evidence is there to show that Anglo-Saxon England was a wealthy place which would be worth invading and controlling?

2   Why do you think that invaders bothered to build churches and look after the Christian religion?

1066 – who were the claimants to the throne?

The Anglo-Saxons

The Anglo-Saxon kings claimed to be descendants of a warrior called Cerdic, who was thought to have led a band of Anglo-Saxon raiders soon after AD 500. During the following five centuries, the Anglo-Saxons created a unified culture in southern England which they called England (Angleland), even though they were in the minority compared to the native Celtic-speaking Britons. The last king from Alfred's line, Edward the Confessor, was the son of King Æthelred and Emma, sister of Duke Robert of Normandy (see family tree).

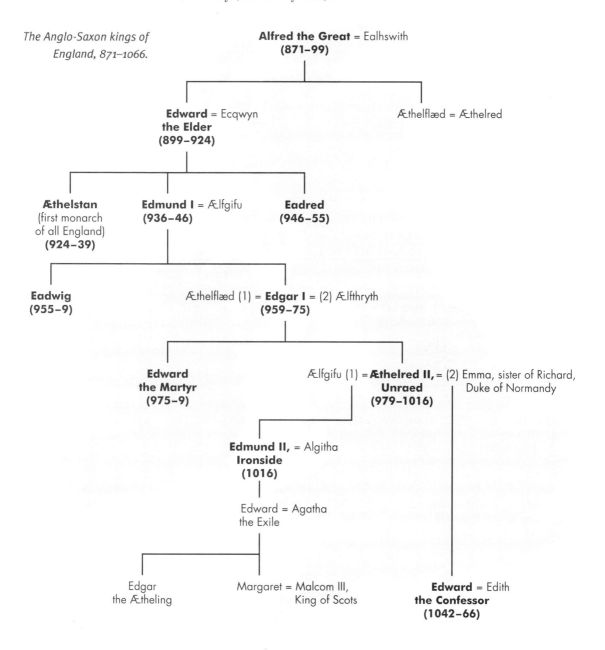

The Anglo-Saxon kings of England, 871–1066.

Alfred the Great = Ealhswith
(871–99)

Edward = Ecqwyn
the Elder
(899–924)

Æthelflæd = Æthelred

Æthelstan
(first monarch
of all England)
(924–39)

Edmund I = Ælfgifu
(936–46)

Eadred
(946–55)

Eadwig
(955–9)

Æthelflæd (1) = **Edgar I** = (2) Ælfthryth
(959–75)

Edward
the Martyr
(975–9)

Ælfgifu (1) = **Æthelred II,** = (2) Emma, sister of Richard,
Unraed Duke of Normandy
(979–1016)

Edmund II, = Algitha
Ironside
(1016)

Edward = Agatha
the Exile

Edgar
the Ætheling

Margaret = Malcom III,
King of Scots

Edward = Edith
the Confessor
(1042–66)

Edward the Confessor had been brought up in Normandy by his mother's family because his father, Æthelred, lost his throne. Edward preferred Norman French as a language, and was attracted to the new Norman ideas that were being introduced when he became King of England in 1042. During his rule, the earls of England advised Edward, and the most powerful and influential of these earls was Earl Godwin of Wessex, whose daughter was married to Edward. When Earl Godwin died in 1053, his son, Harold, became earl and also advised the king. When Edward died in 1066, Earl Harold Godwinson was elected King by the Witan (Council).

The Danes

The Danish kings who ruled England in the early eleventh century were descended from Harold Bluetooth, the first recorded king of Denmark. The Danish King Canute had been chosen by the Witan to be the English king in 1016. This was a good example of how kingship was not only a matter of lineage and royal blood, but also one of having the right qualities for the job. Æthelred had been seen to be a weak king by giving money to the Danes in the hope that they would leave England alone. A strong king had to be seen to defend and be willing to fight for his country.

In 1066, Harald Hardrada, the King of Norway, claimed the English throne through the line of ancestry beginning with Harald Bluetooth.

The Danish kings of England, 984–1066.

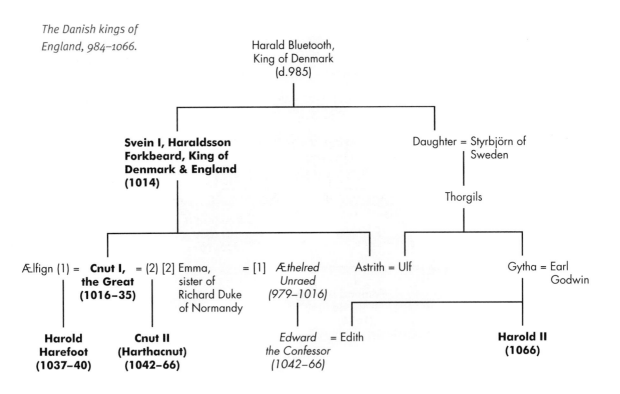

The Normans

William of Normandy was an illegitimate son of Duke Robert of Normandy. He was a good soldier, an efficient administrator, and an ambitious man who had the support of the Pope. William wanted the Normans to gain control of England. William claimed that Edward the Confessor had promised him the throne, and also that Harold Godwinson had sworn an oath to help William gain the throne (after William had rescued Harold from a shipwreck off the Normandy coast in 1064).

When Edward the Confessor died leaving no heir in 1066, the stage was set for a contest for the English throne between three main claimants: Harold Godwinson, an English earl; William, Duke of Normandy; and Harald Hardrada, King of Norway.

Question time

1 Which people claimed the right to the throne in 1066 and what right did they have?

2 Look at the Anglo-Saxon and Danish family trees and try to answer the following questions:

   a If the men in bold were kings, what was particularly important about Edward the Confessor and Harold Godwinson?

   b Why does Harold Godwinson appear to have a good claim to the throne?

   c What other reason could Harold give as to why an Anglo-Saxon should be king?

3 Make a spider diagram 'Target England' showing all the reasons why England was a prime target for invaders in 1066.

4 Use the Internet to find out about King Alfred (871–99). Historians have called him 'King Alfred the Great'. Do you agree that he deserves to be called 'the Great'?

The main players in 1066

Anglo-Saxon England

Anglo-Saxon England was wealthy from trade in wool and natural resources such as minerals. England had come together as a kingdom under Alfred the Great, who had fought and defeated the Danes in 878. However, later kings were not as strong, and the Vikings returned to claim control of England once more. England had been a Christian country for a long time. The king in 1066 was Edward who was nicknamed 'The Confessor' because he spent so much time saying his prayers. Edward died leaving no male heir who might have followed him as king.

Normandy

The Vikings, or Norsemen, settled in the Seine area in 911 because it was an area of plentiful natural resources. These Norsemen became the Normans, gradually becoming more powerful than their neighbours. The creation of a settled and ordered community allowed the Normans to capitalise on their military strengths, and to expand their control. In 1066 the Duke of Normandy was William; he was a very ambitious man who wanted to make his name and reputation as a successful leader.

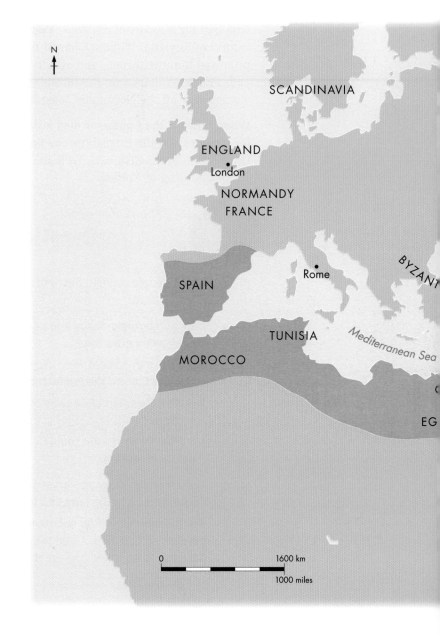

France

The Franks were a successful group who had taken part of the Roman Empire in the mid-fifth century. They established an Empire which was at its height under Charlemagne (Charles the Great, who was crowned by the Pope in 800). However, this did not last much beyond his life. In 987, Hugh Capet came to the throne of France and tried to control the many different parts of his kingdom. Dukes and barons controlled large regions of the kingdom and were supposed to owe loyalty to the king. Many of these dukes and barons, including William Duke of Normandy, were less supportive of the king than they should have been. In 1053, Henry I of France and William Duke of Normandy broke their alliance and, in 1058, Henry ravaged the heart of Normandy. The scene was set for conflict between France and Normandy. Henry did not wish William to become more powerful, as this would put his kingdom of France at risk.

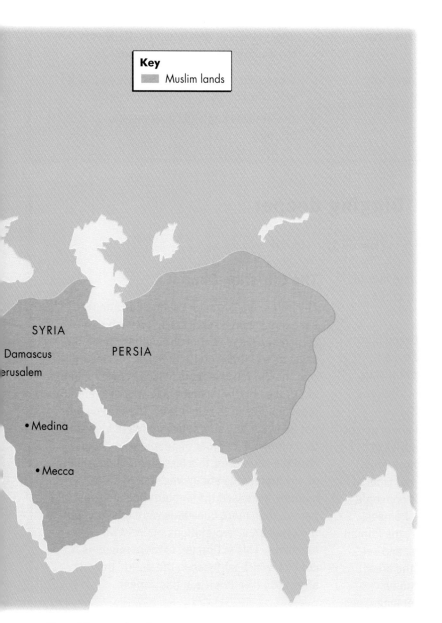

Key
Muslim lands

SYRIA

Damascus

erusalem

PERSIA

• Medina

• Mecca

Map of Europe showing Anglo-Saxon England, Scandinavia, France, Normandy, Rome and the Muslim world.

Scandinavia

The name Viking is used to describe a number of different groups who lived in different areas of Scandinavia. They all had certain features in common. They were sea-faring warriors who travelled far in search of new opportunities. Some of them continued to travel and plunder, but some of them settled in lands where they felt able to build a new life. In this way, the Vikings had an influence in Ireland, England and what became known as Normandy. They journeyed further afield too, reaching Greenland, Iceland and North America, and even Russia. The Scandinavians had a continuing influence in English history, and Harald Hardrada claimed the English throne in 1066 as a result of his Viking ancestry.

The Muslim world

The year of AD 622 is traditionally dated as the start of the Muslim era, with the flight of Muhammad to Medina. From there, gradual expansion and conquest throughout the lands surrounding the Mediterranean occurred. The Muslims conquered most of what had been the eastern part of the Roman Empire. This included North Africa, Spain, the Mediterranean islands, and what is now known as the Middle East. Jerusalem was taken in 638, but was maintained as a joint shrine by Christian and Muslims. The Muslim world had traditionally been tolerant of others. This situation changed because of internal disputes within the Muslim religion, and because of Muslim lands being reconquered by Christians.

The Pope

The Pope lived in Rome, but his influence was felt throughout western Europe. By 1066, Christianity was established in this area as the dominant religion. Once Christianity had been accepted as the official religion of the Roman Empire by Constantine in 312, it stopped being the persecuted religion of a minority group and gradually became dominant. Paganism (worshipping gods other than Christ) was wiped out. The Pope had a representative in all towns in all countries, and he was also seen to have God on his side. He was thus a very powerful person in politics because he was seen to have influence over what happened to a person in the next world, in their life after death.

Question time

1. What advantages did the Normans have from their Viking past?

2. What problem did Hugh Capet have when he tried to rule his kingdom?

3. Why could you argue that the Pope was the most powerful person in Europe?

4. Where did the Muslim Empire extend, and why would this cause potential trouble?

5. Explain why England could be seen as weak in 1066.

Digging deeper

The wider world

If you were a villager living in Yorkshire in 1066, what would you know about the rest of the world? Answer: very little. Why?

There was little communication between places and between people. You could not even have made yourself understood in different places.

The fall of the Romans

The Roman Empire had lasted until about AD 400 in western Europe. Most of the countries in Europe had been under Roman control. After this date countries such as Britain and France were invaded by barbarians, groups of people who had not been controlled by the Romans. The barbarians rejected 'civilisation', the Roman language of Latin, learning and laws, and set about destroying Roman control of the areas they invaded. So, after the end of Roman control, distinct groups with different languages and laws ruled each area of Europe. The Anglo-Saxons, for example, invaded England and helped to create the English language. The Franks helped to create France and the French language.

The only group of people who survived the destruction of the Roman Empire as a European organisation was the Christian Church, which was based in Rome.

The Christian Church

All church officials spoke Latin and Latin was used in all church services. If you went to a church service in York, it should have been the same as a church service in Paris. This meant that the Church was represented in every nation of Europe and that its message was delivered to many nations in the same way. The Church did not allow for any alternative points of view and, by limiting the number of people who could read the scriptures, this lessened the possibility of any arguments about who was right. As learning increased throughout the medieval period, then more questions were raised about the Church's interpretations of Christ's teachings. This in turn led to more religious conflict, which surfaced in the period directly after 1485 (see Book 2 in this series).

Question time

1. What happened to Europe after the fall of the Roman Empire in the East?

2. How did this affect the countries that had been in the Empire?

3. Why was the Christian Church not affected in the same way?

4. Why did the Church still use Latin as its main language?

Assessment section

1   Once the Romans had left, England was invaded by different waves of 'barbarians'. Draw up a grid to show who invaded, what they did in England and why their rule ended.

2   Look carefully at the map and the information on pages 16–17. Who (either individuals or groups) would be:

    a   most likely to want to invade England

    b   least likely to want to invade England?

  Explain why.

3   You have been asked to put together an exhibition called 'England before 1066'. In groups, decide which items you would include in the exhibition, and why. Draw up a plan of the exhibition and write a brief guide for visitors. You may use a word processor and any suitable software to produce a professional brochure.

4   Look back through this chapter and see how many times 'archaeologists' are mentioned. Why are they so important to our understanding of Anglo-Saxon England?

William the Conqueror

In January 1066, Harold Godwinson became King of England. Chosen by Edward the Confessor as he lay dying, elected by the whole Witan and consecrated by Archbishop Ealdred, his rule should have been secure. But in less than a year he was dead, buried beside the Saxon shore he could not defend, and the enemies of Saxon England were beginning their takeover. How had this happened?

The fight for the English throne

The Battle of Stamford Bridge

On 18 September 1066, Harald Hardrada and his army landed on the Yorkshire coast. King Harold Godwinson rushed to meet the invading army. On 25 September the two armies met at Stamford Bridge near York where Harald Hardrada and 7000 of his men were killed in a battle. Almost immediately, on 28 September, news reached Harold Godwinson of another invasion in the south of England. William of Normandy had landed with an army and was advancing towards London. Harold turned his army around and marched towards this new threat.

The Battle of Hastings

On 14 October 1066, William and Harold's armies clashed in a battle near Hastings. The English king, Harold Godwinson, died during the battle. William of Normandy then continued with his army to London where he was crowned King of England. To answer the question 'Why did the Normans win the Battle of Hastings?', we have to look at the facts and interpret them.

- Harold had already fought a battle at Stamford Bridge against Harald Hardrada.

- Harold had rushed from this battle in the North to meet the new threat from the Normans in the South.

- Harold's army was larger than William's, but William had more knights on horseback.

- Harold's army was positioned on top of a hill and waited for William's army to arrive.

- Harold's soldiers used double-handed battle-axes, which were heavy and effective in cutting down the enemy.

- Harold's soldiers used their shields to create a wall which protected Harold against attack. It was difficult to break.

- Harold's plan was to kill the Normans as they attacked. He did not plan to attack. Rather, he intended to stay on the top of the hill and defend his position.

Each of these points could be used to show that Harold was in a winning position, but they could also be used to show why the Normans won the battle. This is because William used a very old trick in order to win the battle.

- William's soldiers ran up the hill to attack Harold, who was surrounded by the shield wall.

- The Normans then turned and ran away down the hill. Harold's men thought they were running away in fear, so some of the shield wall broke off to chase the Normans down the hill.

- At the bottom of the hill, the Normans turned round and massacred Harold's soldiers.

- Because Harold's soldiers had been killed, there were fewer men in the wall around Harold. This allowed the Normans to make a better attack. In the confusion Harold was killed, along with many of his men.

- William of Normandy had won the Battle of Hastings.

SOURCE A

William took Harold by surprise before his men were ready to fight. The English army had a very small space; and many soldiers seeing this difficult position deserted King Harold. Even so, he fought bravely and the enemy's army made little impression on him until, after great killing on both sides, the king fell.

Extract from the Anglo-Saxon Chronicle, *written by English monks, which recorded the English view of what had happened.*

SOURCE B

With the point of the lance, the first knight pierced Harold's shield and then penetrated his chest drenching the ground with his blood which poured out in torrents. With his sword, the second cut off his head just below where his helmet protected him. The third disembowelled him with his javelin. The fourth hacked off his leg at the thigh and hurled it away. Struck down in this way his dead body lay on the ground.

Extract from a poem believed to have been written around 1068 by Guy, Bishop of the French town of Amiens.

SOURCE C

Bayeux Tapestry scene showing Harold being killed by an arrow in his eye. The tapestry was made by Norman women on the orders of Bishop Odo, half-brother to William of Normandy.

Source A gives an English view of what happened at the Battle of Hastings. Even if we accept that this source could be biased in favour of the English, it gives some idea of why later writers and historians wrote about Harold in a favourable way. Very little is known of Harold's life or death, but he is usually portrayed in a positive, romantic way. Sources B and C provide different interpretations of Harold's death. The Bayeux Tapestry tells the story, in words and pictures, of William of Normandy's decision to invade England, and his victory at the Battle of Hastings. It is important not only for the information which is given, but also because it was seen to be very important that William's side of the story was recorded for all to see.

Question time

1 Can you explain why the English might be in favour of the story that Harold was killed by an arrow in his eye?

2 Why would the Normans be more in favour of the story which describes Harold being hacked to death by Norman soldiers?

3 Which story does the Bayeux Tapestry support? Explain your answer carefully.

The Norman rule of England

How to conquer a country?

The Battle of Hastings is often seen as the most important event which decided the fate of the English nation. However, it was really only the start of William's campaign to control England. To defeat an enemy in battle is very different from conquering a country. William of Normandy gained his place in history for being the 'conqueror'. This title meant that he gained total control of England, not something which can be done quickly or easily. Julius Caesar came to England and defeated the Ancient Britons, but he never conquered them. It was left to a much less glorious emperor to do that: Emperor Claudius, who invaded England in AD 43 and conquered the country. He built fortified camps, he created towns and trade, and he brought in laws to rule the people of England. William, Duke of Normandy, used very similar methods to conquer England after the Battle of Hastings in 1066. William used a mixture of technology and efficient soldiering, aiming always to achieve total control. This shows that he understood that the threat of rebellion should never be underestimated.

William establishes control

After the Battle of Hastings, William marched to London; London was the capital of England, and he needed to show his power by controlling it. William also used the journey to London to show off his military strength. He deliberately went through Dover and Canterbury, and forced the English soldiers to surrender. He approached London via Berkhamsted, where he burnt all the crops and built a castle. At Berkhamsted, William met the remaining English earls: Edwin of Mercia and Morcar of Northumbria. They both agreed to serve William – to be in his court and to accept William as king. Some of the important leaders of the English Church also agreed to accept William as king. William then travelled to London and was crowned King of England in Westminster Abbey.

SOURCE A

A section from the Bayeux Tapestry showing Norman soldiers seizing food and cattle.

William started his reign as English king with the support of the Church, some of the English nobles, and – his most important resource – his soldiers. However, William did not have enough soldiers to control a whole country. Furthermore, the army that William brought to invade England did not work for him out of kindness – they expected a reward. William had gathered together a mixture of about 7000 soldiers for his invasion of England. Some of these soldiers were mercenaries – soldiers who fought for any leader as long as they were well paid. Others were barons, who expected to be rewarded for their support with lands and privileges in the newly conquered England.

To develop and maintain his rule as King of England, William needed a better system of control and he needed to reward those who had been loyal to him and had fought for him. By clever organisation, William was able to set up a system that meant he controlled everyone in the land, from baron to peasant. This system was called the feudal system.

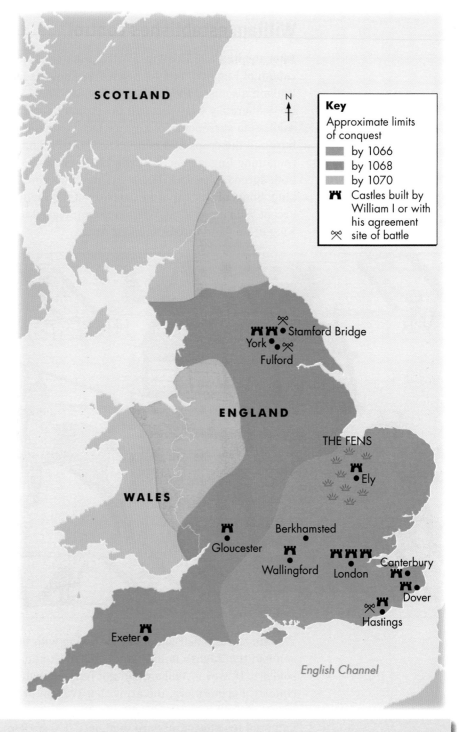

The stages of the Norman conquest, 1066– 70.

Key

Approximate limits of conquest
- by 1066
- by 1068
- by 1070
- 🏰 Castles built by William I or with his agreement
- ⚔ site of battle

SCOTLAND

ENGLAND

THE FENS

WALES

Stamford Bridge
York
Fulford
Ely
Berkhamsted
Gloucester
Wallingford
London
Canterbury
Dover
Hastings
Exeter

English Channel

Question time

1. Why would William need to go to London?

2. Why did William not go straight to London?

3. Why was it important that Edwin and Morcar accepted William as king?

4. What effect would it have on the population of England if the Church gave its support to William?

5. How likely is it that the Saxons in the South of England gave William their support willingly?

The feudal system

William's feudal system was used in Normandy to establish support for the invasion of England. It worked in the following way:

> William claimed all the land in England by right of conquest

> He promised land to the barons who supported him

> The barons then hired soldiers to fight for William

> William won the Battle of Hastings and was crowned King of England

William then used the same plan for the conquest and control of his new land:

> William claimed all the land in England by right of conquest

> He gave land to the barons who supported him and promised to provide soldiers

> The barons then gave smaller amounts of land to knights for their service (as soldiers). These knights, in turn, supported their baron and the king.

> The knights' land was farmed by peasants, who depended on the knights for their homes and land. The peasants supported their knight, the baron and the king.

In this way, William was able to extend his influence throughout the entire country. Every person depended on someone else for their land and their livelihood. They had to be loyal if they were to survive. If you had no job in the Middle Ages, then you had no food, no home and faced almost certain death. It was very important to have a protector, and the feudal system provided a neat pattern of protection.

The division of medieval society

In the Middle Ages, 97 per cent of the population consisted of peasants. However, the land was ruled by the remaining 3 per cent of the population – the king, his barons and the Church. They were the most wealthy members of society, and owned about one third of all the land in England.

In the Middle Ages, there were four different types – or classes – of peasant: freemen, villeins, bordars and cottars, and slaves. Some of the peasants were free, others had very limited freedom. The majority of peasants were given land by their lord in return for loyalty and service.

Freemen

Freemen were, as their name suggests, peasants who were free. They paid rent to their lord for their land. They sometimes had to do some services for their lord, but this was only at very busy times like hay-making and harvest – hence it was called 'boon work'.

Villeins

Villeins were those peasants who worked on the lord's land and did services for him for no pay. They had no freedom and could not leave the lord's land without his permission. They even needed their lord's permission for their daughters and sons to get married! In return for their service, villeins were granted land to farm for themselves.

Bordars and cottars

Bordars and cottars were poorer than villeins. They were given less land by their lord in return for their loyalty and service.

Slaves

About 9 per cent of the population were slaves. These were the lowest kind of peasant. They had no freedom and no land, and had to do whatever the lord demanded.

The amount of land held by different sections of society at the time of the Domesday Book, 1086.

	Per cent of population	Per cent of land
Slaves	9	No land
Bordars/cottars	32	5
Villeins/freemen	56	65
King, barons, Church	3	30

Question time

1. Explain how the feudal system would allow William to control a larger number of people rather than simply putting soldiers in every town.

2. Some of William's followers were rewarded with large amounts of land, but the land was distributed around the country, not in one single area. Why do you think William did this?

3. William gave about one quarter of the land in England to the Church. Why do you think he did this?

Digging deeper

The oath of fealty

William cleverly used religion to back up the feudal system. He made people swear an oath of fealty (faithfulness) when they promised to serve him. This meant people were duty bound to honour their oath. If they broke their oath, then William was entitled to exact a terrible revenge. This was because his subjects had not only broken their word to William, they had broken a pledge to God!

The oath of fealty was passed down from king to lord to knight. Only the peasants did not have to take an oath, because they were assumed to be too unimportant. They had no position in life. Peasants were seen as having no rights, so they didn't count. Besides, if they did disagree with their lord, they could simply be thrown out of their house. Most peasants would not wish that to happen, so they were loyal through fear, if not through honour. However, the idea of being someone's 'man' spread to even the peasant section of the population. Loyalty was therefore encouraged at all levels.

Question time

1. Why was it a good idea to make people take an oath of fealty?

2. Explain why the peasants were not expected to take an oath of loyalty.

3. William also had to swear an oath to be loyal to his barons. Why do you think it was important that he kept that oath?

Defending new lands

Building castles

As part of the deal for gaining land from William, the barons were expected to defend those lands and hold them safe for William. To do this they used the latest method of military technology: the castle.

William had already shown how effective a castle could be in his progress from Hastings to his coronation in London on Christmas Day 1066. As a means of controlling an area, the castle was unrivalled at the time, and William put it to great use.

Some reasons why William chose to have a castle built in a particular place were:

- to establish his position immediately after the Battle of Hastings

- to control the capital city (London)

- to control major towns

- to control the borders with Scotland and Wales (these countries were not conquered by William)

- to spread his control and influence throughout England.

A tool of domination

Added to all this was the fact that these castles, the means of domination, would be built by the very people whom they were intended to conquer. The English built the castles with their forced labour. This created the feeling of subjection, and the finished article completed the picture. The castle would be the highest building in the entire area – very few places had buildings taller than a castle. This also gave the castle an air of mystery and importance. This imposition of the Norman might was particularly felt when castles were built in towns which were already heavily built up. To make room for the new castles, existing householders lost property. Demolition of houses for castle building was recorded at Exeter, Lincoln, Shrewsbury, Canterbury, Cambridge and elsewhere.

SOURCE A

He then went to Nottingham and built a castle there, so from there to York, and there built two castles, in Lincoln, and elsewhere in those parts ... He built castles widely throughout this nation and oppressed the people wretchedly and afterwards it grew much more evil.

An entry in the Anglo-Saxon Chronicle *from 1067.*

It should also be remembered that the land that William gave to his followers had previously belonged to somebody else. It was taken from these original owners, who had owned the land before the Battle of Hastings, and given to William's loyal followers who had sworn to support him. As a result, in both town and country, there were plenty of people who had good reason to resent the coming of the Normans.

Military control

Castles provided a means of military control and this control was linked to those who owned the land. By joining the two together, William created a system which served all his purposes (i.e. the Norman purposes). Inevitably this would not serve the interests of those people who were being conquered, the Anglo-Saxons. Castles therefore had the very real job of providing security in troubled times because rebellion was never very far off in the early days of the Norman conquest.

Motte and bailey castles

A motte and bailey castle.

The first castles were very simple, and were made from wood and earth. The 'motte' was a simple mound, and a hill would be used for the motte if it was in the right position. If there wasn't a hill in a good position, then earth would be dug and piled high to create the mound. On top of this mound there would be a wooden fence, behind which the defenders could group together for a more efficient concentration of firepower.

The 'bailey' was cleared land which allowed a good view of the surrounding area. It prevented anyone from sneaking up in a surprise attack, and gave the defenders a clear area from which to shoot with the deadly crossbow weapon. The advantage of height combined with technology made attacking a motte and bailey castle very dangerous and defence relatively easy. Baileys could also be used as safe places in which people and animals from the surrounding area could shelter during troubled times.

Question time

1 Why would the building of castles help to subdue the English?

2 How did the building of castles fit into William's policy of conquering England?

3 Why would the building of castles in towns be especially resented?

4 The early castles were made from wood and earth. Why would this be helpful to William?

5 Later castles were not just built from wood and earth; stone was used to enclose the outer walls, and the main building (or keep) became a large stone building on the centre of the motte. Explain why the increasing size and strength of castles might pose a threat to William.

Problems facing William

Ruling different lands

Following his coronation in 1066, William redistributed land to his supporters, including those Anglo-Saxons who swore to be loyal to him. It is possible that William began his reign with the hope of uniting Normans and English as equal partners in government. He showed this by his acceptance of the Anglo-Saxon earls, Edwin of Mercia and Morcar of Northumbria (see page 23). William had also accepted Bretons and Flemings into his service and, as long as they were loyal and trustworthy, he saw no problem with this. However, difficulties arose because William was ruling two lands separated by the English Channel: he could not be in both Normandy and England at the same time. Furthermore, as soon as William left England for Normandy, a revolt or rebellion would flare up. Leaving land in Anglo-Saxon hands was therefore a risk – a risk which William took at the beginning of his reign. However, as his reign continued, William took back land from those who went against his rule. By the end of his reign, only Norman lords held land in England.

Squashing rebellion

Between 1067 and 1069, a rebellion broke out in the south-east of England, and William hastily built castles to crush this rebellion. It is interesting to note that the force that put down the rebellion was a combined Anglo-French one. At this time William still had enough supporters to do the job willingly.

The original castles were all built in a hurry as a response to a fresh crisis and threat to William's rule. Castles at Warwick, Nottingham, York, Lincoln, Huntingdon and Cambridge mark the progress of William up to the North and back to the South again in 1068 – each new castle marked a new rebellion. William must have wondered why he bothered to try to establish control in this land of constant rebellion. The South had barely been settled when the North rose against him, and many earls, including Edwin and Morcar, had broken their oath of loyalty to their king. As a result, the first few years of William's reign were fraught with conflict.

The earth and timber from which the original castles were built were easy to find, and so these castles were quick to construct. Later, the first permanent castles were built in London, 'against the fickleness of the vast and fierce populace' according to William of Poitiers, a loyal supporter of King William. The diagram below shows how defensive fortifications improved under the Normans.

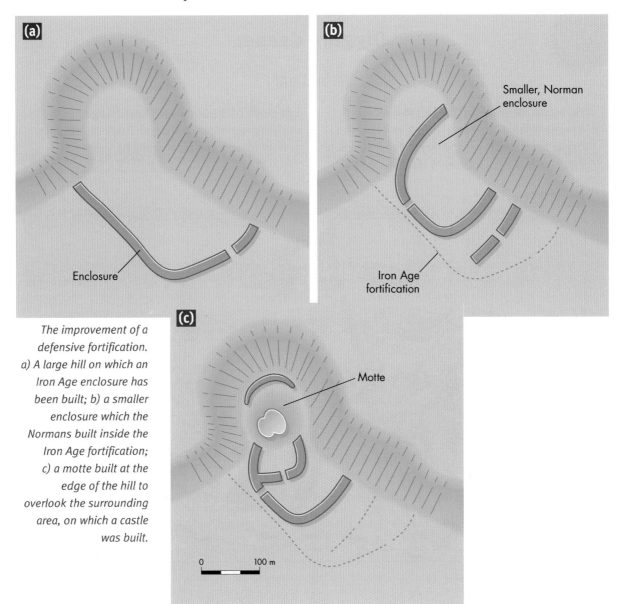

The improvement of a defensive fortification. a) A large hill on which an Iron Age enclosure has been built; b) a smaller enclosure which the Normans built inside the Iron Age fortification; c) a motte built at the edge of the hill to overlook the surrounding area, on which a castle was built.

The Rising of the North

The Rising of the North is seen as the last attempt by Scandinavian claimants to take the English throne. In 1069, Earls Edwin and Morcar, helped by the brother and sons of King Svein of Denmark (see page 14) led a revolt against Norman rule. However, the revolt faced difficulties right from the start, because those opposed to William were not united in their aims, and William was able to use this disagreement to weaken them. Also, through his policy of building castles at strategic points, William gradually extended Norman control and was able to put down the rebellion. He then prevented the possibility of further rebellion by a policy of deliberate destruction, which served as both a punishment and a warning to his enemies. Areas of land between York and Durham were burnt, animals slaughtered and whole villages destroyed in what became known as the 'Harrying of the North'.

Digging deeper

Rebellion!

Hereward the Wake led the last real rebellion against William. Holed up in East Anglia in the city of Ely and surrounded by the Fens – miles of flat, marshy land – Hereward represented the last stand of the oppressed English against the invading Normans. Or did he? Study the sources and try to work out what really happened.

SOURCE A

A nineteenth-century drawing showing Hereward the Wake attacking the Normans.

SOURCE B

1071: Eorl Edwin and eorl Morkere fled away, and fared different ways through woods and fields. Then eorl Morkere came to Ely by ship; eorl Edwin was killed basely by his own men. Bishop Aethelwine, Siward Beam and many hundred men with them came into Ely. When King William found that out, he called out the land-force and the ship-force, surrounded the area, built a causeway and went in, with the ship-force on the sea-side. The outlaws all gave themselves into his hands: that was bishop Aethelwine, eorl Morkere, and all who were with them but Hereward alone, and all who would follow him; he bravely led them out. The king seized ships, weapons and many treasures, and with the men he dealt with as he would. Bishop Aethelwine he sent to Abingdon, and he passed away soon that winter.

Entry in the Anglo-Saxon Chronicle *for the year 1071, written by monks.*

SOURCE C

William faced one last rebel stronghold, in the fens of East Anglia. There, at Ely, a brave band of English rebels had gathered. They were led by a Lincolnshire thane called Hereward, nicknamed 'the Wake' because he was wide-awake and watchful. He was famous for his great strength and his skill as a swordsman.

In the summer of 1071 William set out to conquer the Fens. It was easier said than done. He had to use boats to get his army across the marshes. And even then he could find no way of reaching the rebels until monks from Ely Abbey showed his soldiers a secret pathway. Most of the English were finally rounded up and killed, although Hereward himself probably escaped. Many stories are told about his adventures, but we do not know for certain what happened to him.

From The Middle Ages *by R. J. Cootes, a school textbook published in 1972.*

Question time

1   Look carefully at Source A. The artist wasn't there at the time. How could he have known what happened? Explain your answer.

2   Read Source B. Work out what the following people were doing and whose side they were on:

   a   Eorl Edwin

   b   Eorl Morkere

   c   Bishop Aethelwine

   d   Siward Beam.

3   Read Sources B and C.

   a   List the points on which they agree.

   b   List the points on which they disagree. (Remember that 'disagreement' means saying something different about the same event or person, NOT telling us something extra.)

   c   What does Source B tell us that Source C doesn't?

   d   What does Source C tell us that Source B doesn't?

   e   Why do you think there are differences between the accounts given in Sources B and C?

4   Look back over all three sources. Which source would you trust the most to be giving us an accurate account of what happened in the Fens and Ely in 1071? Why?

William and Edgar the Ætheling

By 1071, of all the English leaders who had been in a position to challenge William, only Edgar the Ætheling remained free; the rest were either dead or imprisoned. William was very careful not to harm Edgar, who was the only male royal descendent from Edward the Confessor's family (see family tree on page 13), and he did not want to resort to murder to establish his claim to the English throne. William granted Edgar lands in 1067, but Edgar joined the northern rebellion in 1069 (see page 32), and was forced to flee to Scotland in 1070. King Malcolm of Scotland was more than happy to offer help to Edgar because this would put William at a disadvantage. In return, Edgar agreed that King Malcolm could marry Margaret, Edgar's sister, thus strengthening the ties between them.

In 1072, William led an army into Scotland and Malcolm made peace with him. Edgar was forced to flee to Flanders (in present-day Belgium). However, by 1074, Edgar was back in Scotland and Malcolm was preparing a huge fleet for an invasion of England. The French King Philip I also provided an army to help. All of William's enemies were working together to remove William from power. Unfortunately for Edgar, the weather destroyed the fleet and he was forced to sue for peace. Edgar accepted some land and a position at William's court. From this time on he was never again seen as a real threat to William.

King Malcolm of Scotland and Edgar's sister Margaret had a daughter, Maud. She was married to Henry, the son of King William. This meant that the Norman and Anglo-Saxon households were joined by marriage.

Question time

1   Explain how the diagrams on page 31 show improved defensive fortifications.

2   Why was speed a vital part of William's castle building?

3   Edgar the Ætheling was a blood relative of Edward the Confessor. Why was William not keen to remove him permanently as a claimant to the throne?

4   Why was Malcolm, King of Scotland, happy to help Edgar?

5   William faced threats to his throne from Scotland, Denmark, France and Flanders. He survived all of them. Was this because of:

a   luck

b   mistakes by his enemies

c   good judgement on his part?

Explain your answer.

Governing England

By 1075, most of William's immediate enemies had been defeated, but he still had to secure his kingdom. Introducing the feudal system and building castles were only part of this plan. There were other ways in which he achieved security. Not only did William change the land with castles and with the feudal system, he also changed the way in which matters were governed in England. He recognised that the system of government had to be Norman. Yet he was sensible enough to also realise that, if this Norman system included the best parts of the Anglo-Saxon system, then it was much more likely to be accepted. In order to govern the country William therefore used a system based on Anglo-Saxon and Norman methods.

The shire system

Local government was run under the 'shire system', with a sheriff in charge of each shire:

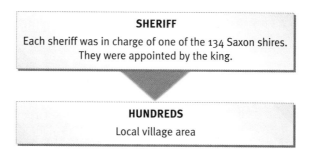

SHERIFF
Each sheriff was in charge of one of the 134 Saxon shires. They were appointed by the king.

HUNDREDS
Local village area

Communities were held responsible for local good order, with occasional visitations by royal commissioners to check that the king's laws were being upheld. Anglo-Saxon laws changed little.

Local customs

William granted a charter to London guaranteeing its local customs. Nothing was to change under the Norman king. William also built the Tower of London – as a symbol of Norman power, which became the centre of administration for the royal court.

The Great Council

William created a Great Council (the Curia Regis), which met three times annually. This replaced the Anglo-Saxon Witan, but had almost the same structure although its members were mostly Norman not Anglo-Saxon. It included:

- tenants-in-chief – William's most important and powerful lords

- a chancellor, in charge of finance

- a justiciar, in charge of justice

- the heads of the royal household staff.

A smaller council, consisting only of some of the tenants-in-chief, also met more frequently. It became known as the Small Council, and was the main advisory and administrative body to the king.

The Church

William used the Church to establish and maintain his supremacy in England.

William was a religious man who felt that the Church in Anglo-Saxon England was in need of reform. He felt it had not kept to the strict teachings of the original Church. He did not believe in married clergy, and he introduced reforms from Cluny in France. Archbishop Stigand and many of the great existing bishops either resigned, were deprived of their bishoprics (the areas over which they had control), or died in prison. They were all replaced by Norman churchmen, who brought in reforms from France. The new Archbishop of Canterbury, Lanfranc, introduced a wave of reforms, including the separation of religious courts and ordinary courts. William then went further in his use of the Church.

- He refused to swear an oath of fealty to the Pope.

- He kept the right to appoint bishops and abbots.

- No papal laws could be put into use in England without the king's permission.

- No tenant-in-chief or royal officer could be excommunicated (thrown out of the Church) without permission of the king.

- Bishops had to attend the Great Council meetings, and were required to do military service or provide the equivalent resources, such as soldiers, for the king.

In this way William made good use of religion to keep control. He was not going to allow the Pope to take control after he had fought so hard to assert his authority.

Question time

1 Construct a chart like the one below which shows what William did to establish his authority, and why his methods were successful.

	What he did	Why it was successful
Administration		
London		
Council		
Church		

Digging deeper

The Domesday Book

In 1085, William decided that it would be good to have an accurate record of the state of his land. He wanted to know who owned what and how much it was worth. He also wanted to know whether the land had changed in the time of his reign. People, land and animals were all counted, so that William could see how wealthy or poor his subjects were.

William sent royal commissioners to all counties to collect this information, which was collected on oath. However, not all counties were represented: records about Lancashire and London do not appear, although there is a large amount of information about most areas of the country.

SOURCE A

The king had great deliberations and very deep speech with his counsellors about this land, how it was occupied and by what men. He then sent his men over all England into each shire, and had it made out how many hides of land were in the shire; what the king himself had in land, and livestock on the land; what dues he had from each property each twelve months from the shire; also he let it be written down how much land his archbishops had, his diocesan bishops, his abbots and his earls – what and how much each man was holding in England, in land, in livestock, and how much money it was worth. So very closely did he let it be searched out that there was not a single hide nor rod of land – nor further, it is shameful to tell though it seemed no shame to him to do it – not an ox, a cow, a pig was left out, that was not set in his documents; and all the documents were brought to him afterwards.

Entry in the Anglo-Saxon Chronicle *for the year 1085.*

The Domesday Book was an important step in the conquest of England because it gave William the information needed to rule the country.

SOURCE B

In the city of York, before 1066 were 6 shires besides the Archbishop's. One of these has been laid waste for the castles. In 5 shires there were 1418 inhabited dwellings. Out of the aforementioned dwellings there are now inhabited in the King's hand, paying customary dues, 400 less 9, both large and small; 400 dwellings not inhabited of which the better ones pay 1 penny and the others less; and 540 dwellings so empty that they pay nothing at all; and the Frenchmen hold 145 dwellings …

A description of York from the Domesday Book.

Question time

1   Make a list of all the information William I wanted his men to collect. Why do you think he wanted this information? How could he use it to strengthen his power?

2   Find out what hides and rods were. (Hint: they are to do with measuring.)

3   Read Source B carefully.

   a   Write a description of York in 1085. Use your own words, not the words of the source.

   b   What can you learn from the source about the ways in which the city had changed since William became king in 1066?

4   This great collection of information, ordered by William the Conqueror, began to be called the 'Domesday Book' quite soon after it was finished. Why do you think that medieval people gave it this name?

5   The 'Domesday Book' was obviously useful to William and his advisers. Explain why it is useful today to historians, geographers, linguists and lawyers.

*Rochester castle in Kent,
built shortly after the
Norman conquest
of England.*

1066 as a turning point

1066 is rightly seen as a turning point in English history. It was the start of what became known as the Norman period. If William had not been a strong king, he might simply have been one more ruler in a line of ever-changing monarchs, as had happened many times before. Although the Scandinavians and the Anglo-Saxons had both ruled England for a number of years, William managed to establish many important changes in England. Indeed, the most important aspect of William's rule was that he changed areas of life which could not easily be changed back, and it was therefore less likely that the population would want to return to Anglo-Saxon ways. The people who opposed William opposed him because he was Norman, but they did not seem to offer any real alternative to his rule. With his new systems that incorporated the old ways, William appeared to offer stability and, therefore, the best of both worlds.

Whilst the feudal system and castles might appear to us today simply as ways of keeping the population under control, they also created an ordered and stable world. In return for this stability and protection, the people of England had to follow William's laws. For the vast majority of people, this was a relatively small price to pay. However, the larger elaborate castles which survive today were not only used to control the population, they were also built for the benefit and glorification of a few lords. In this respect, castles became instruments, not of the king's domination, but of the game of politics between the king and his lords. When this happened, the people really did suffer, as in the later period of 1135–54 when the throne of England was once again disputed – this time between two cousins, Stephen and Matilda (see page 44).

When William died in 1087 he left a prosperous and stable kingdom. The only problem was who should be king next? William had three sons: his eldest son Robert was given rule of Normandy; his second son William inherited the kingdom of England; his third son Henry was given no land, but immense wealth. This division shows that the Normans still thought of Normandy as being more important than England. The strength of the Norman monarchy is shown by the fact that it was able to deal with the problem of succession to the English throne, and continued to prosper after William's death.

William II died in 1100 and his brother Henry became King of England. By 1106, Henry defeated his brother Robert in a battle at Avranches, on 28 September, exactly 40 years after the Battle of Hastings. With Henry's success, England and Normandy were once again united under a single king. Norman rule looked set to continue in England.

Assessment section

1   Make a list of the ways in which William I strengthened his hold and consolidated his power in England. Put them in order of importance, with the most important at the top of the list and the least important at the bottom. Write a paragraph to explain your decisions.

Now compare your list with a partner's list. Are they the same? If they are, find a partner who has a different order. Now discuss why you think differently about the importance of methods William used to consolidate his power.

You could go on like this all round the class, until you have a class list and order with which you agree.

2   Research, using the Internet and reference books, the different weapons and methods that were used to attack castles. Write a few lines describing each one.

Now design a castle that would be capable of resisting attacks from these weapons. Draw up a battle strategy that could swing into place once attackers were sighted.

3   'William I was a ruthless tyrant who cruelly imposed Norman rule on the English people.'

'William I was a good king who brought peace, order and prosperity to England.'

With which of these two opinions do you agree, and why?

4   'History is written by the winners.'

Using all the sources and information in this chapter, say whether you agree that this is true of Norman times. (Remember to take 'written' in its widest sense to include buildings and artefacts.)

5   How different do you think England would have been if Harold had won the Battle of Hastings?

Further reading

Hilda Lewis, *Harold was my King* (Oxford University Press, 1968)

A.E. Marston, *Wolves of Savernake* (Headline, 1994)

Henry Treece, *Hounds of the King* (Longman, 1973)

The monarchy

All successful monarchs are not successful for the same reasons. If we think about the monarchs of England during the Middle Ages, it quickly becomes clear that there is a divide between those who have a reputation as a good monarch, and those who have a reputation as a bad monarch.

Some of them have nicknames:

- William I – 'The Conqueror'
- William II – 'Rufus'
- Henry I – 'Beauclerc'
- Richard I – 'The Lionheart'
- John I – 'Lackland'

It is easy to pick out the ones who have a very positive reputation. Maybe this explains why there has been only one King John!

Question time

1. What qualities should a medieval monarch have? Look at the list below, and pick out five which you think are the most important:

   Determined   **Clever**   **Brave**   **Far-sighted**

   Attractive   **Cunning**   **Ruthless**   **Tactful**

   Devious   **Cruel**   **Honest**   **Arrogant**

2. Compare your list with that of your partner. Are they different? Talk about why, and decide on a list with which you both agree.

3. Now look back at William the Conqueror. Did he display the five qualities on which you have agreed?

   For each of the qualities you have chosen, find something he did that shows how important this quality was in helping him rule successfully.

4. Think about monarchs in the twenty-first century. They have to do a very different job from their ancestors in medieval times. What qualities should modern monarchs have? Are these different from the qualities medieval monarchs needed? Why?

History hall of fame

The monarchs of England, 1066–1216.

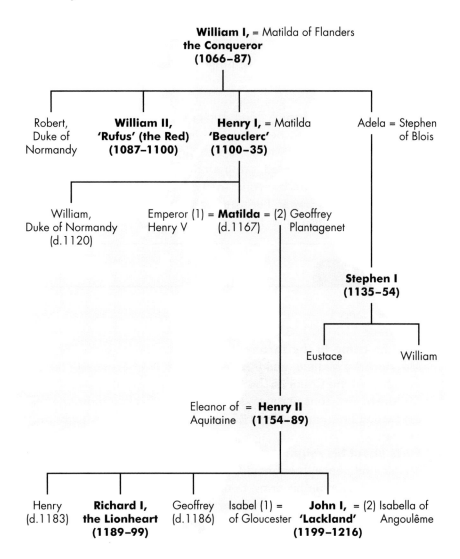

William I, = Matilda of Flanders
the Conqueror
(1066–87)

Robert,
Duke of
Normandy

William II,
'Rufus' (the Red)
(1087–1100)

Henry I, = Matilda
'Beauclerc'
(1100–35)

Adela = Stephen
of Blois

William,
Duke of Normandy
(d.1120)

Emperor (1) = **Matilda** = (2) Geoffrey
Henry V   (d.1167)   Plantagenet

Stephen I
(1135–54)

Eustace   William

Eleanor of = **Henry II**
Aquitaine   **(1154–89)**

Henry
(d.1183)

Richard I,
the Lionheart
(1189–99)

Geoffrey
(d.1186)

Isabel (1) =
of Gloucester

John I, = (2) Isabella of
'Lackland'   Angoulême
(1199–1216)

FACTFILE

Name: William the Conqueror (sometimes William the Bastard)
Reigned: 1066 to 1087
How he came to the throne: Defeated King Harold at the Battle of Hastings, 1066
Married: Matilda of Flanders in 1053
Children: Ten children: six daughters and four sons
Facts about his reign: William is seen as a good king because he was successful. He conquered England, kept control of the country and ruled until the end of his reign in 1087. He established the Norman monarchy in England which lasted for a long time. He brought Norman laws and government systems to England and left sons to rule after him.

Name: William Rufus
Reigned: 1087 to 1100
How he came to the throne: Inherited the throne on his father's death
Married: No
Children: Rumours of one illegitimate son

Facts about his reign: A good soldier and administrator, William ruled England justly and reached workable relations with the kings and princes of Scotland and Wales as well as, eventually, his brother Robert in Normandy. He was, however, opinionated, arrogant and bad tempered and this is where his nickname 'Rufus' (which means 'the Red') comes from. He had little respect for the Church and tried to reduce its power. Because of this the early chronicles, which were written by monks, tend to blacken his name. His death in the New Forest was either an accident or murder.

Name: Henry I
Reigned: 1100 to 1135
How he came to the throne: Inherited the throne on his brother's death
Married: (1) Matilda, daughter of Malcolm III of Scotland and (2) Adeliza, daughter of the Count of Louvain
Children: Two sons and two daughters from his first marriage; none from his second marriage; at least 25 illegitimate children by eight or more other women

Facts about his reign: A highly capable king and successful in warfare. Maintained peace throughout England during his long reign, though he taxed the people heavily to maintain his army. Established the Crown Exchequer – the basis for the later Treasury. A learned man, his nickname was 'Beauclerc' which means 'fine scholar'. His two elder legitimate sons, William and Richard, drowned in 1120 and Henry tried hard to get the barons to recognise his daughter Matilda as his heir. But, after his death, civil war broke out between the supporters of Matilda and her cousin, Stephen, who claimed the throne.

Name: Stephen I
Reigned: 1135 to 1154
How he came to the throne: Inherited the throne on his uncle's death
Married: Matilda, daughter of the Count of Boulogne, in 1125
Children: Three daughters and two sons; five illegitimate children

Facts about his reign: King Stephen was Henry I's nearest male heir. He was accepted as King of England by some nobles, but there was a civil war between Stephen and Henry I's daughter, Matilda, throughout his reign. This war destroyed England's prosperity. Stephen was a weak king because he was too easily persuaded by people, and nobody trusted him. He was replaced as king by Matilda's son, Henry – Henry I's grandson.

FACTFILE

Name: Henry II
Reigned: 1154 to 1189
How he came to the throne: Inherited the throne from Stephen after his uncle was deemed unsuitable to rule as king
Married: Eleanor, daughter of the Duke of Aquitaine, in 1152
Children: Eight children and 12 illegitimate children
Facts about his reign: Henry II is seen as a very successful king. During his reign he built up a huge empire. The land he controlled stretched through all of England, into parts of Wales, Ireland and large areas of France. He had a number of sons, but this proved to be a problem as each of them in turn rebelled against him and worked with Henry's foreign enemies to disrupt his kingdom. By the end of his reign Henry was an unhappy king with sons who warred against each other.

FACTFILE

Name: Richard the Lionheart
Reigned: 1189 to 1199
How he came to the throne: Inherited the throne from his father, Henry II
Married: Berengaria, daughter of the King of Navarre, in 1191
Children: No children
Facts about his reign: Richard the Lionheart is often seen as a good king. He was strong and brave and went to fight for Christianity in the Holy Wars (Crusades) in the Middle East. However, he can also be seen as a bad king because he was away from his country during much of his reign. It is estimated that he spent only seven months of his ten-year-long reign in England. He also had to be ransomed (money paid for his release) when he was held hostage on his return from the Crusades. This money came from taxing the people of England.

FACTFILE

Name: John
Reigned: 1199 to 1216
How he came to the throne: Inherited the throne on his brother, Richard's, death
Married: (1) Isabel, daughter of the Earl of Gloucester in 1189 (divorced); (2) Isabella, daughter of the Count of Angoulême in 1200
Children: None from his first marriage; five from his second marriage; at least 12 illegitimate children
Facts about his reign: Nicknamed 'Lackland' because his elder brothers initially inherited the land in France and England; John was never accepted as king in the French territories. Fair to his English subjects, he worked hard to ensure that the law was properly administered. He created enemies by refusing to take the authority of others seriously, and angered the barons by taxing them heavily. He also angered the Church by refusing to accept the Pope's choice of archbishop. In 1215 the barons forced John to sign the Magna Carta, which guaranteed them and all freemen certain rights. Headstrong, selfish and prone to stir up civil war, many have regarded John as a bad king. His nine-year-old son, Henry III, inherited the throne on his death.

Question time

1 Copy this table into your file and fill it in, using the information in this chapter.

Monarch	Positive points	Bad points
William the Conqueror		
William Rufus		
Henry I		
Stephen		
Henry II		
Richard		
John		

2 a Are there any points which all kings have in common?

b Can you draw any conclusions about what made a good king and what made a bad king in medieval times?

3 a Find out as much as you can about King Stephen. You will need to use the library and the Internet.

b Make a timeline of Stephen's reign.

c Stephen was not a very successful king. Do you think that this was due to bad luck, or was Stephen himself to blame?

Digging deeper

What was wrong with Queen Matilda?

Look back to the royal family tree on page 41. You will see that all of the monarchs of the Middle Ages were men. Indeed, from 1066 until 1553, there were no female monarchs in England. Part of the reason for this is that people had very different ideas about women during that time. Matilda inherited the throne from her father in 1135, and she might have proved a very effective monarch had she not been considered unfit to rule, simply because she was a woman. How did Matilda come to inherit the throne, and why was she seen as being unfit to rule?

Henry had four legitimate children – two sons and two daughters, and so the succession, even after the death of his wife in 1118, must have seemed to him to have been secure. Henry was extremely proud of his elder son, who had fought alongside him in Normandy when only 17 years old, and was seen as the 'rising star' of the royal court. It seemed that William would provide England with a strong monarchy when Henry died. However, this was not to be. In 1120, William and his younger brother Richard were drowned in the English Channel whilst returning from France, in what is known as the White Ship disaster. Some 300 people drowned alongside him, many of them important members of the royal court. It is said that, after King Henry heard of the death of his sons, he never smiled again.

An oath of loyalty to Matilda

With William and Richard dead, Henry was left with no male heir to the throne. Desperate to ensure that the succession continued through his family line, he made the barons swear an oath of allegiance to his daughter Matilda. They promised that, on his death, Matilda would become queen.

To improve her chances as the future queen, Henry next set about finding Matilda a suitable husband. He had married her, when she was 12 years old, to the German Emperor Henry V. Brought up strictly in the German court, Matilda returned to England in 1125 when her husband died. Haughty and arrogant, she knew little of England and English ways. Her father began looking again for a husband for her. His choice was Prince Geoffrey of Anjou and Maine, whom Matilda married in June 1128.

While Geoffrey was blessed with wealthy French lands and a respectable title, this match was not the happiest one for Matilda. Geoffrey was only 14 years old when he married the 24-year-old Matilda. It is also reported that Matilda and Geoffrey never really got on. Despite this lack of affection, their marriage was successful in that Matilda gave birth to three sons in four years. This strengthened the chances of Henry I's royal line continuing after his death.

Stephen claims the English throne

Henry I died in 1135. However, Matilda was in France at the time of her father's death and, before she could officially be crowned as queen, her cousin Stephen claimed the throne for himself.

Stephen had been one of Henry I's favourites, and the king had awarded him lands in both Normandy and England. By the time Henry died, his nephew had become the wealthiest man in the country. While Henry lived, Stephen publicly swore to recognise Matilda as the rightful heir to the English throne. However, secretly he thought her unsuitable to rule because she was a woman, and began gathering support for his claim. There were many men in the realm who shared Stephen's views on women rulers, and it

A picture of Matilda from a medieval manuscript.

was not long before he had the support of the barons and the papacy. On 22 December 1135, Stephen was crowned king in London.

Civil war breaks out

Matilda was not going to give up her claim to the throne without a fight, and set about raising support for her cause. After four years of civil war, Matilda's forces managed to win a victory at the Battle of Lincoln in February 1141, and Stephen was captured. Matilda then claimed the throne for herself, being declared queen, or 'Lady of the English'. However, she made herself very unpopular with her subjects, who hated her for her arrogant manner. The people of London therefore rose up against their new queen, and refused to crown her officially. Instead, they expelled Matilda from London and joined with Stephen's forces. It was not long before Stephen was declared king again.

SOURCE B

Matilda sent for the richest men and demanded from them a huge sum of money, not with gentleness, but with the voice of authority. They complained that they did not have any money left because of the war. When the people said this, Matilda, with a grim look, her forehead wrinkled into a frown, every trace of a woman's gentleness removed from her face, blazed into unbearable fury.

Contemporary description of Queen Matilda.

Queen Matilda had been rejected by the English people, and she returned to France. However, she did not stop plotting against her cousin.

King Stephen was a wealthy man and a nephew of Henry I; in this respect his claim to the English throne was a strong one. However, he proved to be a very weak monarch. Stephen was very mild-mannered and indecisive, and did not stand up to barons who opposed him. During his reign, he failed to keep law and order, and many barons seized property illegally. To avoid creating trouble, Stephen also signed away land in France, Scotland and Wales, and this made him very unpopular.

SOURCE C

In the days of this King there was nothing but strife, evil, and robbery, for quickly the great men who were traitors rose against him. When the traitors saw that Stephen was a good-humoured, kindly, and easy-going man who inflicted no punishment, then they committed all manner of horrible crimes ... And so it lasted for nineteen years while Stephen was King, till the land was all undone and darkened with such deeds, and men said openly that Christ and his angels slept.

The Anglo-Saxon Chronicle *describes England during the reign of King Stephen.*

Who succeeds Stephen?

Stephen and Matilda had fought over the English throne. Both had proved to be unpopular with their subjects. Stephen was seen as a weak king, lacking in authority and considered too much of a push-over. However, he was the preferred choice to Matilda, who was disliked for her arrogance. Matilda was also seen as a weak option simply because she was a woman – as far as her English subjects were concerned, women weren't meant to be monarchs.

Stephen wanted his son Eustace to succeed him as king; Matilda wanted her son Henry to inherit the throne. In the end, Eustace died before Stephen and a compromise was reached. Matilda would not oppose Stephen as king on the condition that her son Henry was named heir to the throne. When Stephen died in 1154, Matilda's son was therefore crowned King Henry II of England.

 Question time

1 Why do you think that women were seen to be unfit to rule during the Middle Ages?

2 Read Source B. The author wanted people to support Stephen. How does the author make Matilda appear in a bad light?

3 What evidence is there that Matilda would have made a good monarch? What evidence is there that Matilda would have made a bad monarch?

4 Read the facts about King Stephen. Why do you think that being mild-mannered was a bad quality for a medieval king?

What makes a good monarch?

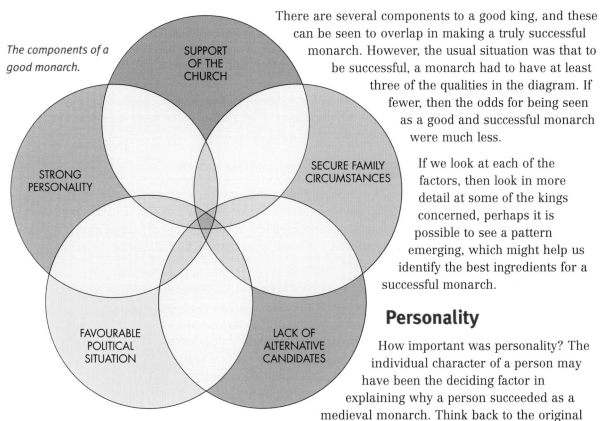

The components of a good monarch.

SUPPORT OF THE CHURCH

STRONG PERSONALITY

SECURE FAMILY CIRCUMSTANCES

FAVOURABLE POLITICAL SITUATION

LACK OF ALTERNATIVE CANDIDATES

There are several components to a good king, and these can be seen to overlap in making a truly successful monarch. However, the usual situation was that to be successful, a monarch had to have at least three of the qualities in the diagram. If fewer, then the odds for being seen as a good and successful monarch were much less.

If we look at each of the factors, then look in more detail at some of the kings concerned, perhaps it is possible to see a pattern emerging, which might help us identify the best ingredients for a successful monarch.

Personality

How important was personality? The individual character of a person may have been the deciding factor in explaining why a person succeeded as a medieval monarch. Think back to the original words which we used to describe those qualities a monarch should have (see page 40). Now look at the list below. Compare the list of positive personal qualities with those that are less attractive. Think how these qualities would make a monarch a successful or a poor ruler.

Good qualities	Bad qualities
Brave	Cowardly
Strong willed	Weak willed
Clever	Lazy
Good with words	Shy
Honest	Deceitful
Attractive	Ruthless
Charming	Greedy

If a monarch was thought to have a bad personality, i.e. was greedy or lazy, then this was often seen as sufficient reason to get rid of him. In many ways, the personality of the king has become more important than what he did. Read the following sources which describe the personal qualities of monarchs. Remember that King John is one monarch who has been portrayed as being a bad king. Even in children's poetry and literature King John is portrayed in a negative light (see Source C). Sources C and D show that the 'badness' of King John is entirely due to his personality. If we look at John's behaviour, however, it was no worse than most leaders of the time; indeed he seems to have behaved better than 'good' King Richard the Lionheart.

SOURCE A

At Pentecost was seen, in a village in Berkshire, blood welling from the earth, as many said who had seen it. Thereafter, on the morning after Lammas, King William [Rufus] at the hunt was shot dead with an arrow by one of his own men, and after brought to Winchester, and buried in that bishopric; that was the thirteenth year that he had the kingdom.

He was very harsh and fierce with his men, his land and all his neighbours, and very much feared. He was ever agreeable to evil men's advice, and through his own greed he was ever vexing [bothering] this nation with force and with unjust taxes. Therefore in his days all justice declined; every injustice arose before God and the world. God's churches he oppressed, and when the heads of bishoprics and abbacies passed on, he either sold all for money or held it in his own hands and let it out for rent, because he meant to be the heir of every man, clerical or lay; so that the day he fell, he had in his own hands the archbishopric of Canterbury and that of Winchester, Salisbury and eleven abbacies, all let out for rent. And though I stretch it out long, all that was hateful to God and just men, all that was customary in his day. Therefore he was to nearly all his people hateful, and abominable to God. So his end revealed, because in the middle of his wrongs, without repentance or any amendment for his deeds, he died.

Extract from the Anglo-Saxon Chronicle, *1100, about William Rufus.*

SOURCE B

Members of the cast from the 1950 film 'Rogues of Sherwood Forest'. Bad Prince John (George Macready) stands on the left next to Maid Marion (Diana Lynn) and Robin Hood (John Derek).

SOURCE C

King John was not a good man – He had his little ways.
And sometimes no one spoke to him for days and days and days.
And men who came across him, When walking in the town, Gave him a supercilious stare,
Or passed with noses in the air –
And bad King John stood dumbly there, Blushing beneath his crown.

King John's Christmas *by A. A. Milne, 1927.*

SOURCE D

King John was probably the worst king ever to mount the English throne. He was cruel and treacherous, a boastful coward; mean and deceitful as a man, utterly untrustworthy as a king. He died loathed by everyone who knew him, regretted by none.

Extract from King John and the Magna Carta *(Wills and Hepworth, 1969).*

Question time

1 Read Source A. Make a list of all the complaints about William Rufus.

2 List all the words or phrases in Source A that suggest William deserved his end.

3 Source A was written by a monk. Does this mean it is telling the truth about William Rufus?

4 How is King John portrayed in Sources C and D? Use words from the sources to support your answer.

Stability under William the Conqueror

England had been conquered by William the Conqueror, and the Norman monarchy had been accepted only after a number of rebellions (see pages 32–4). However, William the Conqueror had ultimately been seen as a just king. His obituary (death notice) in the *Anglo-Saxon Chronicle* reflects the fact that, although he was harsh, he did ensure that law and order prevailed (see Source E).

SOURCE E

Among other things, it is not to be forgotten that good peace he made in this land, so that a man of any account might fare over the kingdom with a bosom full of gold unmolested; and no man dared kill man, even if he had done much evil to him.

Extract from the Anglo-Saxon Chronicle, *1087*

Trouble during the reign of William Rufus

Support for William the Conqueror was very hard won, and was not automatically passed on to his son William Rufus, who inherited the throne of England on the death of his father in 1087. William Rufus was replaced by his brother Henry in 1100, and Henry's reign is portrayed in a more positive light. Perhaps the events of William Rufus's reign can give us clues as to why it tends to be overshadowed by both his father and his brother. Read the timeline below, which shows the events of the reign of William Rufus.

A detailed timeline showing the life of William Rufus.

DATE	EVENT	DETAILS
Sept 1087	Accession and coronation	William II, or William 'Rufus', succeeded his father to the English throne, and was crowned King of England in Westminster Abbey. However, he did not have the full loyalty of the barons because William and his elder brother Robert, who inherited Normandy, were always quarrelling. Barons with land in England and Normandy were torn between loyalty to William and loyalty to Robert.
1088	Rebellion	A number of Anglo-Norman barons rebelled against William Rufus. They believed that, whilst Normandy and England were governed by separate rulers, there would be no stability.
1091	William II and Robert united	Quarrelling between William and Robert stopped as they united against the rebellion of their younger brother Henry.
1093	A new Archbishop of Canterbury	William II was wary of giving Church men too much power, and did not want them meddling in political affairs. In 1093, Anselm of Bec was made Archbishop of Canterbury. This appointment proved to be a disaster for William, since Bec called for Church men to become more politically aware.
1094	Extravagant court life	William was not religious and his court was full of merriment. The court was also full of people hoping to gain the king's favour. Of these, William's favourite was Ranulf Flambard, who used Church money illegally.
1094	Unpopular with the Church	William became very unpopular with the Church. During his reign he increased taxation on the Church, and sold Church positions to the highest bidder rather than filling them by appointment.
1095	Conspiracy	William faced a plot to replace him with his brother Robert Curthose, Duke of Normandy.
1095	Council of Rockingham	Following a ruling by the Pope that all Church men must firstly be loyal to their Pope and put their king second, William called a council – the Council of Rockingham – to deal with the ever increasing problems between himself and his Archbishop of Canterbury, Anselm of Bec.
1096	Curthose leases Normandy to William	William's brother Robert decided that he would like to join the Pope's crusade to recover Jerusalem from the Muslims. To raise the money to equip a force for the crusade, he decided to lease Normandy to William for 10,000 marks.

DATE	EVENT	DETAILS
1096	**William takes Normandy**	Although Robert had only leased Normandy to William, William had no intention of giving the land back. He then made plans to recover more French lands for England – Maine and the Vexin, both of which had been part of William I's Normandy, but had been lost to the French by Robert.
1097	**Anselm of Bec leaves England**	The Archbishop of Canterbury, Anselm of Bec, decided that he had had enough of William Rufus. He sailed from Dover to France, leaving the estates of Canterbury in the king's hands.
1099	**Land gains in Normandy**	William II succeeded in recovering Maine and the Vexin, the land lost by Robert to France.
1099	**Bishop of Durham**	The king's favourite, Ranulf Flambard, was made Bishop of Durham. The appointment of a man who had no respect for the Church to this important position made the people of England angry.
2 Aug 1100	**William II killed**	William was mysteriously killed by an arrow while hunting in the New Forest. The murder is surrounded with mystery. William's younger brother Henry was in the forest at the same time.

Perhaps the most important reason why William II is not seen as being a good king, is because his obituary was written by his enemies. Although Anselm of Bec left England in 1097, which might be seen as a victory for William, their dispute helped to give William Rufus a terrible reputation. This is because, in the eleventh century, it was Church men who wrote biographies of kings. As the information in the timeline shows, William was hated by the Church men of his day – for many reasons. They even disliked his preference for long hair, which they thought was a sign of immorality and effeminacy (the opposite of manliness). They also disapproved of William's tendency for indulgence, frivolity and extravagance, especially because he seemed to think religion so unimportant. Because the biographies of William Rufus were written by Church men, who hated him, they were therefore often extremely biased.

How to be a king according to Henry I

Henry was born to William I and Matilda of Flanders at Selby, Yorkshire, in September 1068. Meanwhile, Henry's brother Robert arrived back from the Crusades and returned to Normandy. When his father died his other brother – William – inherited England. Henry inherited no land on the death of his father, but received £5000 in silver. Jealous of his brothers' positions, he played each of them off against each other, and they subsequently barred him from the succession.

Grab the throne when you can

On 2 August 1100, William II was mysteriously killed by an arrow while hunting in the New Forest. Henry immediately grasped the opportunities his brother's death created. Robert was away on crusade at the time, and Henry immediately rode to Winchester and took control of the treasury. He then gained support by emphasising his Englishness in comparison to his 'Norman' brother Robert. The following day, 3 August 1100, Henry was declared King of England. He was crowned at Winchester on 5 and 6 August. Despite the suspicious circumstances surrounding William's death, nobody accused Henry of the murder of his brother.

Gain popularity

In August 1100, Henry issued a Charter of Liberties criticising William Rufus's oppressive rule and promising a return to good and fair government. That same month, William II's favourite, Ranulf Flambard, was imprisoned for the cruelty he had shown the English people – a very popular move since Ranulf had made many enemies. Then, to gain the support of the barons, Henry recalled from exile Anselm Bec, the Archbishop of Canterbury – though Anselm continued to make problems for the English monarch.

In November 1100, Henry married Matilda, daughter of Malcolm Canmore, King of Scotland, at Westminster Abbey. Matilda's mother Margaret was the sister of Edgar Ætheling, the last royal Saxon descendant, and her father was Malcolm III of Scotland (see family tree on page 13). The marriage represented the union of the Normans and Saxons, and was therefore very popular with the English people. A daughter, Adelaide (Matilda), was born to Henry I in 1102, and a son, William Ætheling, in 1103.

Henry was careful not to upset the Church. In October 1100, he invited the Archbishop of Canterbury, Anselm of Bec, to return from exile, even though he was troublesome for the king. Then, in 1107, he reached an agreement with the Church that meant he gave up appointing Church men. However, Henry insisted that Church men would continue to pay homage to him. In practice the king's wishes were to remain the main factor in the making of bishops, but Henry's co-operation with the Church improved relations between the monarch and the Church. Then, in 1109, Anselm of Bec died. Henry did not replace him so decided to keep the position of Archbishop of Canterbury vacant. After the problems caused by Anselm of Bec, Henry did not want further confrontation with the Church.

Defeat rebellion and win battles

When Henry's brother Robert arrived back from the Crusades, returning to Normandy, he was angered by his brother's usurpation of what should have been his inheritance. Robert landed at Portsmouth in July 1101 to lay claim to the English throne. However, war was avoided after long negotiations, and a peace treaty was signed. The terms of the treaty were that Henry should keep England but pay his brother a pension of 2000 marks per year.

In the following years, Henry managed to remove many of Robert's supporters from England. Then, in September 1106, Henry succeeded in defeating Robert's, army at the Battle of Trenchbrai. Robert was captured and spent the rest of his life as his brother's prisoner. Normandy once again became part of England.

In 1107, Robert's young son, William Clito, was put forward as rightful Duke of Normandy. His claim was backed by Louis VI of France and Count Fulk V of Anjou. Henry was forced to return to Normandy where he successfully defended his claim to be Duke of Normandy. That year, in order to protect his lands, Henry married eight of his illegitimate daughters to princes of lands neighbouring Normandy.

The situation in Normandy remained stable for some time after that, and Henry regularly travelled across the English Channel. However, in 1118, trouble flared up again. Henry spent the whole year in Normandy defending it against attack from the King of France, the Count of Anjou and the Count of Flanders. All this cost money and the people in England were continually taxed all year instead of on special occasions such as harvest.

Show good political sense

Henry was keen to improve relationships with foreign countries through marriage. In 1107, King Alexander of Scotland married Sybilla, the illegitimate daughter of Henry. Then, in January 1114, Henry's legitimate daughter Adelaide married the Emperor of Germany, Henry V, at Mainz in Germany. Her name was changed to Matilda on the same day. She was crowned Empress of Germany as part of the wedding ceremony.

Henry was known as 'Henry Beauclerc' (fine scholar). This suggests that Henry had a good brain, and, indeed, his parents had made sure he had a good education because, as a younger son, he was destined for a career in the Church. One of the most famous changes Henry introduced was in about 1100, when he set up a financial-counting system using a large chequered cloth. The royal treasurer and officials argued general policy and specific expenditure plans across this cloth. It grew into an efficient department for the collection of royal revenues, known as the 'exchequer' – a name still used by politicians today.

Because Henry spent a considerable amount of time in Normandy, he created the position of justiciar. The justiciar was the most trusted of all the king's officials, who took charge of England when the king was away.

Roger of Salisbury was the first justiciar. He helped Henry to set up the Exchequer and, when the king was absent, he led meetings of the Exchequer. Henry also gave other court officials the power to judge local financial disputes and to bring sheriffs into order. In such ways, Henry entrusted his loyal and talented subjects with authority, and this helped him to maintain control of his realm whilst abroad.

Tackle any problems over the succession

On 1 May 1118, Henry's wife Matilda died at the palace of Westminster. She was buried in Westminster Abbey. Two years later, Henry's son, William Æetheling, was created Duke of Normandy. However, disaster struck in November 1120 with the White Ship disaster (see page 44). This ship, carrying a drunken party of 300 noblemen, including William Æetheling, sank with no survivors. When William Æetheling died, along with his brother Richard, Henry had no remaining legitimate male heir to succeed him. In 1121, Henry therefore remarried, to Adelaide of Louvain, in the hope that he would produce a male heir. However, their marriage bore no children, so Henry had to settle his succession elsewhere.

In 1125, the Emperor of Germany died, and Matilda, Henry's only surviving legitimate daughter, was recalled to England. Henry then made the barons swear their allegiance to Matilda as the rightful Queen of England in the event of his death. To secure Matilda's claim to the throne, Henry arranged a marriage alliance between his daughter Matilda and the son of Count Fulk of Anjou, Geoffrey Plantagenet. Matilda was married to the 14-year-old Geoffrey in June 1128 (see page 45). A son, Henry, was born to Matilda and Geoffrey Plantagenet, at Le Mans, Anjou on 5 March 1133. However, relations between Henry I and his daughter and son-in-law were not good. By 1134, Henry I was openly quarrelling with his daughter and son-in-law. Those barons who were loyal to the king thus found themselves in opposition to Henry's chosen heirs.

Henry I died on 1 December 1135. He was 67 years old. He was buried in Reading Abbey, leaving his daughter Matilda to do battle with her cousin Stephen over the English throne (see pages 45–6). Henry's reign had lasted 35 years, which was a good innings for a Norman monarch.

William Rufus and Henry I

The timeline and the information that you have gathered show that a mixture of determination and external events combined to give Henry I the opportunity to become a successful king. William Rufus, on the other hand, seems to have encountered less favourable events during his reign. This, coupled with a less forceful personality, may have resulted in William Rufus being remembered as a bad king.

Question time

1. Look through the events in the timeline for William Rufus and in the life of Henry I. Factors such as war, marriage, unexpected events, religion and the politics of other countries are said to make things happen.

   - Put each factor in the centre of a page and draw a mind map which shows the events related to this factor.

   - For each factor, shade the events with one of two colours; one colour for a positive effect on the monarch and one colour for a negative effect on the monarch.

   - Your diagram should show that neither king had completely positive events in their reign, and neither had completely negative events.

2. Henry I was not fond of his brothers, playing them off against each other, and they barred him from the succession. Henry was with his brother William Rufus when he died in mysterious circumstances, and wasted no time in claiming the throne on his death. Henry then went to war with his eldest brother Robert and eventually imprisoned him.

   Divide into groups. Imagine that you are Henry I. What arguments would you put forward for this ruthless treatment of your brothers? Refer to the events in Henry's life to support your arguments.

Good king, bad king? Richard the Lionheart and King John

Richard was the third son of King Henry II, but although he was born in England, he never spoke the English language, and was really more French than English. At the age of fifteen he became Duke of Aquitaine, a large province in the south of France which had belonged to his mother, Eleanor of Aquitaine.

Richard soon showed that he meant to rule Aquitaine. When his father interfered in these plans, Richard joined with his brothers, Henry and Geoffrey, in revolt. Although Richard was only sixteen, he proved himself so good a soldier that the king had to invade Aquitaine twice to make Richard obey him.

Richard was a large and powerful man, and became known as *Coeur de Lion*, which means lion-hearted. Unfortunately he was also quarrelsome and very quick-tempered. Only two years after the rebellion in Aquitaine, he quarrelled with his elder brother, Henry, who then invaded Aquitaine with an army. Their father, Henry II, came to Richard's aid, but the war ended when Prince Henry suddenly died.

After Henry's death, Richard became heir to the English throne, and King Henry gave orders that his fourth son, John, should become Duke of Aquitaine. Richard objected, and, assisted by his younger brother, again took up arms against his father. The ingratitude of his youngest son is said to have broken King Henry's heart. He died in France whilst Richard, helped by his brother John, was fighting against him.

Extract from Richard the Lionheart, *(Wills and Hepworth, 1965).*

John was the favourite son of King Henry II, and the younger brother of Richard the Lion Heart. Although Henry gave John everything he asked for, including the revenue from six English counties, he rebelled against Henry and joined the French against his own country. His attempted rebellion was not successful, but his treachery is said to have broken his father's heart.

Extract from King John and the Magna Carta, *(Wills and Hepworth, 1969).*

Question time

1   Read Sources A and B. In Source A, Richard is described as showing 'ingratitude'. In Source B, John is said to have shown 'treachery'. What do each of these two words show about the way in which the authors think about the two kings?

2   Create a table like the one shown below. In the table, list the things for which you could criticise Richard and the things which you think that John did wrong.

Richard	John

Digging deeper

Richard and the Crusades

Richard the Lionheart is best known for his fighting ability. As is suggested by his nickname, it is his courage in battle for which he is best remembered. Although he spoke little English, he was popular with the English people because he had an air of glamour about him. He loved poetry, feasting and tournaments, and could control the English lords. However, Richard took little interest in the government of the country, and probably saw the administrative duties of a monarch as being rather dull. Instead, Richard preferred the glory of battle.

Once Richard became king, he set about becoming the leader of a European Christian army. At that time, an army had been called together by the Pope, who wanted to capture Jerusalem from the Turkish Muslims. This religious military expedition was known as a 'crusade'. The Crusades continued, on and off, for approximately 200 years – from 1096 to 1291 – and are covered in more detail in Chapter 9. When Richard came to the throne, the Third Crusade was being set up. The aim of the crusade was to win back Jerusalem – it had been captured by the Christians in 1096, but was recaptured by the Turks in 1187. Richard joined the Third Crusade in 1189, the year that he became king.

Richard saw the Third Crusade as his great chance to prove his skill in battle. He was considered the best military commander of his day, and was famed for being extremely brave in battle – he liked nothing better than to be in the front. Richard's trademark was his large two-handed sword. Once on the crusade, Richard sent word to England for more money and more men. Money for the high expenses of the crusade was obtained by taxing his English subjects, and by selling important positions of state. Richard even said that he would sell the city of London if he could find anyone to buy it, and various towns obtained valuable charters and rights in exchange for contributions to his finances.

SOURCE C

Richard was now King of England, but he took no interest in the government of the country. During the ten years of his reign, he only spent seven months in his kingdom. His whole interest was in war and fighting.

Extract from Richard the Lion Heart, *(Wills and Hepworth, 1965).*

Despite abandoning his duties as King of England, Richard believed that it was natural that he should join the crusade. By the time Richard came to the throne, King Philip of France and King Frederick of Germany had already raised armies to fight for Jerusalem, and he saw no reason why he shouldn't join them. Before the crusade set off, Frederick of Germany died. This was a bitter blow to the crusade because Richard and Philip would probably have accepted him as leader. From that point on, Philip and Richard spent much of their time arguing. They continued to quarrel on the crusade, and eventually Philip returned home, perhaps because he was jealous of Richard's popularity with the English and French soldiers. Later, Richard returned briefly to England and invaded France, before continuing with his foreign travels.

Richard the Lionheart has gone down in history as a good king. However, by the end of his reign, he had bankrupted the country and been absent for nine years out of ten. These qualities are not those usually associated with a good monarch.

 ## Question time

1 What good points and bad points can you find about Richard in the information given?

2 How might Richard have explained the bad points?

SOURCE D

Medieval painting of Richard I fighting King Philip of France at Gisors.

The crimes of King John

As we have seen previously (pages 48–9), King John has gone down in history as a 'bad king'. Below are listed the 'crimes' of which King John has been found guilty.

Betrayal

- He rebelled against his father Henry II.
- When he rebelled, he joined forces with the French against his father and England.
- He divorced his wife to marry Isabella of Angoulême, who was engaged to be married to a French nobleman.

Incompetence

- He lost all the lands in France which his father Henry II had gained.
- He lost Normandy, the land which William the Conqueror had ruled.
- He was defeated by the French at the Battle of Bouvines. John sent hired soldiers to terrorise the lands of those nobles who had refused to serve him in his disastrous war against France.
- He lost the Crown Jewels in an area of marshland called the Wash.

Brutality

- While his brother King Richard I was away fighting in the Crusades, John taxed the people heavily.
- He probably murdered his nephew Arthur because the child had a better claim to the throne.
- He took hostages to guarantee the nobles would do as he wished. He took their wives and children. Some of them died from starvation whilst imprisoned in John's castles.

Arguing with the wrong people

- He had an argument with the Pope, the head of the Catholic Church. The Pope punished John by banning all church services. This included marriages, christenings and funerals. Religion and the Church played a very important role in people's lives in the Middle Ages, so this frightened the people of England, and they hated John for bringing this about.
- He was eventually forced to submit to the Pope. This was very humiliating.

These crimes are many, and some may seem terrible, but they need to be considered in the light of events at the time. We need to consider that, what was considered acceptable behaviour for a monarch in the Middle Ages, might be seen as terrible and immoral behaviour today. Also, when we compare John's actions to those of Richard, he does not appear to be much worse.

Question time

1   Look at the list of crimes of King John. For each of the 'offences', say why this would cause King John to have a poor reputation.

2   Write a speech for the prosecution council which condemns John as a poor king of England.

King Richard v. King John

Was King John such a bad king? What did he do that was so different from other kings?

Typical behaviour?

- Although John rebelled against his father Henry II, so did all the sons of Henry II. Richard I first rebelled against his brother at the age of 16. He often joined forces with his other brothers, and his mother Eleanor of Aquitaine encouraged all her children to revolt against their father.

- When John rebelled, he joined forces with the French against his father. However, Richard was also capable of allying with any group that would help his cause.

- John divorced his wife to marry another woman, Isabella of Angoulême, who was already engaged to be married to a French nobleman. Richard also divorced his wife, because he claimed she had already been his father's mistress.

Double standards?

- While Richard was away fighting in the Crusades, John imposed heavy taxes on the people. However, Richard was just as bad because he obtained money by many illegal taxes and sold even the highest positions of government to pay for his wars.

- It was widely believed that King John murdered his nephew Arthur because he had a better claim to the throne. However, war was a bloodthirsty business and John's personal guilt was never proved. He was accused of killing Arthur by burning out his eyes, but this does not seem a very efficient way of killing him. Killing the claimants to the throne was a time honoured way of easing your path to the throne. (Remember, Henry I was never accused of murdering his brother William Rufus although the circumstances surrounding his death were very suspicious – see page 52.)

- John took hostages to guarantee the nobles would do as he wished. He took their wives and children. Some of them died from starvation in John's castles. However, taking hostages was a normal part of medieval warfare.

- John argued with the head of the Catholic Church, the Pope, but Richard went further and forced the Church to sell its precious objects. Also, the Cistercian monks were forced to give up the whole year's sale of wool to pay for Richard's ransom when he was captured on his return from the Crusades.

- John was eventually forced to submit to the Pope, but then Richard never really had to deal with the Pope because he was always away from England fighting the Crusades. The Pope could hardly fall out with Richard if he was fighting on behalf of Christianity.

People make mistakes

- John lost all the lands in France which his father Henry II had gained, but, while Richard was away fighting in the Crusades, Philip II of France became Richard's sworn enemy. As a result, Philip left the Crusades early, returned to France and invaded Normandy. After the Crusades, Richard returned to England, raised another army and invaded France. He started to reconquer the lands in Normandy, but was killed at Chinon.

- Although John was defeated by the French at the Battle of Bouvines, and sent hired soldiers to terrorise the lands of those nobles who had refused to serve him, Richard also fought a bloody war against Philip in France. French lands were ruined and desolated, and whole areas were burnt to the ground.

- Whereas John lost the Crown Jewels, the cost of Richard's ransom was £100,000. This was a huge sum of money, and taxes were made even higher to pay for it. The treasures of the Church were melted down and sold.

If we compare the actions of King John with those of his elder brother King Richard, then John's actions do not seem as bad. We also gain another view if we compare the consequences of each of the reigns.

The king's legacy?

By the end of his reign, Richard had bankrupted the country and had been absent for nine years out of ten. He had left the rule of his country to the nobles so that he could concentrate on achieving military glory in foreign lands. During Richard's absence, the nobles had therefore ruled their areas without deferring to the king's authority. This meant that their power increased during Richard's reign. On Richard's death, the nobles were not happy with the idea of a king wanting to completely control their decisions again. This meant that the scene was set for a confrontation between the nobles and their new king, Richard's younger brother King John.

During John's reign, the barons came into conflict with the king. By the end of his reign, King John was hated by everybody. The barons, the Church and the general population had all suffered in some way, and it looked as though there might be civil war. The Archbishop of Canterbury, the most important Church man in the country, persuaded the barons that they should join together to try to force King John into agreeing to some changes in the way the country was governed. King John was forced to agree to this, and signed a document known as the Magna Carta in 1215 (this is covered in more detail in Chapter 5). This document granted certain rights and freedoms to the people of England, which have lasted to this day:

- The Magna Carta limited the actions of the king, so that he had to listen to others and he could not imprison or execute people at will (see Source E).

- Taxes were fixed and could not be increased without the permission of the barons and bishops.

- The monarch could no longer demand whatever sum of money he wanted when a baron inherited land. The sum was fixed at £100.

- The monarch was no longer allowed to appoint his favoured supporters to positions in the Church.

The Magna Carta gave the people of England more rights by reducing the power of the monarch. In this way, it can be seen that King John's reign had a more lasting positive effect than King Richard's. Perhaps King John's badness is simply down to the fact that his story was told by those people who did not like what he did – he was not so much bad, as badly reported! Also, Richard was never really around to upset people – he abandoned his country for military glory. However, Richard has been recorded in history as a glamorous king – he was well reported, but the reality is perhaps rather different.

The reputations of people in history change over time. However, a good monarch is one who gives the kind of leadership which is required at the time. As times change through history, and the needs of the population change, then so does the kind of leadership which is required. We cannot assume that King John was a bad monarch if what he did was right for the time and circumstances.

Question time

1 How might King John have defended his actions?

2 Why do you think that so many people have compared King John with King Richard and have reached the conclusion that Richard was a good king and John a bad one?

Assessment section

1 Work in groups of six and set up a balloon debate. In the balloon are William I, William II, Henry I, Henry II, Richard I and King John. Each person chooses to represent one monarch and then prepares an argument as to why they should not be thrown out of the balloon. Each person has a vote as to who should remain.

Who is left in your balloon? Compare your answer with the other groups in your class. Is the same person left each time? If your groups choose different people, work out why.

2 Look back to the work you did on William Rufus. There is a question mark over his death. Can you solve the mystery of who killed the king?

Fact: On 2 August 1100, William went hunting in the New Forest with his younger brother Henry, his close friend Walter Tirel and some companions. In the early evening, William's body was found, with an arrow in his heart.

Clue 1: Walter fled to France; years later he returned to England and was given lands and money by Henry.

Clue 2: Henry left the New Forest and took over the Treasury; three days later he was crowned King of England.

Clue 3: At the time, no one accused Henry of murder.

Opinion 1: In Henry's reign, William of Malmesbury wrote:

The sun was setting, and the King, drawing his bow, let fly an arrow which slightly wounded a stag which passed before him. At this point, Walter aimed at another stag and thus, unknowingly and without the power to prevent it, he pierced the King's breast with a fatal arrow. The King fell to the ground and thus made his death more speedy.

Opinion 2: In 1905, the historian H. W. C. Davies wrote:

The truth was never ascertained. Tirel, it is true, fled the country. But we know that, in later years, when he had nothing to fear from a confession of the truth, he solemnly denied that he was present when the King was slain. The man who benefited was Henry, but Henry's enemies would not have hesitated to tax him with assassination if there had been the faintest possibility of making out a case.

Opinion 3: In 1962, the historian A. L. Poole wrote:

Some facts suggest a plot. Tirel fled immediately across the seas. His two brothers-in-law, Gilbert and Roger of Clare, were members of the hunting party. Henry was also there. His actions seem to have been premeditated; he rode straight to Winchester.

So, who killed William? What do you think is the most likely explanation? How would you check the truth of this explanation?

a What made a good leader in medieval times?

b What makes a good leader today?

c How do you explain the differences between parts a) and b)?

Further reading

Roger Lancelyn Green, *The Adventures of Robin Hood* (Puffin, 1983)

Ellis Peters, *The Virgin in the Ice* (Futura, 1984)

Geoffrey Trease, *Bows against the Barons* (University of London Press, 1968)

4 The expansion of Norman control

The Normans did not stop with the conquest of England in 1066; they expanded their control over Scotland, Ireland, Wales and France, and as far as Sicily in Italy. In history, this extension of control is often presented as the progression of a strong and powerful force. The opposite side to this is the reaction of the people who resisted the expansion of Norman control. This is where the heroes and heroines can change the course of history, or at least make it more interesting! In this chapter we will be looking at the ways in which the Normans expanded their control beyond England after 1066, and those people who have gone down in legend as heroes and heroines for resisting them.

Why did the Normans want to expand their control?

Sometimes it seems that a country may invade another country simply for the sake of leading and winning an invasion. However, there are usually good reasons for such an invasion. These reasons usually involve how useful the neighbouring country could be for economic gain, how big a threat it poses, or whether it is likely to ally with an enemy.

The methods the Normans used to achieve control of Wales, Scotland and Ireland were many and varied. They included:

- force
- organising deals
- getting oaths of loyalty
- joining forces with different groups within the country
- creating the legal system necessary for government.

Some of these methods were successful, others were not.

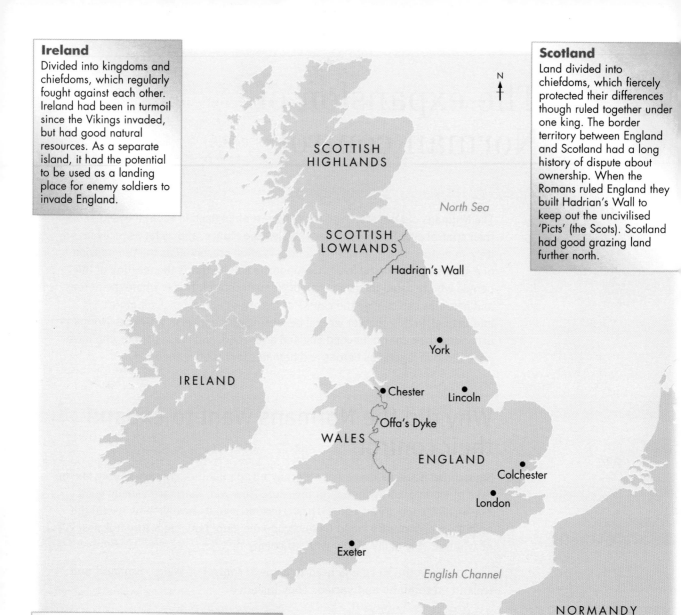

Ireland

Divided into kingdoms and chiefdoms, which regularly fought against each other. Ireland had been in turmoil since the Vikings invaded, but had good natural resources. As a separate island, it had the potential to be used as a landing place for enemy soldiers to invade England.

Scotland

Land divided into chiefdoms, which fiercely protected their differences though ruled together under one king. The border territory between England and Scotland had a long history of dispute about ownership. When the Romans ruled England they built Hadrian's Wall to keep out the uncivilised 'Picts' (the Scots). Scotland had good grazing land further north.

SCOTTISH HIGHLANDS

North Sea

SCOTTISH LOWLANDS

Hadrian's Wall

York

IRELAND

Chester
Lincoln

Offa's Dyke

WALES

ENGLAND

Colchester

London

Exeter

English Channel

NORMANDY

Wales

Divided into kingdoms and principalities with no overall king. Mountains and valleys made it, geographically, a difficult area to control. Rich in minerals and livestock (sheep and cattle). Borders with England made it a refuge for those unhappy with Norman rule in England. Offa's Dyke, thought to have been built in the time of Offa, King of Mercia (757–96), is an earthwork which roughly follows the English/Welsh border.

England

Norman invasion 1066. Control of England gained by dividing land and giving it to Norman barons to control for William. English earls rebelled 1068 and 1071. Gradually all landholders became Norman.

Map of the British Isles in 1066 showing Offa's Dyke and Hadrian's Wall as the main boundaries.

Question time

1   From the labels on the map, list the reasons why the Normans in England might want to invade and control Wales, Scotland and Ireland.

Expansion into Wales

Wales was not conquered by William in the same way as England. As conqueror of England in battle, William claimed all English land and the right to give it to his supporters, whether they were Norman lords or English lords willing to serve William. It was not possible to conquer Wales by one single battle because there was not one single leader. Also, the Welsh mountains prevented a full army invasion. Although William did try a few times to take over north and west Wales using military force, these attempts always failed. At each attempt, the Welsh princes retreated to their mountain hideouts and harassed the English troops until eventually the English withdrew.

To conquer Wales, William decided to use a policy of encroachment. This meant that he hoped to gradually take over Welsh land by placing his supporters in important areas. They would then act in his interests and influence decisions taken in Wales. He distributed land along the Welsh border to the 'Marcher Lords', so called because their lands were on the Welsh Marches, or borders. They were expected to encourage Norman sympathisers to settle in their area, and they tended to guard their lands aggressively.

Castles were built at important geographic positions, such as the junction of rivers or mountain ranges, e.g. Chester and Shrewsbury. Also, thriving markets encouraged Welsh traders and farmers to come into English lands and see what benefits Norman control had brought. Some Norman settlement started in southern and eastern Wales, where the land was fertile and flat, but the northern and western areas were left alone.

Welsh resistance

During the reign of Henry III (1216–72), English control of Wales lapsed because of the many other problems Henry had to deal with. Also, a national revival had set in with a renewed interest in Welsh poetry written by bards (specialists in Welsh language and culture), and this was seen as a way of keeping the old Welsh ideas and stories alive. The Welsh language thus became a symbol of the independence of the Welsh nation. In north Wales, a tribal union was formed with Llywelyn ap Gruffydd (1240–82), ruler of Gwynedd, as their leader. All the Welsh princes agreed to obey him.

Digging deeper

Llywelyn ap Gruffydd (1240–82)

SOURCE B

Llywelyn ap Gruffydd.

of Wales who could effectively challenge English power.

In 1255, Llywelyn ap Gruffydd defeated his brothers, Owain and Dafydd, in a battle at Bryn Derwin. By 1267 he was overlord of Wales and this was recognised by Henry III in the Treaty of Montgomery. As part of this treaty, the English king accepted Llywelyn's homage as Prince of Wales.

Llywelyn gained much from the Treaty of Montgomery but, ten years after his recognition as the Prince of Wales by Henry III, he failed to keep to the terms of the treaty. In 1272 Henry III died and Henry's son Edward became king. Llywelyn refused to pay to Edward I the homage and money payments that were owed under the terms of the treaty, even though the Welsh princes had paid homage to Edward's father Henry III. This was an insult to Edward and was guaranteed to cause trouble. It seemed that Llywelyn was pushing Edward towards a confrontation over the situation between England and Wales.

The Welsh princes of Gwynedd had the difficulty that primogeniture, whereby the eldest son inherits land and title from his father, was not common. When a Welshman died, his land was parcelled out amongst all his sons. So there were lots of small-time lords with small parcels of land. This had led to the division of lands in Wales. Llywelyn wanted to change this, so that Wales could be stronger. He wanted one Prince

To add to the brewing tension, Llywelyn arranged to marry Eleanor, daughter of the rebel English baron Simon de Montfort. He also started building castles, as well as strengthening his grandfather's castles at Criccieth, Ewloe and Dolwyddelan. In 1273, Llywelyn started to build a new castle at Dolforwyn, above the Severn valley. This posed a threat to the royal frontier post at Montgomery.

Llywelyn refused to abandon the building of this castle, even though the potential threat was bound to make the English King Edward I react.

In 1276, Edward decided to act. By August the following year, he had 15,600 troops ready to fight. Against such a large army, Llywelyn had no choice but to sue for peace. The Treaty of Aberconwy which followed represented a complete loss of face for Llywelyn. He was stripped of the overlordship that had been recognised ten years earlier; but worse was to follow.

On 21 March 1282, Llywelyn's brother Dafydd attacked Hawarden Castle. This attack led to the war of 1282–3 and placed Llywelyn in a difficult position. As part of the Treaty of Aberconwy, he had sworn loyalty to Edward I and knew that further rebellion would probably harm Wales even more. However, Llywelyn chose to side with Dafydd, and led the Welsh resistance to the invasion by Edward I. Llywelyn was killed on 11 December 1282 in a brief skirmish with English forces at Irfon Bridge near Builth Wells.

After the death of Llywelyn ap Gruffydd, Dafydd was captured and executed by hanging, drawing and quartering – a public and cruel death. Edward enforced English law and language and divided Wales into seven counties, enforcing the feudal system. Llywelyn's dream of a united Wales had been ruined.

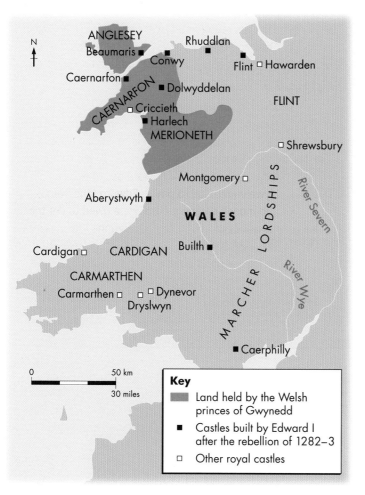

Wales during the Middle Ages.

The Norman conquest of Wales

After successfully defeating the Welsh rebellion of 1282–3, Edward I began a programme of castle building in Wales in places such as Conwy, Caernarfon and Caerphilly. The reasons for this were the same as the reasons for William the Conqueror's castle building in England: to show the might and power of the new king and to protect new lands. Wales was then judged to be totally under English control, and Edward turned his attention to Scotland. However, a nation's spirit is not that easily crushed and, over 100 years later, Welsh nationalism was revived once more.

By the end of the fourteenth century, Richard II was King of England. There had been a great deal of unrest during his reign, and he had been in conflict with Parliament since 1397 over the question of money. Richard wanted more money and Parliament wanted more control over how it was spent. Richard was in conflict with his lords, too. Conditions were right for a coup. In 1399, when Richard was in Ireland, Henry Bolingbroke (who Richard had banished into exile) invaded England. Within six weeks Richard had submitted to him. Parliament decided that Henry should be king.

Although the unpopular monarch, Richard II, had been successfully overthrown, there remained much unrest during the reign of Henry IV. Owain Glyndwr, a Welsh leader, then claimed the title Prince of Wales. Taking advantage of the fact that Henry Bolingbroke was a new and untried king, Owain led a rebellion against the English and took over many of the castles in Wales. He also sought an alliance with the French. In 1405, 2600 French soldiers landed on the coast of Wales, in order to support Owain Glyndwr.

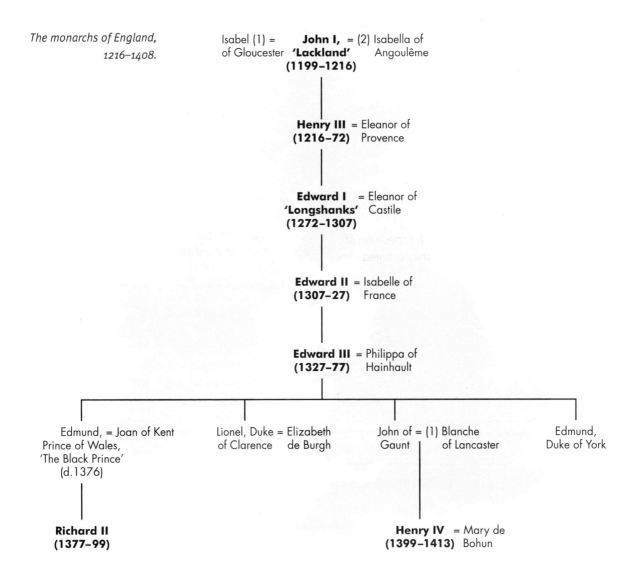

The monarchs of England, 1216–1408.

Isabel (1) = **John I,** = (2) Isabella of
of Gloucester **'Lackland'** Angoulême
(1199–1216)

Henry III = Eleanor of
(1216–72) Provence

Edward I = Eleanor of
'Longshanks' Castile
(1272–1307)

Edward II = Isabelle of
(1307–27) France

Edward III = Philippa of
(1327–77) Hainhault

Edmund, = Joan of Kent
Prince of Wales,
'The Black Prince'
(d.1376)

Lionel, Duke = Elizabeth
of Clarence de Burgh

John of = (1) Blanche
Gaunt of Lancaster

Edmund,
Duke of York

Richard II
(1377–99)

Henry IV = Mary de
(1399–1413) Bohun

Digging deeper

Owain Glyndwr (1359–1415)

This portrait of Owain Glyndwr is based on his seal and was engraved in the nineteenth century by Forrest.

Owain Glyndwr was the last independent Prince of Wales. He is more correctly known as Owain ab Gruffydd, Lord of Glyndyvrdwy in Merioneth.

In 1400, Owain became the leader of a national revolt. The lords of Glyndyvrdwy had a longstanding feud with their English neighbours, the Greys of Ruthin. The Greys had not summoned Owain for the Scottish expedition of 1400, as was his duty, but then they charged him with treason for failing to appear! Owain did not accept this insult lightly, and attacked his English neighbours. When Henry IV returned from Scotland in September, he found north Wales in revolt. A campaign under Henry's command failed to restore the situation. A second campaign by the king in the autumn of 1401 was also defeated. Owain appeared to be in control of the situation in Wales.

Owain called himself Prince of Wales, established a government and called a parliament at Machynlleth. He made an alliance with the French, who sent troops to help fight the English. Soon, Owain gained control of Harlech and Aberystwyth castles.

In spring 1405, the Welsh successes came to an end. They were defeated in March and twice again in May. The English, however, were unable to reinforce these gains because they were dealing with a rebellion in the North of England. Eventually, the capture of Aberystwyth, after a long siege in 1408, marked the end of the Welsh uprising. In February 1409 Harlech was recaptured and during this time Owain's wife, daughter and godchildren were taken prisoner; Owain himself escaped. Owain eventually died in 1415.

Question time

1. Draw a timeline showing the methods used by English monarchs during the Middle Ages to control Wales.

2. Do you think that the English had control of Wales in this period? Explain your answer.

3. Choose three examples of English successes and three examples of English failure in the attempt to control Wales.

4. Llywelyn ap Gruffydd is also known as Ein Llw Olaf (Our Last Leader). He died in battle. Dafydd, Llywelyn's brother, was the last Welsh-born Prince of Wales, and was captured by the English. Why do you think Edward I went to the trouble of a public death by hanging, drawing and quartering?

5. Looking at the family tree, do you think that Henry Bolingbroke had a better claim to the throne than Richard II? Explain your answer.

Expansion into Scotland

Malcolm Canmore, King of Scotland 1058–93, was forced to pay homage to the Norman kings William the Conqueror (1072) and William Rufus (1091). However, this was not the only reason for Norman influences in Scotland. Malcolm married Margaret, sister of Edgar the Ætheling, the last Saxon claimant to the English throne (see page 34). She had a powerful influence on the Scottish court and, because she had been brought up in Normandy, helped to bring Norman influences into Scotland. Norman lords also settled in Scotland, and gradually became Scottish. These new lords included the Balliols, the Bruces, the Lindsays and the Stewarts. They supported the Scottish monarch, but they too introduced Norman ideas from their Norman background.

Scottish independence continued to be a cause of concern for English monarchs because it was always possible that Scotland could ally itself to any enemy of England and invade whilst England was weak – for example, if England was fighting a war against another country. English monarchs also feared that rebellions in Scotland might spill over into England. In 1175, Henry II of England had forced William I of Scotland to pay homage and accept allegiance to England. However, Richard I had spent too little time in England (see page 43), and this allowed England's influence to be weakened in Scotland. King John tried to regain the former position of authority but, because he faced problems in other areas (see page 43), so he left Scotland alone.

Trouble in Scotland

Matters between Scotland and England came to a head when King Alexander III died in 1284, leaving his daughter Margaret to inherit the throne of Scotland. Margaret was pledged to be married to King Edward I's son, to bring about a union of England and Scotland. However, Margaret died, so Edward was asked to judge the claims of those who felt they should be King of Scotland. Edward dismissed the claims of all but two people: Robert Bruce and John Balliol. In 1292, he awarded the throne to John Balliol against the claim of Robert Bruce. Edward felt that Balliol would be more receptive to England's claims of authority than Robert Bruce. He was wrong.

Edward I claims the Scottish throne

The new king, John Balliol, refused to pay homage to Edward I. Then, in 1295, Balliol entered an alliance with France, England's old enemy. Edward saw this as treason (a crime against the monarch) and invaded Scotland. His army consisted of well-disciplined cavalry and some new longbowmen, whom he had seen in action in his campaigns in Wales. They fought well and his army was successful: Edward defeated Balliol at the Battle of Dunbar in 1296, and promptly declared himself King of Scotland. He received oaths of allegiance from the nobles, and took away the Coronation Stone (a symbol of Scotland's independence) from the Palace of Scone.

In this way, Edward sought to end any claims which the Scots might have for independence. To this end, Edward tried to impose his will upon the Scottish people and harsh laws were passed and brutally enforced by English soldiers. However, this quickly led to a rising of the people against Edward's rule. It also led to Edward being known as the 'hammer of the Scots'.

The monarchs of Scotland, 1057–1306.

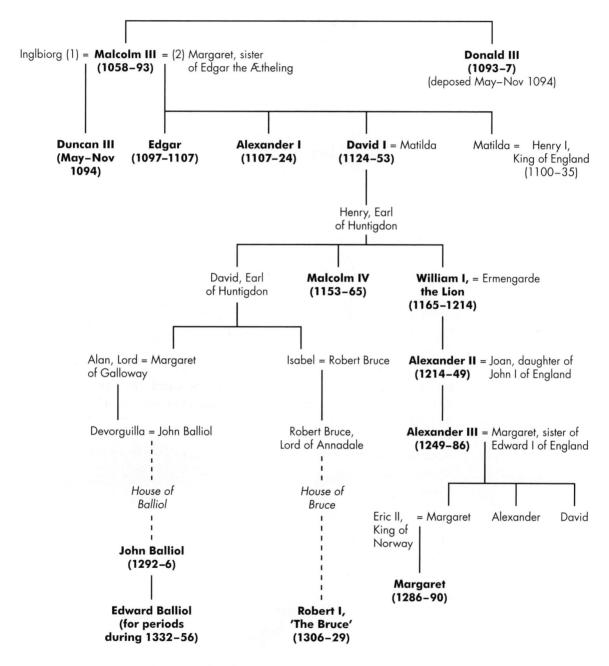

At this time, a Scottish knight called William Wallace became a popular hero. He rebelled against English rule, winning a famous battle at Stirling in September 1297, but this made Edward more determined to regain control. Edward eventually defeated Wallace at the Battle of Falkirk in 1298. Wallace was forced to go into exile and Edward continued his campaign to conquer Scotland. By 1304 the conquest was complete – Wallace was captured and Edward reinforced his control in several ways:

- Wallace was publicly executed in 1305.

- Scotland was incorporated under the English Crown.

- Scottish nobles were forced to give up their fortresses.

- An English lieutenant (representative of the king) was sent to rule Scotland. He was to be in charge of a council with the power to amend Scottish laws.

Digging deeper

William Wallace (1270–1305)

Sir William Wallace is known to have gone against the law at an early age, when he was charged with killing the son of the governor of Dundee. It is said that Wallace took out his dagger and killed him. Wallace was declared a traitor, outlawed and forced to flee.

Wallace soon came to be the leader of those who opposed English rule. He and his supporters lived mainly by attacking convoys of English people, and retreating to the woods when pursued. Wallace also visited garrisoned towns in disguise, to see for himself the strength and condition of the enemy. His heroic exploits became legendary and, following the heavy Scottish defeat at the Battle of Dunbar in 1296, he became the focus of hope for many Scots who wanted independence from England.

Sir William of Heslope, the English sheriff of Lanark, became one of Wallace's victims when he was put to death for killing the heiress of Lamington (Wallace's sweetheart). The people of Lanark rose in support of Wallace and his men and drove out the English garrison. After taking Glasgow, Wallace marched to Scone in May 1297. The speed of the attack took Ormsby, the English justiciary, by surprise, making the English forces flee. Wallace's successes made him a very popular figure and he became the focus for all those who hated English rule. He was joined by a number of the nobility, including the future king, Robert Bruce.

When Edward I heard about Wallace's success, he sent a force of 40,000 foot soldiers and 300 horsemen under Sir Henry Percy and Sir Robert Clifford to deal with Wallace and bring an end to the problems he and his supporters were causing the English in Scotland.

SOURCE A

A statue of William Wallace in Aberdeen.

Many Scottish nobles were unhappy about being led by Wallace because he was of low birth, and was therefore inferior to them in status. Most of the Scottish nobles decided to switch sides and support the English, although Sir Andrew Moray and Sir John the Graham continued to support Wallace. As a result of this, Wallace retreated to the North, without battle. Sir Henry Percy and Sir Robert Clifford assumed that this retreat marked the end of the problem and returned south, only to be followed by Wallace and Moray. Wallace and Moray divided their forces and, in a short time, again forced the English south. While laying siege to the English-held Dundee Castle, Wallace heard that an English army was again advancing north, under the Earl of Surrey. The siege was abandoned to halt the advance of the English army and, at the Abbey of Cambuskenneth, Wallace and his men faced the strength of the English invading army.

Though hugely outnumbered the Scots refused to negotiate with the invaders, stating that they were there to show the English that Scotland was free. The English, under Cressingham, advanced to cross Stirling Bridge but, when only half of them were across, the Scots attacked, killing thousands. Those English who had still not crossed the bridge saw their fellow soldiers being slaughtered and retreated in panic, leaving their leader Cressingham among the many dead. This was an amazing feat – a small army had defeated a much larger and more experienced one. This defeat on 11 September 1297 was followed by the surrender of Dundee Castle and the total expulsion of the English from Scotland.

In March 1298, Wallace was knighted and elected as Regent of Scotland. He continued raiding England as far south as Newcastle. Edward I heard of these raids and, in retaliation, gathered an army of 100,000 foot soldiers and 8000 horses. Wallace retreated, using a 'scorched earth' policy: destroying all cattle and crops as he withdrew. This tactic slowed down the English and they were on the point of giving up, when Wallace was betrayed by two Scottish nobles: Patrick, Earl of Dunbar, and Umfraville, Earl of Angus.

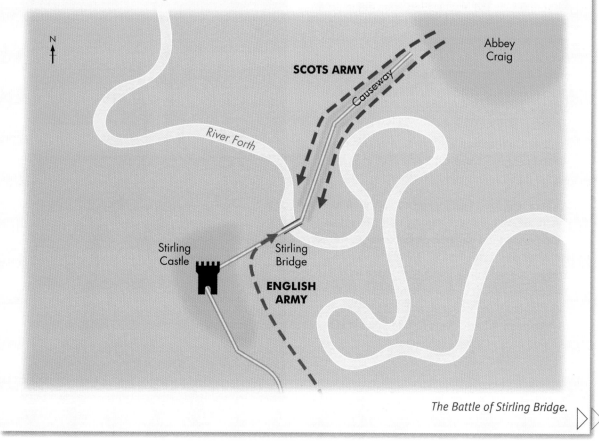

The Battle of Stirling Bridge.

Edward immediately ordered his army to advance on the Scottish army. The two sides met at Falkirk. The Scots were heavily outnumbered (the Scottish army was less than one third the size of the English one) and were caught off guard. This time the Scottish army was no match for the English cavalry, and they scattered. Defeat became certain when Comyn, Lord of Badenoch, leader of a large part of the Scots army, turned his banners and marched off the field with his men. Wallace retreated and managed to escape from the English. However, by destroying the land in and around Stirling, Wallace forced the English to retreat because they had no way of getting fresh supplies.

Wallace realised that the Scottish nobles would not support him, and resigned the Regency. He left for France to get help from the King of France. However, this mission proved unsuccessful and so Wallace returned to Scotland in 1303. He started harassing the English once more with a few of his supporters.

Edward I had made most of the Scottish nobles submit to him, but Wallace had escaped capture and became a heroic figure to the Scots. To put an end to Wallace's freedom, Edward offered a ransom of 300 marks for Wallace's capture, and orders were issued to use every means to capture him and send him in chains to London. Wallace was eventually betrayed by one of his servants, Jack Short, and handed over to the English. On reaching London he was taken to Westminster Hall and, on 23 August 1305, accused of treason and other crimes.

Wallace was found guilty and condemned to death. He was dragged through the streets of London and then hanged, drawn and quartered. His head was placed on a pole on London Bridge; his right arm above the bridge in Newcastle; his left arm was sent to Berwick; his right foot and leg to Perth; and his left quarter to Aberdeen, where it was buried in what is now the wall of St Machars Cathedral.

SOURCE C

The William Wallace monument in Stirling.

Robert Bruce

The murder of William Wallace was very unpopular in Scotland and led to an uprising under Robert Bruce, grandson of the original claimant to the Scottish throne (see page 70). Robert Bruce was crowned King of Scotland in 1306 and Edward was forced to resume his wars against the Scots. Edward I, 'the hammer of the Scots', died on a last campaign against Robert Bruce in 1307. His son, Edward II, was then crowned king (see family tree on page 68).

The Scots fight back

Robert Bruce was a very skilful soldier. He had seen that the English army was better equipped and would therefore win in pitched battles, so he chose to use guerrilla tactics. This meant that, instead of fighting battles, his soldiers ambushed English soldiers in small skirmishes and destroyed crops so that the English army was not able to feed itself off the land. These tactics eventually forced the English to retreat from Scotland. By 1314, Bruce had gathered his forces and started to besiege Stirling Castle, the only castle still in English control.

Edward II, on the other hand, was not a very successful soldier. He was reluctant to wage war but realised that he must deal with the increasing threat in Scotland. He had sent 25,000 English soldiers to fight 7000 Scots, yet the Scots still won the Battle of Bannockburn in June 1314. The battle was very bloody, with many casualties, but the English had been totally humiliated and Edward II had fled.

After success at Bannockburn, Robert Bruce was able to further establish himself as King of Scotland. The Treaty of Northampton in 1323 confirmed English recognition of Robert Bruce as Scottish king, and arranged for the marriage of Robert's son David to Edward II's daughter Joan. However, Edward II still refused to recognise Scotland's independence and the border between Scotland and England remained a trouble spot. Raiders from both sides crossed to steal cattle and murder each other. Other areas of conflict remained as well, such as the exact placing of the border, and the difficulty of conflicting loyalties which occurred when a noble owned land in both England and Scotland. However, the main clashes usually came about when power struggles in either country allowed different groups to develop: then rival groups in Scotland would seek support in England, and vice versa.

No English king seriously tried to invade and conquer Scotland after this time. Scotland and England had the same monarch after 1603, when King James VI of Scotland became King James I of England. He happened to have the best claim to both the thrones of England and Scotland by right of birth and he was a candidate who did not offend too many people. It was not until 1707 that the governments of England and Scotland were united.

Question time

1. Draw a timeline showing the methods used by Norman monarchs to try to control Scotland. Try to explain why these different tactics were used.

2. How successful were the Normans in achieving control of Scotland?

3. Choose three examples of English successes and three examples of English failure to control Scotland.

- Find out who was on the English throne at the time.
- Find out what problems, if any, there were during his monarchy.

4. Draw a chart comparing the success of the English in Wales against their performance in Scotland.

5. Why do you think the English managed to control Wales but not Scotland?

Expansion into Ireland

Before the Normans came to Ireland, there had been a period of anarchy. This civil unrest followed the death of Brian of Munster. He had been accepted as overall leader, so his death in 1014 at the Battle of Clontarf, where he defeated the Vikings, left the rival clans in disarray and they fought each other bitterly.

Pope Adrian IV sent the English King Henry II a letter in 1155 granting him Lordship of Ireland. However, it wasn't until the 1160s that Dermot Macmurrough, a clan leader in Ireland, came to Henry for help in establishing order in Ireland. Henry agreed to the appeal, and Richard of Clare, Earl of Pembroke, agreed to supply men and arms in return for land. Richard of Clare's nickname was Strongbow, and he invaded Ireland and made the Irish leaders swear an oath of loyalty to Henry. Strongbow settled in Ireland, and soon a thriving colony was established under the Norman king.

Ireland under the Norman kings

In 1171 Henry II went to Ireland to assert his supremacy. At the Synod of Cashel, Henry's sovereignty was acknowledged, and he also introduced English laws and customs. Pembroke and his Norman followers had settled in the most fertile areas, forcing the Irish people off the land. However, Henry left orders that he wished the Irish to be treated fairly so that they would not rebel. This only served to create more problems because the Norman settlers wanted to use the land for their own interests, and behaved badly towards the Irish. This meant that the viceroy who ruled on behalf of the king was unpopular with both the Irish for staying in Ireland, and the settlers for not supporting them against the Irish. As a result, Ireland was not a settled place.

In 1213 King John gave England and Ireland to the Pope, in a bid to escape the difficulties which he was having with his barons. He thought this was a clever plan to outsmart them: if England and Ireland were held by the Pope, then the barons owed their loyalty to the Pope and could not disobey him.

However, this situation did not last long. The Pope returned England and Ireland to the English crown. English interest and investment in Ireland continued to develop during Henry III's reign (1216–72), when bridges and castles were built, new towns created, and trade and industry prospered – but only in the area of Norman colonisation.

Between 1272 and 1307, Edward I allowed prosperity to continue in Ireland, but the widening difference between the areas under Norman control and the rest of Ireland, which was still under the control of the native clans, was becoming apparent. The area which was actually governed by the English was very small. Most Irish land was still in the hands of native lords who refused to accept any English rule. Also, English involvement in the wars against France meant that England was too busy fighting to try to bring the situation in Ireland under control.

Map of Ireland, showing Norman territory and castles, about 1250.

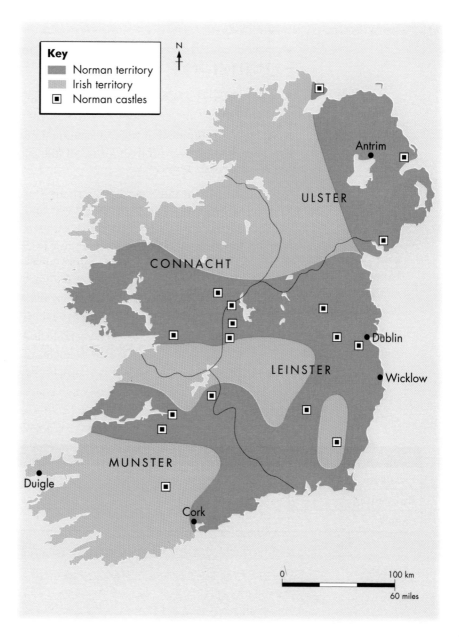

Trouble in Ireland

By 1398 Ireland was seen as out of control. Richard II went on two expeditions to try to get full control of Ireland, but these expeditions cost a lot of money and both failed. During Henry V's reign (1413–22), the situation in Ireland deteriorated, and it is estimated that about half of the colonists returned to England. Richard of York arrived in Ireland in 1449 and appeared to have a good relationship with both the colonists and the Irish. He returned to Ireland in 1450 and set in motion a policy which gave Ireland a degree of independence. This included separate coinage and an Irish Parliament. However, Edward IV (1461–83) reverted to a policy of harsh repression. In 1485, Richard III was killed at the Battle of Bosworth and the new monarch Henry Tudor was keen to exert his authority. In 1494 he introduced the Statute of Drogheda which stated that:

- No Irish Parliament could be held without the consent of the King of England.

- No bill could be brought forward in Parliament without the King of England's consent.

- All recent laws passed in the English Parliament should also hold true in Ireland.

However, by 1500 most of Ireland remained out of English control. Ireland was governed by over 60 Irish lords, all independent of the English monarch.

Question time

1 Look back at the measures used to control Wales and Scotland on pages 65–75. Which methods were also used in Ireland? Use the text to back up your answer.

2 How successful were the English in controlling Ireland?

3 Wales, Ireland and Scotland resisted English domination by the following means:
   - outright rebellion
   - passive resistance (outwardly agreeing but waiting for an opportunity to revolt)
   - keeping a national identity with culture (language, stories, family ties etc.).

Draw a table like the one below. Complete it with examples of Welsh, Scottish and Irish resistance to the English.

Method	Wales	Scotland	Ireland
Rebellion			
Resistance			
Culture			

Expansion into France

William the Conqueror was also Duke of Normandy, and held lands in both England and Normandy. The subsequent English control of lands in mainland France depended on the strength and nature of the king. Strong, military leaders extended English control, while weaker monarchs, who had more problems at home, tended to lose French lands.

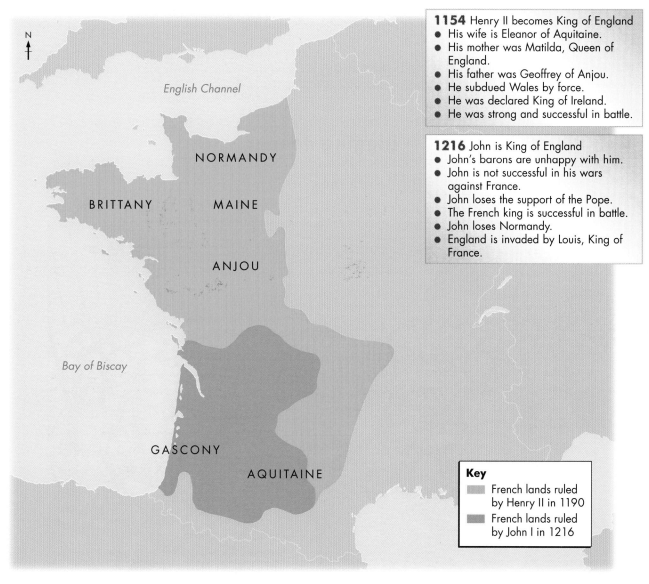

1154 Henry II becomes King of England
- His wife is Eleanor of Aquitaine.
- His mother was Matilda, Queen of England.
- His father was Geoffrey of Anjou.
- He subdued Wales by force.
- He was declared King of Ireland.
- He was strong and successful in battle.

1216 John is King of England
- John's barons are unhappy with him.
- John is not successful in his wars against France.
- John loses the support of the Pope.
- The French king is successful in battle.
- John loses Normandy.
- England is invaded by Louis, King of France.

English Channel

NORMANDY

BRITTANY

MAINE

ANJOU

Bay of Biscay

GASCONY

AQUITAINE

Key
French lands ruled by Henry II in 1190
French lands ruled by John I in 1216

The extent of English control in France during the reign of Henry II and after King John.

It was not going to be easy to extend English control beyond the Channel into France, particularly as the kings of France were also trying to extend control within France. The kings of France not only wanted to get rid of the English, they also wanted better control of all the lands in France. The conflict between England and France had periods of great success for England, but in the end the kings of France achieved control over the vast majority of the area which we now call France. The various wars between England and France over a long period of time are called the Hundred Years War.

The Hundred Years War, 1337–1453

King Charles IV of France died in 1328. He was succeeded by Philip of Valois, who was crowned King Philip VI of France. However, Edward III refused to recognise the French king as his overlord and, in retaliation for Edward's rebuttal, Philip tried to remove all English control from Aquitaine (see map on page 79). By 1337, Philip had declared Edward's lands in France forfeit – that is, the French king declared that they were in fact French lands once again. This was effectively a declaration of war from Philip, since it amounted to stealing land away from the English king. Therefore, later in 1337, Edward attacked Philip's lands in northern France and, in 1338, he formally claimed the French crown for himself. England and France were now in full-blown conflict.

Digging deeper

The Battle of Crécy, 26 August 1346

SOURCE A

A contemporary painting of the Battle of Crécy.

Before we can begin to understand the importance of the Battle of Crécy, we have to go back six years to the first big battle of the Hundred Years War – the sea battle of Sluys. An English fleet of 200 ships, carrying hundreds of soldiers, was about to land near Sluys, in Flanders. Spotting a much larger French fleet, the English attacked. Most of the French ships were anchored and so their crews were easily picked off by English longbowmen. By the end of the day, the French fleet was almost destroyed and the English had control of the English Channel. This meant, firstly, that England was safe from invasion and, secondly, that the English could attack the north coast of France, safely, at any time they chose.

The English had short, summer campaigns in northern France, hitting the French quickly with raiding parties and getting back across the Channel before they had to fight a full-scale battle. But, in August 1346, things went badly wrong. After a raid in Normandy, Edward III and his troops were caught by a much larger French army and had to stand and fight. Edward had about 12,000 archers and 2400 cavalry. His son and heir, the Black Prince, was also fighting with him. There was much to be lost. The French army, led by Philip VI, was made up of about 12,000 cavalry, 20,000 town militiamen and 6000 crossbowmen, plus some foot soldiers and a cavalry division under John of Bohemia.

There didn't seem much doubt about the outcome, even when the English took up a defensive position on a hillside outside the village of Crécy, forcing the French to fight uphill. Philip's archers used crossbows which fired iron-tipped bolts. The bolts were deadly, but crossbows took time to reload and couldn't fire as far as the English longbows. Firing at a rate of six arrows a minute, English archers forced the advancing French cavalry to turn back, trampling their own troops underfoot in a hail of arrows that brought horses and men crashing to the ground. The French knights charged 16 times, but by midnight it was all over. 1500 French knights lay dead and the English marched on Calais.

Calais was long renowned for being the home of pirates who preyed on English shipping. Edward laid siege to the town but had to continue through the winter before the starving citizens surrendered. They were driven out and English families installed in their place. Calais became a base for English merchants and an important stronghold on continental Europe.

The Battle of Crécy is important, however, not only because it delivered Calais to the English, but also because it showed, for the first time in continental warfare, that the longbow was a superior weapon to the crossbow.

 ## Question time

1   What does Source A tell us about the Battle of Crécy?

2   Which would you trust to give a more accurate view of what happened – Source A or this account? Why?

The Black Prince

After the success of Crécy, the English continued to win military battles in France under the leadership of the Black Prince. Only 16 years old at the time of Crécy, the Black Prince became one of the most feared medieval warriors. He was called the Black Prince because of the colour of his armour: he stood out on any battlefield, which made him a rallying point for his men and a target for his enemies. In 1355 the Black Prince invaded Bordeaux. He defeated the French in 1356 at the Battle of Poitiers, and captured the French king John II. In 1360, Calais and Aquitaine were returned to England by the Treaty of Brétigny. This caused renewed fighting by 1369.

The tide turns ...

In 1370, the Black Prince returned to England. He was ill, and was replaced in France by his brother John of Gaunt. However, John was not an able soldier and Poitou and Brittany were soon taken back by the French. By 1373, the French had won back nearly all of the territory that they had lost to the English. In 1375, with the Black Prince in poor health and Edward III nearing the end of his reign, the English decided to call a truce with France – they no longer had the upper hand.

In 1376, the Black Prince died. This was a great blow to the English, who believed that Edward would have proved a great king. When Edward III died the following year, the English throne passed to his grandson Richard. Although he was the son of the Black Prince, Richard was not an impressive military leader – he was only ten years old when he inherited the throne and was led by John of Gaunt during his minority. By 1380, English control in France had diminished, and England now controlled only Bordeaux, Calais, Bayonne, Cherbourg, Valais and some of their surrounding areas.

Richard II proved a weak monarch, and there was much unrest in England during his reign. This meant that the English king was too preoccupied with troubles in his own realm to start creating troubles abroad. In 1396, England and France signed the Twenty-Year Truce. This guaranteed peace between the two nations; as part of the agreement Richard married the daughter of King Charles VI of France – Isabelle.

Despite making peace with the French, Richard II could not settle affairs in his own country and, in 1399, Henry of Lancaster seized the English throne, becoming Henry IV (see page 68). There followed a period of civil unrest during which French troops intervened in English affairs: in 1405, French troops landed in Wales to support Owain Glyndwr's rebellion (see page 69), and, in 1407, they attacked Aquitaine.

Henry V renews the French campaign

Henry IV died in 1413. His reign had been troubled by internal rebellion, and he therefore had little time to concentrate on fighting battles in France. However, his son Henry V had different ideas. In 1415, Henry V sailed for France for a season of campaigning

Digging deeper

The Battle of Agincourt, 25 October 1415

Henry V's spring campaign lasted longer than expected, but eventually the siege of the French town of Harfleur was successful and Henry was able to turn for Calais and home. Unexpectedly, the French gathered their forces together and blocked his way. French soldiers, with cavalry on their flanks, stretched in three densely packed lines across the ploughed fields between the villages of Agincourt and Tramecourt – and waited. The English forces were outnumbered three to one, weary after the long siege and anxious to get home – they seemed doomed.

Painting of the Battle of Agincourt showing the use of the longbow. From a fifteenth-century manuscript by Froissart.

Henry V ordered the English forces to advance until the French were just within the range of their longbows. The first round of arrow fire started the French cavalry charge. However, the fields across which the horses galloped were little more than thick, slippery mud, and into these the English had hammered long wooden stakes. Consequently, the French cavalry charge collapsed. Next came the French footsoldiers. Exhausted from their struggle through the mud, the French troops made for the English nobles. They were not ordered to wipe out the archers and their deadly fire; there was, after all, greater glory to be gained from killing an English nobleman than a lowly archer. This mistake, and divisions in the French command, proved fatal for the French troops. The constant firing of the longbows killed hundreds of French soldiers, weighed down with heavy armour and struggling in deep mud. In contrast, the lightly armoured Englishmen fired on and on relentlessly, and the battle turned into a rout. By the end, thousands of French lay dead yet only a few hundred Englishmen were killed in the battle.

After the success of the Battle of Agincourt, Henry V was able to retake Normandy and advance as far as Rouen, tightening his grip on France. Peace followed in 1420 when the English and French signed the Treaty of Troyes. England kept all conquests as far south as the river Loire; Catherine, daughter of the French King Charles V, was shipped off to England as Henry V's wife, and Henry was recognised as heir to the French throne (see also Chapter 6).

The English had secured a tremendous inheritance in France. However, the tide once again turned in 1422 when Henry died at the young age of 35. Although the English continued to win victories in France under the Duke of Bedford, the new monarch – Henry VI – proved a weak military leader.

Breaking the siege of Orléans

In 1422, English forces under the Duke of Bedford lay siege to the French city of Orléans. By 1429, with support from allies in Burgundy, the English controlled nearly all the French lands north of the river Loire. However, they were met with effective resistance from an unlikely source – a young woman. After a vision in which she led the French armies to victory against the English, Joan of Arc travelled to Chinon to see the French King Charles VI and persuaded him to lead troops against the siege of Orléans. True to her vision, Joan successfully led the troops to victory (see Digging Deeper on pages 85–6).

After successfully lifting the siege of Orléans, the French continued to win back control in France. In 1436, Charles VII captured Paris; in 1449, Normandy was retaken by the French; and, in 1451, Bordeaux and Bayonne returned once more to French control. From 1453, only Calais remained in English hands – and continued to do so until 1558, when it was returned to the French during the reign of Mary Tudor. After 1453, England accepted that France belonged to the French, and no further attempts were made to conquer it.

Map showing the extent of English control in France by 1422, and by 1453.

Digging deeper

Joan of Arc (1412–31)

Painting of Joan of Arc from a French manuscript c. 1505 by Antoine du Four.

Just as the battles against England created national heroes for Wales, Scotland and Ireland, so France had its own heroine in Joan of Arc.

Joan was born into a relatively poor peasant family. From a young age she was witness to the turmoil created by the Hundred Years War, and had to move from her home several times to avoid the fighting. When she was 13 years old, Joan began to have visions. She claimed that these visions came directly from God, who gave her instructions about what to do. At first Joan was told that she should simply lead a good life and worship regularly, but when she was 16 she had a vision in which she was told to help crown the French prince (the dauphin) as king, and to lead French troops against the English. The timeline below reveals the strange events which followed.

February 1429	Joan leaves home without telling her parents and travels to Chinon. There she tells the French king, Charles VI, that she has had a vision in which she will lead the French armies to a victorious relief of the siege of Orléans.
June 1429	Joan leads the French to victory over the English, successfully lifting the siege of Orléans. The French dauphin is crowned King Charles VII of France at Reims. Joan attends the coronation, standing by the new king's throne.
August 1429	The French army moves towards Paris.
March to May 1430	Joan conquers Compiegne, but is then captured when the drawbridge is raised too hastily. She is handed over to Bishop Pierre Cauchon, who is in the pay of the English.
May to November 1430	Joan is imprisoned.
January 1431	Opening of Joan's condemnation trial for heresy.
May 1431	Joan is found guilty of witchcraft and heresy by the French clergy, supported by the English. Joan is burnt alive at Rouen's old market square, the Place du Vieux Marché.
April 1909	Joan of Arc beatified by the Catholic Church.
1920	Joan of Arc canonised (made a saint) by the Pope.

A timeline of Joan of Arc's life.

After her capture in 1430 and her imprisonment, Joan of Arc was tried by a French religious court for the crime of heresy. Charles VII, whom she had helped to become king, did not intervene in her trial and instead left her to her fate. Joan was accused of having acted against the accepted religious ideas and principles of the day. In particular, she was accused of inventing visions and angels, and of wearing men's clothes. For these crimes, she was tried and convicted, sentenced to death and burnt at the stake. Twenty-five years later she was declared innocent, and nearly 500 years later she was made a saint.

SOURCE D

'I have but now resumed the dress of a man and put off the woman's dress.'

'Why did you take it, and who made you?'

'I took it of my own free will: I prefer a man's dress to a woman's dress.'

'Why have you resumed it?'

'I have resumed it because the promise made to me has not been kept; that is to say, that I should go to Mass and should receive my Saviour and that I should be taken out of irons.'

'Did you not promise not to resume this dress?'

'If I am allowed to go to Mass, and am taken out of irons and put into a gracious prison ... I will be good, and do as the church wills.'

Transcript of the questions asked by the Prosecution at Joan of Arc's trial.

SOURCE E

Joan was thirteen-years-old when the Archangel Michael, as she states, appeared, and urged her to be pure and holy and religious. Later on St Catherine (the Virgin) and St Margaret appeared to her, and told her that the Lord ordered her to go into France and relieve Orléans. In her examination she tells these things with great particularity, meeting all questions as to age, size, voice, dress, language, and surroundings of the angels, with a simple directness which carries conviction of her absolute truthfulness.

Extract from a history book published in 1903.

SOURCE F

... that you have been on the subject of thy pretended divine revelations and apparitions lying, seducing, pernicious, presumptuous, lightly believing, rash, superstitious, a divineless and blasphemer towards God and the Saints, a despiser of God Himself in His Sacraments; a prevaricator of the Divine Law, of sacred doctrine and of ecclesiastical sanctions; erring on many points of our Faith, and by all these means rashly guilty towards God and Holy Church. And also, because that often, very often ... you have been sufficiently warned to correct thyself, and have always obstinately refused to do ... for these causes we declare thee of right excommunicate and heretic.

The sentence passed on Joan of Arc, 30 May 1431.

 Question time

1 Why was it important that Joan claimed that she was on a mission from God? How would this help her efforts to help the French king?

2 Why do you think the Church was so upset by Joan wearing men's clothes?

3 Read Sources D, E and F.

   a What impressions of Joan does each source give?

   b Why do you think they give such different impressions?

4 Why do you think Joan of Arc was tried, convicted and then executed? The main characters involved in her conviction include:
   - Joan herself
   - the English king
   - the French king
   - the French nobles
   - the French priests.

Write an argument justifying each of their positions concerning the conviction of Joan of Arc.

4 Assessment section

1 Medieval monarchs did not have to explain themselves to anyone! But, in private meetings with their advisers, they probably did talk through various courses of action.

   a How might Edward I have explain why he acted as he did towards Wales and Scotland?

   b How might Richard II have explained why he acted as he did towards Ireland?

2 Owain Glyndwr and William Wallace were both regarded as heroes by their own people. Which man, in your estimate, did most for his country?

3 Find out all that you can about longbows and crossbows.

   a Draw a clear working diagram of each one. What was their range? In what sort of battle conditions did each work best?

   b Why did the French continue to use crossbows after the Battle of Crécy?

4 William Shakespeare wrote a series of plays about the kings of England. In 1599 he wrote *King Henry the Fifth*. In Act IV scene III of this play, he has Henry V make a speech in the English camp just before the Battle of Agincourt. If you have time, look up the speech yourself.

This day is call'd the feast of Crispian:
He that outlives this day, and comes to safe home,
Will stand a tip-toe when this day is nam'd,
And rouse him at the name of Crispian.
He that shall live this day, and see old age,
Will yearly on the vigil feast his neighbours,
And say, 'Tomorrow is Saint Crispian':
Then he will strip his sleeve and show his scars,
And say, 'These wounds I had on Crispian's Day'.

Old men forget: yet all shall be forgot,
But he'll remember with advantages
What feats he did that day. Then shall our names,
Familiar in his mouth as household words,
Harry the King, Bedford and Exeter,
Warwick and Talbot, Salisbury and Gloucester,
Be in their flowing cups freshly remember'd.
This story shall the good man teach his son;
And Crispin Crispian shall ne'er go by,
From this day to the ending of the world,
But we in it shall be remembered;
We few, we happy few, we band of brothers;
For he today that sheds his blood with me
Shall be my brother; be he ne'er so vile
This day shall gentle his condition:
And gentlemen in England now a-bed
Shall think themselves accurs'd they were not here,
And hold their manhoods cheap whiles any speaks
That fought with us upon Saint Crispin's day.

   a Why do you think Shakespeare's Henry V made this speech?

   b There is no evidence at all that the real Henry V ever said anything like this to the English troops before the Battle of Agincourt. Does this mean, therefore, that Shakespeare's history plays are of no use to a historian?

Further reading

P. Clarke, *The Boy with the Erpingham Hood* (Faber, 1956)

William Shakespeare, *Henry V*

Rosemary Sutcliff, *The Shield Ring* (Penguin, 1956)

5 Challenging the monarchy: power to the people?

If the monarch was all-powerful in the Middle Ages, what happened when he or she wasn't? What happened when this power was challenged? Most monarchs faced challenges to their power at some time during their reign. For a few those challenges changed the power of the monarchy and changed the relationship between the ruler and the ruled.

The challenges to King John

King John is seen as one king whose power was challenged in a big way. From the beginning of his reign, John faced threats to his throne and made decisions which made him unpopular with his subjects:

- Richard I died on 6 April 1199 and his brother John became King of England (see page 43). However, there was another claimant to the throne – John's nephew, Arthur of Brittany. Arthur was the son of John's elder brother Geoffrey, and on this basis had a better claim to the throne of England than John. John's Angevin lands in France, stirred up by Arthur and Philip II the King of France, began a formidable revolt against him.

Contemporary illustration of King John hunting.

- John angered the English people by divorcing his first wife, Isabel of Gloucester, a year after his coronation. He then made enemies in France by marrying Isabella of Angoulême, who had been promised in marriage to Hugh de Lusignan. Hugh was extremely angry at this and complained to the French king Philip II. Philip summoned John to appear before him, to answer for what he had done, but John refused and so Philip promptly confiscated all John's lands in France.

- John began defending his French lands in the spring of 1202. All was going well for the English until John made a terrible mistake. He captured and imprisoned his nephew Arthur of Brittany, and Arthur's sister Eleanor. Arthur was never seen again. By Easter 1202, there were reports that his mutilated body had been seen in the river

Seine and strong rumours began circulating that John had killed him. Distrust of John increased and French barons previously loyal to John began to turn against him. By 1206 John had to surrender all his lands in France north of the Loire.

- Some of John's barons in England held land in France as well. They were angry with John because he had also managed to lose their French lands.

King John spent a lot of his time arguing with important people: the Pope, the King of France and his barons. For England, the most important of these people were the barons, because their resentment would lead to serious trouble for everyone.

Argument with the Pope

In 1205, John's chancellor and Archbishop of Canterbury, Hubert Walter, died. Walter had been a good adviser to the king and his advice was sorely missed. His death brought about a crisis in the English Church when John refused to accept the Pope's choice for the new archbishop, Stephen Langton. He did not want an archbishop who put loyalty to the Pope above loyalty to his monarch! The Pope, angry that a mere king would defy him, put all England under an interdict. This meant that no masses could be held and there could be no church ceremonies, such as marriages and burials. Although these ceremonies could go ahead, they would be without the rituals and blessing of the Church. All a priest could do was baptise babies and hear the confessions of the dying. This frightened many people because they believed that, without regular attendance at mass and without making their confessions regularly to their priest, their souls would go to hell when they died.

John was not specially worried by this, even though the Pope had excommunicated him. He simply confiscated Church revenues and threw the monks out of Canterbury. He then used the money to fund his campaigns in Scotland, Ireland and Wales. This calmed down the barons for a short time because it gave them the opportunity to gain land to replace that which John had lost for them in France.

But the tide was turning against John. The Pope threatened to depose John and support an invasion of England by Philip II. A murder plot was uncovered and the barons became restless. Under such circumstances, John had no choice but to try to patch things up with the Pope. In this, at least, he was successful. John agreed to hold his lands as a fiefdom from the Pope, which meant that he acknowledged the Pope's authority. In return, the Pope lifted the interdict he had placed on England and supported John in his actions against the barons and Philip II.

John now had the money and the Pope's support to begin regaining his lost French lands. At first he was successful, but eventually had to agree to a peace treaty which the barons saw as a defeat.

The barons revolt

The barons had had enough. They had put up with many judgements in favour of their tenants that King John had made against them, and with the heavy taxes they had had to pay to John. The most hated tax was scutage, which was really a fine they had to pay if they did not fight for John when he asked them to. As the barons grew less and less inclined to support John in war, the scutage tax increased further. In addition to these complaints, the peace treaty with France and the apparent impossibility of getting back any of their French lands whilst John was King of England was, for the barons, the final straw. They rebelled openly and civil war broke out in May 1215.

London fell to the barons in June 1215 and John was forced to meet them at Runnymede, by the River Thames, to agree terms. On 15 June 1215 John was forced to agree to the barons' demands. He ordered his seal to be set to the *Magna Carta*, the Latin term for Great Charter.

The Magna Carta was intended, as you have seen, to be nothing more than a way of bringing about peace between John and his rebellious barons. People at the time certainly didn't see it as anything more. However, later generations have viewed the Magna Carta as a timeless declaration of the rights of the individual against the state. They have read into it what they wanted to read and what suited their purposes.

Question time

1   Copy the grid below into your file.

Who challenged King John?	Why did they challenge King John?	How did they challenge King John?	What was the outcome?
Arthur of Brittany			
Philip II of France			
Pope Innocent III			
The barons			

Did King John emerge from these challenges as a stronger or a weaker monarch?

2   Do you think King John's troubles were of his own making?

3   This is the beginning of a short story:

The night was still and the stars bright. A wolf howled in the distance. A horse kicked over its water bucket and a stable-lad swore under his breath and burrowed back into the straw to sleep. Inside the castle's great hall, the candles guttered and the lights flickered as first one and then another great baron gently pushed aside the tapestry over the doorway and softly stepped inside. Treachery was in the air and on their minds. When six of them were comfortably seated, Ranulf stood up. 'We are agreed that enough is enough. What are we now to do with this man John who calls himself our king?'

a   What do the plotters decide to do?

b   How do they carry out their plans?

c   What happens to them in the end?

d   Finish the story, remembering to be true to the history and to what was possible in the thirteenth century.

Digging deeper

Examining the Magna Carta

SOURCE B

Part of the Magna Carta.

Magna Carta is often seen as the first real statement about the rights and liberties of the English people and the foundation stone of British constitutional government. Three sections (called chapters) of Magna Carta are seen as being especially important:

- Chapter 12 says that 'No extraordinary tax shall be imposed except by common counsel of the kingdom'. This can be seen as an early statement that no one should be taxed without his agreement.

- Chapter 14 describes the Great Council, a group of men that are to meet to discuss weighty matters and to give advice to the king. This Great Council can be seen as the beginnings of Parliament.

- Chapter 39 says that 'No freeman shall be seized or imprisoned or stripped of his rights or possessions except by the lawful judgement of his peers and by the law of the land'. This can be seen as the beginnings of people's right to a trial by jury.

The last chapter was a determined effort to ensure that the Magna Carta would be upheld. Twenty-five barons were to sit in judgement, with the right to go to war against the king, if they thought that he had gone back on any of the liberties that he had guaranteed.

SOURCE C

... the English church shall be free, and shall have her rights entire, and her liberties unchecked and unchanged ...

This extract from the Magna Carta asserts the freedoms of the Church.

SOURCE D

No widow shall be compelled to marry, so long as she prefers to live without a husband; provided always that she promises not to marry without our consent, or without the consent of the lord who is responsible for her.

Extract from the Magna Carta dealing with the rights of widowhood.

SOURCE E

No scutage shall be imposed on our kingdom, unless by common counsel of our kingdom, except for ransoming our person, for making our eldest son a knight, and for once marrying our eldest daughter; and for these there shall not be levied more than a reasonable aid.

The barons would have been pleased with this section of the Magna Carta on scutage tax!

SOURCE F

And the city of London shall have all its ancient liberties and free customs, as well by land as by water; furthermore, we decree and grant that all other cities, boroughs, towns, and ports shall have all their liberties and free customs.

No freemen shall be taken or imprisoned or dispossessed or exiled or in any way destroyed, nor will we go upon him nor send upon him, except by the lawful judgement of his peers or by the law of the land.

Sections of the Magna Carta dealing with civil liberties.

SOURCE G

All merchants shall have safe and secure exit from England, and entry to England, with the right to tarry there and to move about as well by land as by water, for buying and selling by the ancient and right customs, quit from all evil tolls, except (in time of war) such merchants as are of the land at war with us.

The Magna Carta on the rights of merchants.

SOURCE H

And all the will, hatreds, and bitterness that have arisen between us and our men, clergy and lay, from the date of the quarrel, we have completely remitted and pardoned to everyone ...

Wherefore we will and firmly order that the English church be free, and that the men in our kingdom have and hold all the aforesaid liberties, rights, and concessions, well and peaceably, freely and quietly, fully and wholly, for themselves and their heirs, of us and our heirs, in all respects and in all places forever, as is aforesaid. An oath, moreover, has been taken, as well on our part as on the part of the barons, that all these conditions aforesaid shall be kept in good faith and without evil intent ...

The Magna Carta concludes with an assertion of good will towards, and of liberties for, all peoples of England.

Question time

1   Read through the extracts from the Magna Carta. Explain why these concessions have been extracted from John.

2   Use your school library or the Internet to find a poem called 'What say the Reeds at Runnymede' by Rudyard Kipling.

    a   How far do you think the poem is historically accurate?

    b   Does it matter whether the poem is historically accurate or not?

3   Magna Carta was concerned with setting down the rights of freemen, not the mass of ordinary people. Why, then, do you think people today look on it as the basis of our freedoms?

4   In groups, research the role which the monarch has today within the British system of government. Once you have done this, write a charter for today's monarch explaining what their role should be in the running of the country. Be careful to link it to what you feel the people's needs are.

The challenges to Henry III

Henry III inherited the English throne on the death of his father King John in 1216. He was only nine years old when he was crowned at Westminster Abbey. Henry's reign began in turmoil because he inherited the troubles from his father's reign (see pages 88–9), when the barons had rebelled and the Magna Carta had been agreed. At the start of Henry's reign there remained problems with the barons, especially in the northern regions, and only those in the Midlands and the southwest expressed their loyalty to the boy king.

During the years when he was too young to rule, Henry III had two regents. The first was William the Marshal, who governed for two years until his death in 1219; he was replaced by Hubert de Burgh, who governed until Henry was 20 years old. Until Henry was old enough to rule by himself, the barons tried to limit the monarch's power. To this effect, the Magna Carta was reissued twice in the early years of Henry's reign, in 1216 and 1217. In addition to written restrictions on royal authority in the Magna Carta, the barons also wanted to be consulted on matters of state. They therefore called together a Great Council (see page 91). The Great Council enabled the most important nobles and barons to meet to discuss the government of the country, to monitor taxes and spending, and to give advice to the monarch.

SOURCE A

Portrait of Henry III from a contemporary manuscript.

An unpopular ruler

Henry III is remembered as a weak king who favoured foreigners, much to the annoyance of his English subjects. Henry even preferred to speak and write in French! In January 1236, Henry married Eleanor of Provence. His marriage proved unpopular because he allowed himself to be governed by the relatives of his French wife. The barons, in particular, with their desire for influence in government, hated Henry for ruling according to the advice of his friends from southern France.

Henry's tutor was also a Frenchman, Peter des Roches, who was Bishop of Winchester. Under his influence, Henry grew up to be very pious and developed close ties with the papacy. Whilst Henry's religious devotion might be seen as a good thing for an English monarch, it only increased his unpopularity when he allowed the Bishop of Winchester to introduce a number of Frenchmen into the government. Papal influence in Britain also increased during Henry's reign. He allowed many Italians to enter English society to fill Church positions, and increased payments to the Church in Rome, to support the Pope's officials living throughout Europe. English subjects were subsequently prevented from entering vacant positions in the Church, and clergymen lost any chance of promotion. What made matters worse was that many of the foreign churchmen never even visited their parishes. Such moves infuriated the barons, who saw that Henry was not only denying them influence, but was also giving his power and money away to foreigners! England, they believed, was coming under foreign rule.

Simon de Montfort wins power and influence

The de Montforts were one of the Norman families who first came to England with William the Conqueror in 1066. Simon was born in France in 1208. His father was one of the great nobles of the time and a successful general. On his father's death, Simon inherited the earldom of Leicester from his grandmother and, in 1229, settled in England.

King Henry III was known to favour foreigners, and Simon soon became one of the king's favourite advisers. In 1231, Henry recognised Simon's earldom and he was officially created Earl of Leicester. Then, in January 1238, Simon married Henry's sister Eleanor. However, the marriage took place in secret and Henry was furious with Simon when he heard about it. In 1240, Simon achieved glory on crusade in Palestine under the king's brother Richard, Duke of Cornwall.

The Gascon campaigns

In 1227, Henry was old enough to rule without a regent and was given full powers as king. In 1230, he led an unsuccessful expedition to Gascony and Brittany, in the attempt to win back some of the French lands that had been lost during his father's reign (see page 88). The campaign was again repeated in 1242, when Henry was accompanied by Simon de Montfort. This Gascon campaign was, once again, defeated by Louis IX of France.

In 1248, while Simon was preparing to go on a new crusade, Henry again sent him to Gascony, where there were feudal wars and small uprisings.

Simon was given unlimited powers to crush these rebellions and, with a combination of both military skill and ruthlessness, was able to defeat the Gascon barons and establish order. Although successful in this mission, the people of Gascon complained bitterly about Simon's use of force. By 1252 these complaints had reached the king's ears. Ever-sympathetic to the French, Henry called Simon to an inquiry in England, where he was accused of unjust administration. Simon was furious, and a bitter quarrel with the king followed. Simon was eventually found innocent of all charges and returned to Gascony, but was then called back a second time, during the middle of a campaign, when Henry ordered Simon to allow his son, the young Prince Edward, to take charge. Believing that Henry had now twice betrayed him, Simon returned to England. His friendship with the king never fully recovered.

The barons oppose the king

By 1254, the relationship between Henry III and his barons was deteriorating. The barons were angered by several of Henry's schemes, and particularly his refusal to listen to their advice. These schemes included:

- the rebuilding of Westminster Abbey, and the building of other churches, at great expense

- a crippling rise in taxes, to pay for war debts

- the cost of the failed campaigns in France, which meant Henry had to sell off many of his possessions in France

- the offer to make one of Henry's younger sons, Edmund, King of Sicily. This had been suggested by the Pope, who wanted Henry to provide him with financial and military support for his war against the Hohenstaufen dynasty in Sicily. The Pope had run up huge debts in this fruitless war, and wanted Henry to take them on

- the proposal that the king's brother Richard of Cornwall should seek election as Holy Roman Emperor. This venture required huge funds, and Richard asked the Great Council for one third of all English revenues for the Pope.

Richard of Cornwall's request was made at a time when England was experiencing great economic distress and hardship. To the Great Council, it simply added insult to injury. The English barons were increasingly frustrated by Henry's subservience to the Pope and his willingness to be influenced by foreigners. When Henry agreed to take on the Pope's debts in his war against Sicily, it was the final straw. In protest at Henry's kingship, and angry at his unwillingness to consult them when making decisions, the barons refused to give him the necessary funds.

Henry III now faced a crisis on two fronts. Not only was he threatened with excommunication from the Pope, he also faced a crisis in government. As a religious man, excommunication would have been intolerable for Henry. He had thus been forced into a situation where he needed the support of his barons, who were now led by his old favourite Simon de Montfort.

The Provisions of Oxford, 1258

Angered by Henry's refusal to respect the Great Council, the barons, led by Simon de Montfort, held two meetings of the Great Council in 1258. They concluded that Henry III had not been ruling properly, and pushed him into accepting their proposal for government reform. This proposal stated that a committee of 24 barons should meet to draft a scheme for constitutional reform. Of this committee, half of the representatives were to be chosen by the king; the remainder was to be chosen by members of the Great Council.

The scheme for constitutional reform was drawn up in Oxford in June 1258, under the leadership of Simon de Montfort. It was known as the Provisions of Oxford. Its main points are:

- There would be a council consisting of 15 elected members to advise the king, with a majority rule and a right to veto (see Source B). In other words, the king's decision was not final.

- The council would meet three times a year to consult with representatives of the realm, with or without the presence of the king (see Source B).

- The council would have authority over the officers of the state – the treasurer, justiciar and the chancellor. The chancellor would not be able to use the royal seal without the council's knowledge (see Source C).

- Committees would be chosen through an electoral system among members of the council.

- There would be reforms to the royal household, and foreign members were to be banished.

- There would be changes in local administration so that taxes were decided locally, and not by the king.

- All castles were to be held by native-born Englishmen, not by foreigners.

- Each county would appoint a sheriff, who would be elected annually by the men of that county.

- All officials, including the king, would take an oath of loyalty to maintain the provisions.

SOURCE B

There are to be three parliaments a year: the first on the octave of Michaelmas; the second on the morrow of Candelmas; the third on the first Holy day of June, that is to say, three weeks before St John's day.

To these three parliaments shall come the chosen councillors of the King, even if they are not summoned, to view the state of the kingdom and to treat of the common business of the kingdom and of the King likewise ...

And they [the council] are to have authority to advise the King in good faith on the government of the kingdom, and authority to amend and redress all the things they see need to be redressed and amended. And if they cannot all be present, what the majority does shall be firm and established.

This section of the Provisions of Oxford states the role of the council.

The Chancellor of England ... will not seal any writ without the order of the King and of the councillors who are present.

The powers of the chancellor as described in the Provisions of Oxford.

A king without authority

The Provisions of Oxford effectively placed the barons in control of the country. They could make decisions whether or not the king was present at their meetings, and without his approval. Also, the king could no longer make decisions without the council's knowledge and approval.

Initially, the council managed to govern efficiently. It refused Henry permission to honour some of his commitments to the Pope, dismissed foreign advisers, and forced the king into a treaty with France. In addition, Henry's foreign relatives – who had once been so influential – now left England. The council also took steps to provide for merchants, the poor and widows. However, it was not very long before the council members started bickering among themselves.

There were also divisions among the barons in general. Younger barons, who had not been elected onto the council, had lost influence and were resentful of this. They wanted a return to their traditional role as adviser to the king. Older barons, who feared the consequences of the reforms in government, actually turned to the king for support in returning to the traditional feudal system.

It was these divisions among the barons that eventually enabled Henry to bring an end to the Provisions of Oxford, and to reassert his authority. In 1261, only three years after agreeing to the Provisions of Oxford, the king obtained a release from the Pope for the oaths he had taken to uphold the provisions. He then replaced the 15 members of the council, of which barons were in the majority, with his own nominees. Simon de Montfort left England in disgust.

Question time

1 Why do you think the Magna Carta was reissued in 1216 and 1217?

2 Why did Henry III start to fall out with his barons?

3 Why did the barons decide that they no longer wanted to support the call for reform of parliament?

The Barons' War, 1263–7

A group of nobles on the border of England and Wales fell out with Henry in 1263. They demanded the reforms of the Provisions of Oxford, and called Simon de Montfort back from France, to lead them in military action against the king. England was plunged once more into civil war.

Master of England?

The Barons' War started well for Simon, who won a great victory at the Battle of Lewes in 1264. He captured Henry and successfully forced the king to reaffirm his oath to the Provisions of Oxford. With the king in his custody, Simon became 'master of England'. He set out to govern England according to the guidelines set out in the Provisions of Oxford. However, the king was hardly going to play the game according to Simon's plan, and it became impossible for Simon to rule according to the Provisions of Oxford, which were based on the presence of a co-operative monarch. In the end, despite many years spent fighting for fair government, Simon de Montfort behaved more like a ruthless military dictator.

SOURCE D

To the most excellent lord Henry, by the grace of God, king of England ... we wish your excellency to know that we wish to preserve the safety and security of your person with all our might, as the fidelity which we owe to you demands, proposing to overthrow, to the utmost of our power, all those who are not our enemies but yours too, and the foes of the whole of your kingdom; and if any other statement is made to you respecting these matters, do not believe it; for we shall always be found your faithful subjects.

Letter from Simon de Montfort to Henry III before the Battle of Lewes, 1264.

SOURCE E

Since, from the war and general confusion existing in our kingdom, which has all been caused by you, and by the conflagrations and other lawless mischiefs, it is distinctly visible that you do not preserve the fidelity which you owe to us, and that you have in no respect any regard for the safety of our person, since you have wickedly attacked our nobles and others our faithful subjects, who have constantly preserved their fidelity to us, and since you still design to injure them as far as in your power ... we do not care for your safety or for your affection, but defy you, as the enemies of us and them.

The reply which Henry gave to Simon's letter (Source D).

The first parliament

By 1265, Simon de Montfort was losing the support of the barons, some of whom were beginning to side with Henry. Foreign powers also began offering Henry their support. To increase the amount of support in his name, Simon now summoned two knights from every shire, and two citizens from each town to a meeting in 1265. This meeting of government was the first in which the commons was represented – before, only the most important nobles, or barons, in the country had attended. It therefore marks what is considered to be the first true parliament. However, though Simon called this parliament in order to rally national support, by representing the common people he actually upset many of the barons, who feared a loss of status.

The Battle of Evesham, 1265

Simon de Montfort was eventually beaten at the Battle of Evesham in 1265. This decisive victory was led by the heir to the throne, Prince Edward, and came after the Welsh Marchers (Englishmen along the Welsh border) rose in the king's name. Once captured, Simon de Montfort suffered a cruel death. His head and genitals were cut from his body, and his limbs were severed and sent to different parts of the country.

SOURCE G

And a wonderful conflict took place, there being slain on the part of the lord Edward only one knight of moderate prowess, and two esquires. On the other side there fell on the field of battle Simon, earl of Leicester, whose head, and hands, and feet were cut off, and Henry, his son, Hugh Despenser, justiciary of England, Peter de Montfort, William de Mandeville, Radulph Basset, Roger St John, Walter de Despigny, William of York, and Robert Tregos, all very powerful knights and barons, and besides all the guards and warlike cavalry fell in the battle, with the exception of ten or twelve nobles, who were taken prisoners …

Extract from the chronicle of Matthew of Westminster which describes Prince Edward's victory at the Battle of Evesham.

By 1267, the barons had backed down and the civil war was over. The Provisions of Oxford and Westmister were revoked and the king was able, once more, to choose his own councillors. However, after the many trials and tribulations of his reign, Henry III ruled as monarch only in name. Instead, it was his son Prince Edward who actually ruled the realm. Unlike his father, Edward was aware of the need for government reform in England. The events of Henry's reign helped to pave the way for the constitutional developments during the reign of Edward I.

Question time

1   Read Source D. Why is Simon de Montfort very keen to stress his lack of personal hatred for the king? Who does he say he is really fighting?

2   What is the tone of Henry's letter in Source E? How does this help explain why he is in difficulties with his barons?

3   Read Source G. What information suggests that support for Simon came not only from the nobles, but from other areas of the country?

Digging deeper

Simon de Montfort: hero or villain?

Simon de Montfort is a controversial character in English history. Historians are divided as to whether Simon's actions were noble or selfish. They also question the extent to which Simon's actions changed the history of both the monarchy and government in Britain. Present-day authors are equally divided about Simon's position in history.

SOURCE H

A French-born English patriot, lordly champion of the commons, an honourable adventurer, he continues to be as controversial a figure in our time as he was in his own. Men have been arguing about the man, his motivations, and his legacy for the past seven hundred years. To an admiring Winston Churchill, 'de Montfort had lighted a fire never to be quenched in English history'. But the historian Sir F. M. Powicke, while grudgingly according Simon a certain 'murky greatness', also saw him as a 'dark force'. Victorian historians in particular tended to overestimate Simon's contribution to constitutional government, lauding him as 'the father of the English parliament', ascribing to him sentiments and ambitions no medieval man could have imagined. Simon's admirers and his critics do find some common meeting ground, all agreeing that Simon was able, arrogant, courageous, hot-tempered, and charismatic. Opinions then begin to diverge widely ... History's judgement upon Simon de Montfort has been fluid, fluctuating over the centuries in accordance with prevailing political winds, for each age interprets the past in the light of its own biases. But the verdict that lingers in the imagination is that of Simon's contemporaries, the medieval villagers who flocked to his grave, the steadfast Londoners, the poor and the powerless, who believed in him, who did not forget him.

This is what one modern writer has to say about Simon de Montfort.

SOURCE I

After Simon de Montfort's death there were miracles alleged to have happened in his name. Many sought his canonisation but the English crown was hostile to this idea. Simon's son Amaury succeeded in winning the pope's support and Simon's mutilated body was reinterred before the High Altar in the Abbey of Evesham, where the last battle had been fought. Although the abbey was demolished during the reformation in the 16th century, in 1965, 700 years after his death, a memorial was erected on the site of his grave. The inscription reads thus:

Here were buried the remains of Simon de Montfort, Earl of Leicester, pioneer of representative government...

Extract from Falls the Shadow, *an historical novel based on the life of Simon de Montfort by Sharon K. Penman.*

Activity time

1   You are an investigative reporter. Your task is to produce a report on Simon de Montfort which looks at both sides of the issue and highlights the main points of the argument. Use the evidence of Sources A–G.

- The monarch's side will argue that Simon de Montfort and his ideas were wrong and dangerous.

- Simon de Montfort and the reformers will argue that they do not intend to harm the monarchy, merely to strengthen it by making greater links with the people of the country.

Where do you think the barons will stand on this one? It could be that you can find barons willing to stand on either side of the argument. You might even find ones who will stand on both sides at the same time!

Edward I and Parliament

Edward I was a clever ruler and a great legislator. He surrounded himself with able ministers and lawyers. He regularly consulted with knights and townsmen, although not always in parliament. Parliament met frequently during his reign and there seems to have been a good connection between the crown and public opinion. In this way, although there were disagreements between England, Scotland and Wales during Edward's reign, negotiations were always started soon enough to prevent serious trouble. The institutions of the English state began to take shape, including the membership of parliament and its function:

- In 1275, Parliament granted an increase in the export duty on wool and leather to the king. This was to meet the increasing cost of government. Previously, the king had simply taken the money for himself without asking; now Parliament 'granted it'.

- In 1295 a formal request to attend Parliament, known as the Writs of Summons, was issued to bishops, abbots, earls, barons, knights, burgesses and representatives of the parishes. It contained the Latin phrase *quod omnes tangit ab omnibus approbetur,* which means 'Let that which touches all be approved by all.' In other words, matters of government which affect the people should be approved by representatives of the people – not simply decided by the monarch.

The Confirmation of Charters

In 1297, as a result of pressure from his subjects, Edward agreed to the Confirmation of Charters. This document covered all the provisions of the Magna Carta plus some extra ones. It now became law that no tax could be imposed on the English people by the monarch without parliamentary approval. Pressure to approve the charter had been placed on Edward by a group consisting of:

- barons, who were resentful at the high level of taxation

- merchants, who were resentful of high taxation and trade restrictions.

Together, the barons and the merchants made a strong force with which to petition the king for reform. In 1303, another charter was signed – the Carta Mercatoria – which granted merchants even more rights. They were now entitled to full freedom of trade in exchange for accepting a new system of taxes called custom dues, which were put on imported goods.

Question time

1 In what ways did Edward I show he intended to govern with the consent of the people?

2 Do you think that Edward's actions here showed that he was a weak king or a strong one?

Challenging the monarch: the Peasants' Revolt, 1381

The Peasants' Revolt in 1381 was a desperate and determined attempt to limit the power of the monarchy. The revolt was led by a peasant named Wat Tyler, and its immediate cause was the peasants' refusal to pay the hated poll tax. However, the Peasants' Revolt also reflects dangerous new ideas about the way in which society and the Church should be structured. In 1381 the king, nobles and the Church all feared the changes which were actually happening, and wanted to stop the changes and maintain the status quo.

Causes of the Peasants' Revolt

The peasant uprisings were a result of a number of causes:

- social change because of the Black Death (see below) and the consequent shortage of peasant labour

- disenchantment with nobles and the monarchy as a result of failure in foreign wars

- poor administration, incompetence and bribery in government leading to the government's loss of reputation

- lack of a strong monarch – Richard II was only ten years old when he came to the throne in 1377. This meant he had to rely heavily on advisers

- growth of critical views about religion

- the poll tax – a tax set at the same level for all people.

All of these factors increased the tension between those who were governed – the peasants – and those who ruled – the nobles and the monarch. These tensions had been accumulating for some time. Eventually, the revolt was triggered by the introduction of the poll tax. This meant that both rich and poor people had to pay the same amount, and was obviously unfair to the peasants, who were least able to pay.

The Black Death and social change

The Black Death arrived in England in the 1340s and proceeded to devastate the country (this is covered in more detail in Chapter 11). If the same proportion of people was affected today, about 20 million people would die. The first deaths occurred in 1348–53 when between one third and one half of the population died. Because so many people, particularly peasants, died of the disease, a shortage of labour occurred. As a result, landowners were forced to pay more to each peasant worker in order to keep them on their land. Some peasants started to leave their own lords to search for better pay elsewhere. The feudal system was breaking down.

This labour shortage led to a rise in the worth of labour as landowners were keen to find people to work on the land. The government tried to stop this new development by issuing the Statute of Labourers in 1351 to every county in the kingdom (see Source A).

The Statute of Labourers:

- set maximum pay rates (set at 1346–7 rates), so that peasants could no longer bargain for the best possible pay

- reaffirmed the rights of lords to claim certain services of peasants, such as free labour

- made arrangements for runaway peasants to return to their original manors

SOURCE A

Due to the number of people killed by the pestilence, and seeing that the landowners have limited workers to help, the king ordains the following:

1 Every able person under the age of 36 who is not a craftsman must work for his lord for the same wages as before the plague.
2 Any worker or servant leaving his lord's services without cause or licence should be imprisoned.
3 A man must not pay his servant more than the above wages, on pain of a fine of twice the labourer's wage.
4 A lord of town or manor must not pay his servant more than the above wages, on pain of a fine of thrice the labourer's wage.
5 Any craftsman charging more for his goods or service than pre-plague levels should be imprisoned.
6 Traders and merchants overcharging for their goods will pay a fine of three times the amount.
7 Anyone giving alms to the poor or gifts to beggars will be imprisoned. This is to ensure that they carry out rightful employment.

Part of the Statute of Labourers, 1351.

For about 25 years the statute achieved its objective: the protection of the interests of employers of labour, particularly the lords of the manor. These laws did have an effect on wages but, as time went on, further developments made these restrictions appear even more unfair to the peasants. By 1377, the peasants' dissatisfaction was great enough for a petition to be presented by the commons in Parliament noting that, in many areas, peasants were refusing to serve their lords. The peasants were demanding an end to slavery.

Foreign wars

The Hundred Years War played its part in the Peasants' Revolt. It had started well for England (see pages 80–1). Success in the Battle of Crécy in 1346 and the Battle of Poitiers in 1356 marked a period of glory, with associated war booty being used to invest in the building of splendid manors and churches. By 1360, France seemed to have accepted English sovereignty in many areas of the country. By 1375, however, only Calais, Cherbourg, Brest, Bayonne and Bordeaux remained in English hands. This series of military humiliations in France was followed by raids on the English coast. This brought the war uncomfortably close to the population of England, who had benefited from the victories in France but who now felt threatened and humiliated by England's losses. They feared for their homes and their livelihoods.

Poor administration of government

Sir Richard Waldegrave, the Speaker in Parliament in 1381, reinforced the view that the peasant rebels were reacting against bad government. He spoke to Parliament about the extravagance of the court, the weakness of the ministers, the burden of taxation and the mess made in national defence as reasons for the uprisings. Certainly the peasants were aware of how badly England was being run and knew who to blame for it. During the revolt they targeted the lands and possessions of those who were responsible. They blamed the king's advisers, not just the king himself. Richard was only ten years old, and therefore too young to be held responsible.

Lack of a strong monarch

Edward III reigned from 1327 to 1377. He was a strong, popular monarch. He initially gave generous concessions to the barons and recognised the complaints of the middle-class traders, since he understood the importance of trade in creating wealth. Edward was fond of war and during his reign the Hundred Years War was viewed favourably by his subjects. The successes of the early stages of the war (see pages 80–1) helped to increase his personal popularity, as well as bring in valuable income for all sections of society. Edward also resisted the Pope's demands for money and influence in England. In 1362, English became the language of the law, and in 1375 it was taught in schools. Edward III's successes and the changes that occurred during his reign made him a popular and successful king.

By the last part of his reign, Edward III was old and senile. His son, the Black Prince, was popular and had had many successes in battle (see page 81), but when he returned from France in 1371 he was ill. With the king and his eldest son in an unfit state to rule, there was a lack of influence at court, which allowed John of Gaunt, Edward III's third son, to increase his power and influence (see page 82).

Edward the Black Prince died in 1376. This meant that, on the death of Edward III in 1377, Richard II, son of the Black Prince, inherited the throne. He was only ten years old. Richard's council was dominated by men such as John of Gaunt. A regency government (where advisers take all the decisions until a monarch is old enough) always carries the problem of possible corruption when the leader of the governing body acts more for personal reasons and ambitions than for the good of the country. The lack of a strong king was certainly seen as helping to allow social and political problems to fester.

Religion

This period saw different ideas developing in religion. Some of these ideas went against the teachings and traditions of the Church. Many people found these new ideas shocking, and accused those spreading them of heresy. The most renowned of these English medieval heretics was John Wyclif, who made his criticisms of the Church in the period leading up to the Peasants' Revolt. He said that the early Christian Church had not had property or wealth, so argued that neither should the medieval Church. He also believed that only the individual could make their peace with God; he did not believe that the Church should be making money from selling pardons for sins. However, Wyclif's message had not spread far outside the Church by the time of the uprising, and his ideas were to have much greater impact in later years.

There were others in the Church who had more impact on the peasants because they were preachers who wandered from town to town. They linked a strongly Christian message to arguments in favour of freedom for the poor. Many of these priests who saw the living conditions of the peasants felt an enormous sympathy for them.

One such preacher was John Ball. He travelled the countryside, preaching the equality of all before God. This was dangerous stuff indeed, and in 1366 the Church formally forbade him to preach and then excommunicated him. But this didn't stop John Ball. He became part of a sort of religious underworld figurehead, hated by those in power yet respected and even loved by the peasants. His illegal preaching eventually landed him in Maidstone gaol from where, in 1381, the peasants released him. When the Peasants' Revolt collapsed, John Ball was captured, imprisoned and, on 15 June 1381, hanged, drawn and quartered.

SOURCE C

When Adam delved and Eve span
Who then was the gentleman?

This was used by John Ball as the text for one of his sermons at the start of the Peasants' Revolt in 1381. He adapted it from a poem by Richard Rolle de Hampole written earlier in the fourteenth century.

SOURCE D

My good friends, things cannot go well in England until everyone is equal. They are dressed in velvet while we are forced to wear rags. They have wines, spices and fine bread, while we have only black bread. When we drink, it must be water.

Extract from one of John Ball's speeches, quoted in Froissart's Chronicle, which dates from 1460.

SOURCE E

John Ball saint mary priest, greteth well all maner of men, and biddeth them in the name of the trinitie father, son, and holy ghost, stand manlike together in truth, and helpes truth, and truth shal helpe you:
Now reigneth pride in price,
couetise is holde wyse,
lechery without shame,
glotony without blame:
envy reigneth with treason,
and slouth is taken in great season.
God doe boote, for nowe is time!
Amen.

John Ball's letter of June 1381.

The poll tax

The poll tax was the spark which ignited the Peasants' Revolt.

- Early in the 1370s, in order to pay for the Hundred Years War, the government had started demanding heavy taxes.

- In 1377, to raise still more money, the first poll tax was imposed, at a rate of 4d per person. This tax was the same for every person over 14 years of age, regardless of how much money they earned.

- In 1379 another poll tax was introduced, in an attempt to link the amount of tax paid to the amount of income earned.

- In 1380 yet another poll tax was introduced, at a rate three times higher than in 1377. This poll tax was the same for everyone. Even the chronicler of the time, the Monk of Westminster, generally unsympathetic to the peasants, described this taxation as 'rapacious' (excessively greedy).

Those who administered the government and supervised the collection of the taxes were blamed for the unfairness of the poll tax, especially the Chancellor and Archbishop of Canterbury, Simon Sudbury, and Sir Robert Hales, the Treasurer. Property belonging to these men and their associates was a particular target of the rebel peasants during the revolt, and both Sudbury and Hales were beheaded by the angry peasants.

The Peasants' Revolt begins

The economic, political, social and religious problems which had been building up during the reign of Richard II came to a head in mid-1381. Many peasants refused to pay the poll tax, and in some villages the tax collectors were beaten up. Large, noisy groups of peasants gathered in various parts of south-east England. They elected leaders and grouped together for common objectives, and were the basis of the uprisings of 1381. Source F describes how the Essex village of Fobbing rose up, led by one man, and encouraged other villages to join in. This marked the start of the Peasants' Revolt, and the rioting spread quickly from Essex into Kent.

SOURCE F

Then others joined them, and then each of them sent messages ... from village to village, district to district, seeking advice and asking them to bring prompt help ... And so they began to gather together in companies with great show of jubilation ...

Henry Knighton of Leicester describes the events arising from the actions of one man in the Essex village of Fobbing in 1381.

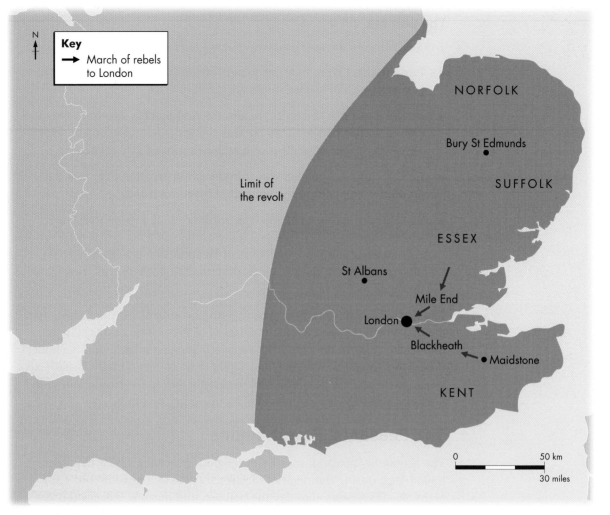

The spread of the Peasants' Revolt, 1381.

Many of the groups of peasants came to London where, with the poor of the city, it is estimated there were some 100,000 rebels. The peasants' discontent was expressed in the demands from the main body of the rebels, who participated in the events in and around London in June 1381. These demands were first expressed at Maidstone in early June and had four elements:

- allegiance to the king and the commons
- to have no king named John
- to accept no tax but the traditional levy of one fifteenth of moveable wealth
- to be ready to act when called upon.

By the time the rebels met with King Richard at Mile End in London on 14 June, the aims had become:

- the handing over of 'traitors'
- the end of serfdom (slavery)
- the right to hire out at fair wages
- the right to rent land at a cheap rate.

Digging deeper

The events of the Peasants' Revolt, 1381

May

A tax collector arrives at the Essex village of Fobbing to find out why the people there have not paid their poll tax. He is thrown out by the villagers.

June

Soldiers arrive in Fobbing to establish law and order. They too are thrown out and many other local villages in Essex join the rebels. One man emerges as leader of the peasants, Wat Tyler from Kent.

7 June

Tyler and his followers take possession of Canterbury. There, they open up Maidstone prison and liberate John Ball, a lapsed priest who had been arrested shortly before by the Bishop of Canterbury. The rebels march towards London, attracting followers along the way.

10 June

Throughout the country, peasants march towards London. As the peasants from Kent march to London, they destroy tax records and tax registers. Buildings which house government records are burned down.

11 June

The peasants in Norwich rebel, under the leadership of Geoffrey Litster. However, the peasants are not effective as soldiers and their enemy, Bishop Henry Despenser, defeats them in a bloody battle. The bishop and his troops also kill many of the city's workers after the battle.

Nearly 100,000 peasants arrive in London and wait to present their demands to the king.

12 June

The rebels get into the city of London when the people there open the gates to them. They burn John of Gaunt's London palace, the Savoy, along with Fleet prison and the Hospital of St John.

14 June

The Tower of London is taken by the peasants. The Chancellor and Archbishop of Canterbury, Simon Sudbury, and Sir Robert Hales, the Treasurer, are killed on Tower Hill (near the Tower of London). King Richard II escapes and agrees to negotiations with the peasants, and to meet the rebels at Mile End in London. At this meeting, Richard II listens to the rebels' demands, which include free labour contracts and the right to rent land at four pence an acre. Richard promises them justice, gives the peasants all they ask for and asks that they go home in peace. Some do, but Richard II spends the night in hiding for fear of his life.

15 June

Richard II meets the rebels again. Wat Tyler then presents the king with his list of demands, to which the king readily agrees. Suddenly, one of the king's lords (Walworth or Standish) approaches from behind with a sword and kills Wat Tyler. This is the signal for the king's troops (8000 men) to attack the peasants: 1500 of them are killed.

Historians cannot be sure about what happened at the meeting on 15 June between Richard II and Wat Tyler because the only people who could write about it were on the side of the king, and so their evidence might be biased. However, we do know that the Peasants' Revolt did not last long. The death of Tyler, and another promise by Richard to give the peasants what they asked for, was enough to send them home. But Richard betrayed them and, in so doing, betrayed their trust in the crown and in the monarchy.

A contemporary illustration of events at Smithfield, 15 June 1381. On the left Walworth has drawn his sword and is striking Tyler. On the right, Richard II rides over to speak to the peasants.

SOURCE H

Afterwards the king sent out his messengers to capture the malefactors and put them to death. And many were taken and hanged at London, and they set up many gallows around the City of London, and in other cities and boroughs of the south country. At last, as it pleased God, the king seeing that too many of his liege subjects would be undone, and too much blood spilt, took pity in his heart, and granted them all pardon, on condition that they should never rise again, under pain of losing life or members, and that each of them should get his charter of pardon, and pay the king as fee for his seal twenty shillings, to make him rich. And so finished this wicked war.

A contemporary account of the punishment of the rebels.

By the summer of 1381, the revolt was over. All the main leaders had been hanged (see Source H). Richard did not keep any of his promises, claiming that they were made under threat and were therefore not valid in law. The poll tax was withdrawn, but the peasants were forced back into their old way of life, under the control of the lord of the manor.

 Question time

1 How helpful is Source G to historians investigating events at Smithfield in 1381?

2 Read Source H. Is the author more sympathetic to the rebels or to the king?

Richard II survived as monarch until 1399. He was then deposed in favour of Henry Bolingbroke, son of John of Gaunt. If you look back at the events of Richard's reign, you can see that he committed the same crimes that many medieval monarchs had committed before him. He had failed to be successful in France, he had married a French princess, and he had offended one too many of his barons. Richard paid the price with his throne and his life. He died mysteriously in Pontefract Castle.

Question time

1   Draw a spider diagram to show all the causes of the Peasants' Revolt. Highlight the three causes you think are the most important. Write a paragraph for each one, explaining why.

2   Compare the list of final demands which Wat Tyler read to the king with the original demands of the peasants. What differences can you find in these demands? Can you suggest reasons why this should be?

3   Think about Richard II's behaviour.
   a   Why did he lie to the peasants?
   b   Is it right that a monarch should lie to his subjects?
   c   Why did he treat the peasants so harshly?

4   Was the Peasants' Revolt doomed from the start?

Digging deeper

Popular voices

We know quite a lot about what the rich and famous in medieval England thought and felt. But we know little about ordinary people's thoughts and hopes and feelings. Sometimes we can catch a glimpse of what it must have been like for them.

SOURCE 1

A Haberdasher, a Dyer, a Carpenter,
A Weaver and a Carpet-maker were
Among our ranks, all in the livery
of one impressive guild fraternity.
They were so trim and fresh their gear would pass
For new. Their knives were not tricked out with brass
But wrought with purest silver, which avouches
A like display on girdles and on pouches.
Each seemed a worthy burgess, fit to grace
A guild-hall with a seat upon the dais.
Their wisdom would have justified a plan
To make each one of them an alderman;
They had the capital and revenue,
beside their wives declared it was their due.

An extract from The Canterbury Tales, *a rhyming story written by Geoffrey Chaucer in about 1375.*

Geoffrey Chaucer reading his poems to the court of Richard II. Illustration from a contemporary manuscript.

SOURCE K

A faire feeld ful of folk I ther bitwene
Of alle manere of men, the mene and the riche,
Werchynge and wandrynge as the world asketh
Whan alle tresors arn tried, Truthe is the beste.
Brewsters and baksters, bochiers and cokes
For thise are men on this molde that moost
    harm wercheth
To the povere peple.

An extract from 'The Vision of Piers Plowman', a poem written by William Langland in about 1340.

SOURCE L

Right worshipful husband, I commend myself to you. This is to let you know that I sent your eldest son to Lady Morley to find out what entertainment was put on in her house the Christmas after the death of her husband. And she said there was no disguisings or harping or lute-playing or singing and no noisy amusements, but backgammon and chess and cards; these were the games she allowed her people to play, and no others.

Please also send me a pot of treacle very soon, for both I and your daughter have not been at all well since you left here. And one of the tallest young men of this parish is ill, and has very bad catarrh; what will become of him, God knows.

Sir Harry Inglose has passed to God tonight, on whose soul God have mercy, and was carried to St Faith's at nine o'clock today, where he is to be buried. If you want to buy any of his things, please let me know quickly and I will speak to Robert Inglose and to Witchingham about it. I think they are the executors.

As for cloth for my gown, I cannot get anything better than the sample I am sending you, which is, I think, too poor in both cloth and colour, so please buy me $3\frac{3}{4}$ yards of whatever you think is suitable for me, of what colour you like, for I have really searched all the drapers' shops in this town, and there is a very poor choice. Please buy a loaf of good sugar as well, and half a pound of whole cinnamon for there is no good cinnamon in this town.

Extracts from Margaret Paston's letters written to her husband John in the 1450s.

Question time

1 Why do you think it is so difficult to find out how ordinary people lived in the Middle Ages?

2 What can you find out about everyday life from these sources?

3 How complete a picture do these sources give us of everyday life in the Middle Ages?

1 A weak king was the curse of medieval England. Barons saw an opportunity to increase their power and challenged each other and the monarch.

King John and King Henry III both had problems with their barons.

a What were the similarities and what were the differences in the opposition John and Henry III faced from their barons?

b Did they face opposition because they were weak kings?

c Why was Edward I more successful in dealing with challenges to his power than John and Henry III?

2 Geoffrey Chaucer was a writer who lived in London in the 1380s. He wrote *The Canterbury Tales* in about 1375, a story about various different people who went on a pilgrimage to Canterbury. You can read an extract from his *Canterbury Tales* on page 111.

Sadly, Geoffrey Chaucer didn't write about the Peasants' Revolt. That is, as far as we know. But what if a manuscript was discovered at the back of ancient shelving in an old library that *did* tell a story about the Peasants' Revolt? What might it say?

Your task is to write up the story of the Peasants' Revolt as it might have been written on this lost manuscript. You will write of the different people who were involved: peasants and nobles, the king and priests, people from London and people from other parts of the country. Each person will be very keen to tell their side of the story, and the part they played in the revolt.

You will need to decide which characters you will write about. You may work in a group and take one character each, putting them together to produce an epic work.

Further reading

Geoffrey Chaucer, *The Canterbury Tales*

Sharon Penman, *The Reckoning* (Penguin, 1991)

A. Phillips, *The Peace Child* (Oxford University Press, 1988)

Geoffrey Trease, *Baron's Hostage* (Heinemann Educational, 1975)

The Wars of the Roses

Where are we now? We're moving rapidly towards what is traditionally accepted as the end of the medieval period. 1485 is seen as marking the end of the Middle Ages and the start of the modern period of history. Why is this? If changes in the pattern of history are the reason, then there are several possible answers.

Let's start with the change of monarch in that year. Richard III was defeated in battle and Henry VII became king. Nothing too unusual in that: Richard was one of four crowned monarchs who lost their thrones other than by natural death in the preceding 160 years. And that's without counting the mysterious disappearance of the two princes in the Tower who never even made it to be crowned (see page 130).

Richard III's death in 1485 at the Battle of Bosworth was the last time an English king died in battle trying to save his throne. He was the last member of his family, the Lancastrians, to be king. The new king, Henry VII, was part of a different family – the Tudors – although there was a distant connection with the house of Lancaster.

The royal family tree, showing links between the families of Lancaster and York, 1327–1485.

Edward III = Philippa of
(1327–77) Hainhault

Edward, = Joan of Kent
Prince of Wales
'The Black Prince'
(d.1376)

Richard II
(1377–99)

Lionel, Duke = Elizabeth
of Clarence | de Burgh

Edmund = Philippa
Mortimer |

Eleanor = Roger
| Mortimer

*Richard, Earl = Anne
of Cambridge | Mortimer

Cecily Neville = Richard Plantagenet,
(granddaughter   Duke of York and
of John of Gaunt) Protector of England

Edward IV = Elizabeth
(1461–83) | Woodville

Edward V
(never crowned)
(d.1483)

George, Duke
of Clarence

Richard,
Duke of York
(d.1483)

John of = (1) Blanche
Gaunt | of Lancaster

Henry IV = Mary de
(1399–1413) Bohum

Henry V = (1) Catherine = (2) Owen
(1413–22) of Valois   Tudor

Henry VI = Margaret
(1422–61) of Anjou
(1470–1)

Richard III = Anne
(1483–5) Neville

= (3) Katherine
Swynford

John = Margaret
Beaufort |

John, Duke = Margaret
of Somerset

Edmund = Margaret
Tudor | Beaufort

Elizabeth of York = **Henry VII**
(1485–1509)

Edmund,
Duke of York

Richard, Earl
of Cambridge*

The Lancaster and York families

In 1485, Henry VII saw the need to unite and control the nobles, so that divisions did not become too great and lead to open warfare. Although the checks on the king's power which had developed during the Middle Ages remained in place, Henry created a monarchy with a much stronger grip on everything. He became much more of an absolute monarch. This means that he had total control of finances, politics and the lives of the nobles who served him. This method of working helped to ensure that no real threat arose to either Henry VII or his heirs.

After 1485, despite the many changes in fortune for the monarchy, including the lack of a suitable heir, Charles I is the only monarch who loses his life by being on the wrong side at the wrong time. By looking at the pattern of monarchs it would seem that a change in monarch was not always the dramatic event it once had been, perhaps because the monarch did not hold the place of importance which he or she once had. 1485 is often seen as the beginning of a more civilised approach to government with less fighting, at least in public.

Whatever the reasons, Henry VII's reign is often seen to mark both a change and a transition between the old ways of the Middle Ages, and the new modern approach. It only leaves the question why did this happen at that time? As ever, we need to look back to the period before Henry VII for the answers.

Power struggles

Before Henry VII came to power, the monarchy in England had gradually became more and more unsettled, starting with the reign of Edward III. The ideal situation for any monarch was to have one or two healthy, intelligent and militarily capable sons. This meant there would be one son as heir to the throne, and one son 'to spare'. Edward III had many sons, and this created problems, especially as Edward himself lived to a ripe old age. This problem had been evident since William the Conqueror and his three sons. If there were too many sons, one or more of them could feel excluded from power. Certainly the lands of England could not be divided up too much, or the monarch would lose power.

The story of these years is one of a power struggle between the Lancaster and York families for control of the throne of England. Known during the period as the wars between Lancaster and York, it was not until much later that it was noticed that the symbol of the House of York was the white rose and that the coat of arms of the House of Lancaster included a red rose. Shakespeare made much of this in his historical plays about the period, and it is from this that we take the modern name for the wars: the Wars of the Roses.

A painting by Henry A. Payne in 1921 called 'Choosing the Red and White Roses'. It shows nobles picking red and white roses, based on a scene from Shakespeare's play about Henry VI.

Question time

1 Look at the family tree for the Lancaster and York families 1327–1485.

a Find and list the kings in chronological order.

b Underline or block in red the kings who were descended from John of Gaunt. These were known as the Lancastrians because John of Gaunt was the Duke of Lancaster.

c Underline or block in white the kings who were descended from Edmund, Duke of York. They were known as Yorkists.

2 Henry VII married Elizabeth of York in 1486. Using the evidence of this family tree only, can you suggest why he did this?

3 Look at Source A, which was painted in 1921, over 400 years after the Wars of the Roses.

a Explain whether or not you think it likely that the nobles really chose sides in this way.

b The artist had a very definite reason for painting this scene. Research in your local library or the Internet to find out why. (Hint: your English teacher may be able to help.)

Henry IV

The Wars of the Roses started in 1399 when Richard II (the grandson of Edward III) was forced off the throne by Henry Bolingbroke, Duke of Lancaster. Henry Bolingbroke was Richard's cousin and also a grandson of Edward III. Richard died mysteriously at Pontefract Castle (see page 111). Richard had certainly not been a popular king, particularly towards the end of his reign, and you might think that a change of king would be seen as a good thing all round. The difficulty was that if one king can be disposed of so easily, it becomes easy to get rid of any king who doesn't quite match up to requirements.

Henry Bolingbroke had himself crowned as Henry IV, thus establishing the Lancastrian family on the throne. His reign was troubled by unrest and occasional rebellion. The Welsh, the Scots and the North of England all rose against the king at one time or another during his reign. He did survive long enough, however, to pass the crown to his son, Henry of Monmouth.

Portrait of Henry IV. Date and artist unknown.

Henry V

Henry V began his reign in 1413 at the age of 26. There were those who felt he would not be a suitable king because his exploits as a young man were reckless and immoral. However, he had seen the chaos of rebellion in his father's reign and had been part of the fighting which had finally settled the country.

When he became king, Henry established good government and, perhaps more importantly, he succeeded in taking attention away from the problems in England. He did this by invading France and winning the famous Battle of Agincourt in 1415 (see pages 82–3). Success at Agincourt marked the beginning of the English conquest of large parts of France and this led to a surge in national pride. By 1420, the Treaty of Troyes acknowledged English gains across northern France and recognised Henry V as the heir to the throne of France.

Portrait of Henry V. Date and artist unknown.

Henry V's wars in France helped make England a stable country because:

- Success in war is helpful to a king: it boosts his personal image.

- The wars in France also meant that many of Henry's barons were engaged in fighting, so they had little time for plotting rebellion.

- The gains in France meant there were rewards for the barons, and these made them pleased that they had linked themselves to Henry V.

- Even the peasants who fought in the armies of England benefited from the booty which they brought home from France.

- Henry V married Catherine, daughter of the King of France, ensuring that there would be peace between the two countries.

- Henry V appeared as a good king, was well supported, and everything looked secure for the Lancastrian line.

However, Henry soon became a victim of his success. Exhausted by constant campaigning, he caught dysentery and died in 1422. Although England held most of western France, the difficulty now lay in the fact that Henry V's son, Henry of Windsor, was less than one-year-old. The infant Henry was proclaimed King Henry VI, although it was agreed that a committee of his uncles would rule as regent until he was old enough to rule alone.

Henry VI

Henry VI, just nine months old, was proclaimed King of England and France. His uncles assumed responsibility for governing: the Duke of Gloucester became regent in England, and the Duke of Bedford became regent in France.

Troubles in France hit England

Despite all that Henry V had done, the Hundred Years' War (see pages 80–4) continued. But where Henry's fighting in France had had a good effect in England, continued fighting under the leadership of the Duke of Bedford most definitely did not. This was because:

- The cost of keeping garrisons in France in order to control Henry V's conquests meant that English people had to pay higher taxes.

- The French adopted different tactics against the English. Instead of set battles they began guerrilla warfare, swooping on English supply convoys and constantly harassing the soldiers. This led to disillusionment among the troops and morale crashed.

- Falling morale continued when the French began winning back more and more land. By 1453, only Calais remained in English hands.

Question time

1 How did events in France mean that Henry V could keep England peaceful?

2 Why was England a troubled country during the years of Henry VI's reign?

Digging deeper

Henry VI

What do we know about Henry VI? Let's start with some basic facts.

- He was born in Windsor Castle on 6 December 1421.

- He ruled England officially from 1 September 1422 to 4 March 1461, when he was deposed.

- Henry was proclaimed King of France and crowned in the Cathedral of Notre Dame de Paris on 16 December 1431

- He declared himself of age (able to rule by himself) in November 1437. Before then, England had been ruled in his name by his uncle Humphrey, who was the Duke of Gloucester, and his uncle John, who was the Duke of Bedford.

- Though deposed in 1461, Henry was restored to the throne on 3 October 1470. He was then deposed again, for the final time, on 11 April 1471.

- Henry was crowned in Westminster Abbey on 6 November 1429, and for the second time in St Paul's Cathedral on 6 October 1470.

- On 22 April 1445 he married Margaret, the daughter of the Duke of Anjou, in Titchfield Abbey. They had one son.

- Henry was murdered in the Tower of London on or about 21 May 1471.

But these are only the bare bones of Henry's life. What else do we know about him as a person?

- He devoted himself to Christian contemplation and prayer.

SOURCE D

Portrait of Henry VI. Date and artist unknown.

- When Henry was a child, his uncles made sure that they held as much power as possible. So, by the time Henry was able to take over running the kingdom himself, he had become the pawn of two powerful men. Also, he was too weak willed to assert himself.

- Henry gave power and authority to people he trusted and, because he was a man of poor judgement, chose unsuitable men like the Duke of Suffolk and the Duke of Somerset.

- After about August 1453 Henry began suffering from bouts of mental instability and deep depression. During those times when he was clearly unfit to reign, Richard of York was made 'Protector of the Realm'. Henry's wife Margaret also did her best to look after his interests during these times.

Sources E–G reveal what some historians have said about Henry VI. As you read through the rest of this chapter, think about whether you agree with these historians, or not.

SOURCE E

Henry VI was the youngest king ever to ascend the throne; the only king to know what it was like not to be king; the only one ever to be crowned King of France, and arguably the worst, who inherited two kingdoms and lost them both.

In another age, and another society, a man who turned his back on vainglorious war and whose greatest achievements were the promotion of education through the founding of Eton College and King's College Cambridge, might have been highly regarded. But in fifteenth-century England, a king like Henry VI was a public disaster.

Professor Anthony James Pollard writing about Henry VI in 1988.

SOURCE F

Henry VI is a prime example of the wrong king at the wrong time, and that made for a very tragic reign. Had Margaret been the queen of a stronger king, they would have made a remarkable pair and doubtless ruled with considerable effect, but she had the misfortune to be married to a king who began weak and sank into mental decline.

The historian Mike Ashley writing in 1998.

SOURCE G

Undoubtedly his life had been tragic, but for his subjects his reign was calamitous. He stood helplessly by as England slid into the Wars of the Roses, and as well as losing the throne of England twice, he witnessed from afar the loss of all his dominions in France except for Calais.

Professor John Gillingham writing about Henry VI in 1981.

Question time

1. Work out how old Henry was when the major events of his life happened.

2. Find out who Henry VI's son was, when he was born, and when and how he died.

3. Research Henry VI's wife, Margaret of Anjou, and find out what she did during the Wars of the Roses.

Profiteering from war

Farming was no longer being done simply to support the workforce, but to make a profit for the landowner. Many nobles had also grown rich with the booty from the successful wars in France during Henry V's reign, and benefited from the new wealth from the woollen industry. These wealthy landowners started to protect their lands with increasing numbers of private armies. Each noble family produced its own coat of arms so that their soldiers and land could be recognised.

Digging deeper

Heraldry

Sports teams – rugby and football, hockey, lacrosse and basketball – can all be recognised by their supporters because of the colours they wear. At the time of the Wars of the Roses, royal, noble and powerful families could also be recognised and distinguished from one another by their coats of arms. Each of these families had their own colours and symbols, called *devices*. There was nothing really new in this. The Roman eagle, the Viking raven and the dragon of Wessex had been seen in England hundreds of years before the Norman conquest. But these belonged to different peoples – Saxons, Vikings and Romans – rather than to individuals. By the time William of Normandy began rewarding his loyal Norman followers with lands and titles, devices had become more personal and were beginning to belong to individual families rather than to larger groups of people.

Heraldic devices

In the twelfth century the golden lions of the Plantagenets were among the first to appear as hereditary (inherited) heraldic devices. In 1127, Count Geoffrey Plantagenet of Anjou had several lions on his shield; his son King Henry II stuck to just two such lions. By 1198, however, the Plantagenets had settled on three lions, and these still form part of the British coat of arms.

During the twelfth century, developments in armour made the use of heraldic devices vital. Knights wore new-style helmets that completely covered their heads. This made them unrecognisable in tournaments and battles, so they had devices emblazoned on their helmets, shields, tunics (called surcoats) and the trappings on their horses. In battle it was essential that allies and enemies could be recognised in a couple of seconds, and so devices first of all tended to be simple and bold: stripes, chevrons, squares and heraldic beasts.

Heralds

As devices became more complicated, specialist 'heralds' supervised opponents in tournaments and picked out enemies during battles. During a battle, by recognising different coats of arms heralds were able to tell their lord who his opponents were, how many knights they had put into the field and who had left or joined the battle. At the Battle of Agincourt in 1415, French and English heralds watched events together and, at the end, reported to King Henry V of England that he had won. Heralds identified captives: rich and important captives were held for ransom; poorer ones were killed. They also identified the dead, which was not always an easy task. When knights charged into battle on huge warhorses, wielding heavy axes, swords and lances, they did a lot of damage to each other. Often, for the heralds, it was a question of finding the right bits and putting them together before they could decide who had died!

The Plantagenet banner. Three gold lions were on the shield of Geoffrey Plantagenet, Duke of Anjou, and on the shields of the Plantagenet kings.

Coats of arms

By the end of the thirteenth century it became fashionable to have a coat of arms. Any rich and important family of note had its own set of devices that could be distinguished from those of another family. Coats of arms were used to show how families were united by marriage and which monarchs owned what tracts of land. Edward III, for example, put the arms of France on one quarter of his shield (doing this is called quartering) to emphasise his claim to the French throne.

At great social events, like tournaments, those taking part would let everyone know they were there by hanging their shields outside their lodgings. On the day of the tournament, coats of arms were painted on tents and marquees, banners and flags, as well as on shields, surcoats and horse trappings. Pages, dressed in bright costumes, carried their knights' shields; those watching wore their own armorial bearings and cheered on the knights they supported.

Heraldic arms, because they were unique to a person, came to have great symbolism. To insult someone's shield was to insult the person. When Edward II's favourites, the Despenser family, fell from favour, they were mockingly dressed in their surcoats as they were taken to the block to be beheaded. In 1377, when the London mob rioted against John of Gaunt, they hung his arms upside down – this was considered the greatest insult possible.

By the middle of the fourteenth century, heraldry had spread to decorate tombs, castle doorways and manuscripts. Everyone could see who was rich and powerful.

SOURCE H

The Turberville window in Bere Regis Church in Dorset. It shows the Turberville arms combined with those of their wives.

To govern effectively the king's council relied on these so-called great families to uphold royal authority, particularly in remote areas of England. These great dynasties existed as mini-kingdoms, were allowed to raise troops in times of war, held court in great castles, and were answerable to the king alone. This gave the nobles tremendous power. Henry V had made it clear that he would tolerate no opposition to his authority. Henry VI was a very different king.

Families such as the Yorks, the Percys, the Nevilles and the Beauforts enjoyed enormous wealth and power. At this time the king was more than a figurehead to his people. He was expected to be a good general, policy-maker, ambassador and law-giver. He was also expected to balance the ambitions of the nobility, but at the same time maintain a clear policy of his own. This required a king with a very strong personality and excellent political skills. Henry V had been such a king but, unfortunately, his son Henry VI was not.

Jack Cade's Rebellion

Henry VI's weakness in ruling and the loss of lands in France began to have a direct effect on the people in England. In 1450, matters came to a head. A revolt of about 30,000 men from Kent and Sussex, including many respectable landowners, marched to London to demand reform in government and the restoration of the Duke of York as main adviser. There were reports of riots in Kent, Wiltshire and the west of England.

In July 1450, a mob of several thousand men, led by Jack Cade, entered London and murdered two crown officials. Although the mob then dispersed, the king's prestige and standing had been dealt a serious blow – the weakness of his rule and his government's lack of power had been ruthlessly exposed. Suffolk, now an earl, was blamed for the government's failure and accused of treason. He was murdered as he fled into exile.

Re-enter Richard, Duke of York

One of the demands made by Jack Cade and his followers had been for the restoration of Richard, Duke of York as the king's chief adviser. The collapse of the rebellion did not, however, mean that this demand had simply gone away. Seeing the country in a state of unrest and confusion, some of the great families began wondering whether the return of the Duke of York might actually be a good move. Certainly, Henry VI was in no state to give the country the strong leadership it needed. However, the Yorkists had not forgotten events in 1399, when the Duke of Lancaster had seized the throne from Richard II and proclaimed himself King Henry IV (see page 111), so the risk factor was high. Maybe, with the weak Lancastrian king, Henry VI, on the throne, the Yorkists would try to stage a comeback.

Richard, Duke of York, had ambitions which didn't seem to stop at being the king's chief adviser – he wanted to become king himself! Initially, Richard had hoped to gain the crown peacefully: Henry VI and Queen Margaret had no children and so on Henry's death the crown could simply pass peacefully to the Yorkists. But in 1453 disaster struck – Margaret of Anjou gave birth to a son and Henry VI suffered a paralysing mental breakdown. A son made the Lancastrian succession seem secure, but a mentally ill monarch with a baby as his heir gave Richard his last chance at claiming the throne.

Richard acted quickly. He returned from exile in Ireland and demanded that the king's council accept him as a member. He then negotiated, bribed, dragooned (forced into submission using violent measures) and persuaded the Council to make him Lord Protector. Once in office, Richard ran the country competently and to everyone's satisfaction – except, that is, to the satisfaction of the hardcore Lancastrians and the queen. Queen Margaret was the real force behind the monarch, and would defend her husband's throne and her son's inheritance fiercely.

The Wars of the Roses begin

The first battle of the Wars of the Roses happened, not because Henry VI went insane, but because he became sane again. Recovering his sanity, Henry dismissed Richard of York from his position as Lord Protector, and reinstated the hated and incompetent Somerset as his chief adviser. This was too much for the ambitious Duke of York to bear. He gathered his army of 3000 experienced soldiers and set off for London.

Question time

1   Who do you think was to blame for the start of the Wars of the Roses?

The Battle of St Albans, 22 May 1455

Approximately 3000 Yorkist supporters reached St Albans on 22 May 1455. The Lancastrians were ready for them and had barricaded the streets of the town, even though they could muster about 2000 soldiers. At first, both sides negotiated. The Yorkists maintained that they were loyal to the king, but wanted the unpopular Duke of Somerset and his henchmen to be handed over to them. The Lancastrians refused, hoisting the king's standard to emphasise that they had the monarch's right on their side. But this was the sign the Yorkists were waiting for. The Duke of York and his men stormed the barricades, while the Duke of Warwick broke into the town through the back lanes and alleys, coming up behind the Lancastrians. Fierce hand-to-hand fighting followed, with knights forced to dismount and men slashing, hacking and stabbing each other. The Lancastrian Duke of Somerset was killed, probably by the Duke of Warwick. The king didn't fight and didn't even put on his armour. He watched the street-fighting from a distance but was wounded in the neck by an arrow and so was quickly taken to the safety of a tanner's cottage. (The king was too great a prize to lose at this stage.)

After just 30 minutes' fighting, the Yorkists won the day. The Duke of York came to King Henry VI to beg forgiveness, which was duly given. But the important thing about the Battle of St Albans was that the Yorkists' objective had been gained – the powerful Duke of Somerset was gone, and with him the influence he had held over the king. The Yorkists had also demonstrated that the king ruled because they chose to let him do so.

After the Battle of St Albans, Richard of York became Protector again, though only for a year, and Queen Margaret plotted her revenge. She was determined to remove the Duke of York and his heirs from the scene, so that the strongest claim to the English throne was that of her husband Henry VI and their son Edward. For the time being, however, Margaret had to wait while battles and skirmishes were fought between Yorkists and Lancastrians, each winning by turns. At one point, after the Battle of Ludford Bridge in 1459, the Yorkist leaders were forced to flee abroad, only to return in July of the following year to trounce the Lancastrians at Northampton.

The Battle of Northampton put the Duke of York in control of Henry VI and therefore in an extremely powerful position. But neither Parliament nor the judges would agree to Richard replacing the anointed king, Henry VI. Richard had to be satisfied with ruling the kingdom in Henry's name, and with being named as his heir. This arrangement was most certainly not to Queen Margaret's liking. She fled to the North, where the Lancastrians had the support of great and powerful families – the Percys, the Nevilles and the Cliffords. With their help, she raised an army of more than 10,000 fighting men, intent on challenging and defeating the Yorkists once and for all.

The battles of the Wars of the Roses

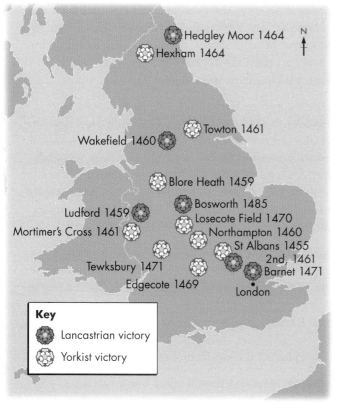

St Albans (1455) won by the House of York.

Blore Heath (1459) won by the House of York.

Ludford Bridge (1459) won by the House of Lancaster.

Northampton (1460) won by the House of York.

Wakefield (1460) won by the House of Lancaster.

Mortimer's Cross (1461) won by the House of York.

2nd St Albans (1461) won by the House of York.

Towton (1461) won by the House of York.

Edward IV (House of York) becomes king in 1461.

Hedgley Moor (1464) won by the House of Lancaster.

Hexham (1464) won by the House of York.

Edgecote (1469) won by the House of Lancaster.

Edward is forced into exile and Henry VI (House of Lancaster) is briefly reinstated in 1470.

Losecote Field (1470) won by the House of York.

Barnet (1471) won by the House of York.

Tewkesbury (1471) won by the House of York.

Henry VI dies in the Tower of London in 1471.

Bosworth (1485) won by the House of Lancaster.

The battles of the Wars of the Roses.

The Battle of Wakefield, 31 December 1460

It was at Wakefield that Queen Margaret had her terrible revenge. Richard, Duke of York, had assembled a force of some 6000 men and had set out from London on 9 December, confident of a successful winter campaign. He was heading for Sandal Castle, two miles south of Wakefield. The Lancastrians, however, had anticipated Richard's plan and had sized up the situation. They knew that the heavily fortified Sandal Castle could not feed and support a garrison of 8000 soldiers and so made sure that the Yorkists would be unable to get much food from the surrounding countryside. Richard, however, wasn't worried. Having arrived at the castle, he simply sat tight and waited for reinforcements to come with his son Edward, who was marching from the Welsh border.

Lancastrian tactics

Well out of sight of the Yorkists, the Lancastrians created a diversion. They secretly split their army in two. One half moved into a wood close to Sandal Castle where they quietly took up their positions. The other half marched boldly towards Sandal Castle. Faced with a far smaller force than he had been expecting, Richard of York marched out to meet the Lancastrians, confident of an easy victory. And at first, the Yorkists appeared to be on the winning foot – the Lancastrians retreated, time and again, drawing the Yorkists away from Sandal Castle. However, once the Yorkist forces were a fair distance from the security of the castle, the Lancastrians turned and gave battle. Then, once the Yorkists were fully locked in combat, the second half of the Lancastrian army surged out of the woods and surprised the Yorkists from behind. Unable to retreat to Sandal Castle, the Yorkist forces were defeated in 30 minutes.

Revenge was sweet. The young Yorkist Earl of Rutland, on his knees and begging for his life, was told by the Duke of Clifford: 'Your father killed mine, so now I shall kill you.' And so he did. Richard, Duke of York, was also killed, though whether he died during or after the battle remains unclear. Certainly Margaret exacted a chilling revenge: Richard's corpse was beheaded, stuck on a spike outside the gates of the city of York, and crowned with a paper crown. Ironically, Richard was probably the most stable and statesmanlike figure to be involved in the complicated crises that were the Wars of the Roses.

After the Battle of Wakefield, the Lancastrians seemed poised for total victory. Although Edward, Richard of York's eldest son, defeated Lancastrian forces at Mortimer's Cross at the beginning of February 1461, Yorkist forces led by the Earl of Warwick received a crushing blow ten days later at the Second Battle of St Albans. Here, Queen Margaret allowed her seven-year-old son to decide whether the prisoners should be killed by axe, sword or rope. A new brutality was replacing the old-fashioned ideas of chivalry.

Verged on the brink of success, Margaret then made a crucial mistake. London lay open to her and Henry VI, but she chose to move north, to her power base, taking her hapless husband with her. This gave Edward of York sufficient time to travel to London and rally the Yorkists. After the death of Richard, Duke of York (Edward's father), the Yorkists could no longer claim to be ruling in the name of Henry VI (see page 125) and so proclaimed Edward as king. The Yorkists' aim was now clear – to depose Henry VI.

The Battle of Towton, 29 March 1461

Edward gathered a large army and moved north during March 1461, in pursuit of Margaret and the Lancastrians. Yorkist recruits poured in, sickened by the cruelty of the Lancastrian soldiers, and anxious to be on what they clearly thought would be the winning side. Little did they know that they would shortly be engaged in the bloodiest battle ever to be fought on British soil.

The two armies, each numbering about 50,000 men, met in a swirling snowstorm outside the village of Towton, 15 kilometres (10 miles) north of Tadcaster. Both armies were drawn up in parallel lines, facing each other across a shallow muddy gully that sloped towards a sluggish river.

- The Duke of Somerset was overall commander of the Lancastrian army, with the Earls of Northumberland and Exeter commanding the right and left flanks.

- Edward, the man whom the Yorkists had proclaimed king, commanded the Yorkists. Although he was only 19 years old, he was strong, six foot four inches tall, and loved by his men. Fauconberg and Warwick commanded the Yorkist flanks.

The Yorkists, as challengers, advanced slowly. The battle began with a series of arrow flights from both sides and quickly moved to close fighting. Men fought as they had done at Agincourt (see pages 82–3) – climbing over piles of bodies to get at the enemy. The turning point came in the afternoon when the Duke of Norfolk finally caught up with his Yorkist allies. The Yorkists now fell upon the Lancastrians with fresh troops and the whole battle was pushed down the slope into the flooded river, where it turned into a bloodbath. It didn't take long for the river to become blocked with thousands of corpses. Contemporary accounts record that the waters ran red with blood for six miles downstream.

So who won? The battle lasted from dawn to dusk and at the end the Lancastrian army broke ranks and fled. The Yorkists were triumphant. Edward took down his father's head from the gates of York and replaced it with the heads of Lancastrian nobles. Henry VI and Queen Margaret fled to Scotland with their son and the remnants of their supporters. In June 1461, Edward was crowned King Edward IV of England.

Question time

1. Long-drawn out wars, like the Wars of the Roses, have turning points where a certain battle, or other event, changes the whole direction of the war. In what sense were the Battles of St Albans, Wakefield and Towton, turning points in the Wars of the Roses?

2. a. What tactics used by the winning side in the Battles of St Albans, Wakefield and Towton led to success?

   b. Research, using your library and the Internet, tactics used in other medieval battles. How typical were the tactics used in these three?

Edward IV: the first Yorkist king

After the Battle of Towton, Parliament declared the last three Lancastrian kings to have been 'usurpers': this meant that they had wrongly come to the throne. Edward, Duke of York, was crowned King Edward IV in June 1461. He addressed the House of Commons, and thanked them for their support.

Henry VI's reign had left England in a state of lawlessness. Most people wanted an end to the fighting and to live in peace. Edward IV offered them this and they gave him their support. But his marriage to a commoner, Elizabeth Woodville (whose first husband had been killed in the Wars of the Roses) offended many powerful Yorkist families. By marrying outside the powerful noble families who surrounded and advised him, Edward had created a new nobility which owed allegiance to him only, and who had no 'old scores' to settle.

Warwick, 'the Kingmaker', switches sides

The Duke of Warwick, who had been a prime mover in making Edward king, was deeply angry. He had found a suitable bride for Edward, only to be told of Edward's secret marriage to Elizabeth Woodville. Edward was, perhaps, trying to show Warwick that he could act independently and didn't always need his advice. However, Warwick's reaction to Edward's marriage was extreme: he switched sides. Taken off guard, Edward was forced to flee abroad and Henry VI became king again, but only temporarily.

The Battle of Barnet, 14 April 1471

SOURCE 1

A contemporary painting of the Battle of Tewkesbury, 1471.

The exiled Edward wasted no time in putting together an army while he was in Europe. He landed once again on English soil early in 1471, at Spurnhead in Yorkshire. From there he marched to London, taking the city, and Henry VI once again became Edward's prisoner. Now Edward had to defeat Warwick and his new allies, the Lancastrians.

With the return of Edward, Warwick and the Lancastrian army approached London, determined to throw Edward out and keep Henry VI on the throne. The two armies met at Barnet, 20 kilometres (13 miles) north of London. Warwick had around 15,000 soldiers; Edward slightly fewer.

Both armies fought on foot – even the leaders, although they had tethered their horses on the edge of the battlefield. This was common practice. Ordinary soldiers, kept from fleeing the battlefield by a ring of 'reserve' knights, often complained that this meant their leaders could flee a battle if things began to go wrong, while they were forced to stay to the bitter end and often their own deaths. The fighting, which began in thick fog early in the morning, was confused. Soldiers had problems seeing who was a friend and who was an enemy, and there were many cases of mistaken identity and cries of 'treason'.

Edward eventually won the Battle of Barnet; Warwick, trying to escape, was cornered in a nearby wood by Yorkist soldiers and killed in cold blood. However, Edward still had to capture Henry VI and put an end to Margaret's plotting and scheming. Three weeks' later, Edward made his position secure beyond doubt by a crushing victory over the Lancastrians at the Battle of Tewkesbury. Edward, Henry VI's son and Prince of Wales, was killed; Queen Margaret was captured and allowed to return to France; and Henry VI was imprisoned in the Tower of London and murdered there. The Lancastrian cause was over.

Question time

1. The Earl of Warwick is often called 'Warwick the Kingmaker'. Use the information in this section to explain why.

2. This chapter has been about skirmishes and battles. In groups, research the weapons, armour and different sorts of soldiers that would have been used. Make a large collage of a medieval battle, with all the fighters correctly dressed and armed. Pin the collage onto a display board, with information around it explaining the armoury and weaponry used. You could use the picture of the Battle of Tewkesbury as a starting point.

Unrest, uncertainty and treachery

Edward IV was 41 years old when he died, leaving a wife and seven children. Of these, two were sons: Edward, aged 12, and Richard, aged nine. Control needed to be in the hands of responsible people until the elder boy was of an age to rule alone. There were two candidates: Richard, Duke of Gloucester, the only surviving brother of the dead king and uncle to the boys; or Anthony Woodville, Earl Rivers, who was the queen's eldest brother.

After Edward's death, the royal council started to organise a coronation for his eldest son.

- Some historians believe that this was what Edward IV wished.

- Other historians point to the fact that, because Richard had been absolutely loyal to his brother during his lifetime, Edward would have wanted Richard to act as Protector until his eldest son was old enough to rule.

- Edward IV had shamelessly advanced his wife's relatives (the Woodville family) during his reign, and the aspiring Woodvilles now wanted to retain their power base. Richard of Gloucester's loyalties did not lie with the Woodville family. Perhaps the powerful Woodville family pressurised the council to agree to the coronation in order to keep Richard from power.

- After several years of political struggle and civil war, perhaps the council simply wanted to prevent a power struggle breaking out between noble families by crowning Edward as king.

When Edward IV died, Richard of Gloucester was in Yorkshire, and Earl Rivers was in Ludlow with the young Prince Edward. Receiving news of the forthcoming coronation, both men immediately left for London.

Their paths crossed at Stoney Stratford, where Richard promptly seized Prince Edward and arrested Earl Rivers on charges of treason. Richard's control of the prince gave the Council no choice but the allow him to rule the country as Protector. What happened next is open to interpretation.

- On 10 June 1483, Richard wrote to the city of York asking for military help against a Woodville conspiracy.

- On 13 June, Richard charged William, Lord Hastings and one of Edward IV's closest friends, with treason and he was promptly beheaded.

- On 16 June, Richard persuaded Elizabeth Woodville to send her younger son Richard to the Tower, where Edward was also being kept. Richard argued that the young Duke of York would be needed for his brother's coronation later in the month.

- Richard then proceeded to declare that, because he had previously pledged himself to another woman, Edward IV's marriage to Elizabeth Woodville was bigamous. By this charge, all of the children of Edward IV and Elizabeth Woodville were declared illegitimate.

- On 26 June, Richard claimed the throne as King Richard III. The princes were never seen again.

Had Richard planned all along to take the throne from his brother's son? Or, having discovered the illegitimacy of the boy supposed to be king, was he simply acting quickly in order to avoid unrest?

The Battle of Bosworth, 21 August 1485

The Wars of the Roses did not stop with Richard III. Henry Tudor, son of Edmund Tudor and Margaret Beaufort, remained the last hope of the Lancastrians. He had been brought up in Brittany, in safety and away from the dangers of civil war. In August 1485, Henry decided his time had come. He landed with a force of about 2000 soldiers at Milford Haven in south Wales. As he marched toward the Midlands, men trickled to join him and, by the time he faced Richard III at Bosworth field in August, he had 5000 men to Richard's 15,000. There must have been times when he wondered what on earth he was doing, facing an experienced soldier king in his own country.

Fortunately for Henry Tudor, Richard's forces were uncertain and disloyalty was in the air. The Earl of Northumberland, for example, wasn't going to commit his forces until he saw on which side Lord Stanley was fighting. As the battle progressed, the Duke of Norfolk's men pushed hard at the centre of Henry's battle lines and Henry himself became isolated. It is said that, upon seeing this, Richard galloped into battle, determined to kill his challenger in single combat. However, at this point Stanley finally decided to commit his troops to the opposing side. Richard is said to have decided to die in battle rather than lose his kingdom. Whatever the truth of the matter, it is certain that Richard III took to the battle with disastrous results: he was brutally killed and his naked corpse was slung over a horse. Richard's crown was found in a thorn bush and placed triumphantly on the head of Henry Tudor, now King Henry VII.

Question time

1. Some newspapers today have 'In Memoriam' columns. This is where people can post messages in memory of a dead friend or relative. On 21 August a notice regularly appears. It says 'Richard III, King of England 1483–5, treacherously slain on Bosworth Field'. Do you agree that Richard was treacherously slain?

Digging deeper

What part did women play in the Wars of the Roses?

Women, during the Wars of the Roses, did the various chores that women have always done. They scrubbed clothes and swept floors, milked cows and collected eggs, gave birth and laid out the dead. Some were good and some were wicked; most just muddled through as best they could. But there were some women who, either by birth or by chance, stood out from the rest. You have already read a lot about Margaret of Anjou, wife to Henry VI. Let us now look at the lives of some other women.

Margaret Beaufort (1443–1509)

Margaret was the daughter of John Beaufort, Duke of Somerset, and Margaret Beauchamp. Her father died in 1444, leaving her heiress to the Suffolk fortunes and therefore a very desirable bride for young men seeking a fortune or looking to consolidate their power and influence. In 1455, aged 11, Margaret married Edmund Tudor, the Earl of Richmond. Almost immediately she conceived a son, Henry, who was to be their only child; Edmund died in November 1456 when Margaret was six months pregnant. Edmund's brother Jasper took Margaret, and later her son, into his care and protection. Margaret married twice more: in 1464, to Henry Stafford, son of the Duke of Buckingham; and in 1473, to Thomas Stanley, 1st Earl of Derby. She outlived both her husbands, but had no more children.

So what of Margaret's only child? Margaret was first separated from Henry Tudor when he was four years old, and then reunited with him in 1470 only to lose him again soon afterwards. This was because, after the Battle of Tewkesbury (see page 129), Henry was the best hope of the Lancastrians and he had to be kept safe abroad. The next time that Margaret saw her son, he would be King of England.

While Henry was abroad, Margaret threw herself into working for her son's cause. She was completing arrangements for his return to England when Edward IV died unexpectedly and his brother Richard became king (see pages 129–30). Caught unawares, Margaret could do nothing immediately. However, she was undoubtedly part of the conspiracy that ended with Henry Tudor's victory on Bosworth field in 1485 (see page 130).

After Henry was crowned, Margaret, as mother of the king, wielded enormous influence. Indeed, people at the time believed that she was the only person of whom Henry VII took any real notice! She played a leading part in negotiating Henry's marriage to Elizabeth of York, the eldest daughter of Edward IV. Outliving her son, she also made certain that the succession of her grandson, Henry VIII, was secure; she died a fortnight after his coronation in 1509.

Margaret Beaufort had power and influence during Henry VII's reign, not simply because she was the mother of a king, but because she was a very capable woman. She backed large fen-drainage schemes (in order to reclaim land), was the patron of the poet William Caxton, and founded Christ's College and St John's College at Cambridge. The first women's college at Oxford, Lady Margaret Hall, was named after her.

Elizabeth Woodville (1437–92)

Elizabeth was the daughter of Richard Woodville (later made Earl Rivers) and Jacquetta of Luxembourg, who had been married to Henry V's brother, the Duke of Bedford. Elizabeth's first husband, Sir John Grey, was killed at the Battle of St Albans in 1455 whilst fighting the Lancastrians. No one knows when Elizabeth met Edward IV, but on 1 May 1464 he secretly married her at the Woodville family home in Grafton Regis. Edward's advisers, his court and parliament were all furious when they found out. They had proposed several high-born and wealthy brides for Edward but he had rejected every one. For a king to marry one of his subjects – and a subject with two sons by a previous marriage, as well as countless relatives, all of whom would expect favours and advancement – was unheard of. Indeed, Edward's council was bold enough to say that 'she was not his match, however good and fair she might be, and he must know well that she was no wife for a prince such as himself'. Not a good start to any marriage!

Once his secret marriage was known about, Edward gave Elizabeth a lavish coronation and made an appropriate dowry for her. Elizabeth spent this wisely and never lived beyond her means. Elizabeth Woodville's five brothers, seven unmarried sisters and two sons were well provided for by Edward, not so much with titles and lands, but with good marriages that had to be carefully negotiated.

There were many children of Elizabeth's marriage to Edward: three sons and seven daughters. Elizabeth never interfered in politics, but contented herself with negotiating advancements for her large family. This didn't make her very popular – or them, and was one of the reasons that the Earl of Warwick changed sides (see page 128). It was the anger of those pushed out of power and favour by the Woodvilles that was partly to blame for Richard III's smooth takeover of the Crown (see pages 129–30) and, ultimately, for the deaths of her sons, Edward V and his brother Richard. However, although Richard III declared Elizabeth's marriage to Edward invalid and her children illegitimate, he gave Elizabeth a pension that allowed her to live comfortably.

The disappearance of her two sons, whom she eventually must have assumed dead, didn't stop Elizabeth from continuing to promote the Woodville family. Together with Margaret Beaufort, she plotted and planned a marriage between her eldest daughter Elizabeth and Margaret's son Henry Tudor. Elizabeth lived to see her daughter marry Henry VII and, after spending a short time at their court, retired to Bermondsey Abbey.

Jane Shore (died 1527)

It was common for medieval kings openly to have mistresses, usually with the knowledge (if not the agreement) of their wives. In an age when royal marriages were usually made for political reasons, love – if it came at all – followed later. At court, where rich and powerful young men were surrounded by pretty and available young women, these 'alternative' arrangements were hardly surprising.

Jane Shore was the most well known of Edward IV's many mistresses. She was the daughter of a wealthy London merchant and had married a goldsmith, but then she caught the attention of the king. Edward IV didn't worry whether a woman was married or not, and in 1470 she became his mistress. Thomas More called Jane Shore 'the king's merry harlot', adding that her husband 'put her aside' because of her relationship with the king. A wife was expected to put up with her husband's mistress, but it didn't always work the other way round!

The official story is a little different: the marriage of Jane and William Shore was annulled, because of William's 'impotency'. It was clear, at least to Thomas More, that Jane was special to Edward. 'Many he had', More explained, 'but he loved her.' Contemporary records describe Jane as witty, lively, of 'pleasant behaviour' and, most importantly, she could read and write as well.

Jane's relationship with Edward continued until his death in 1483. Mistresses, especially royal ones, could exercise quite a lot of power and patronage. But they are dependent on their lovers for protection. Once this is removed, for whatever reason, the discarded mistress becomes instantly vulnerable. But Jane was lucky. She was taken into the protection of one of Edward's close friends, William, Lord Hastings.

All might have continued well for Jane had the new Protector, Richard, Duke of Gloucester, not had Hastings arrested and charged with treason. Jane was accused with him, was arrested too and had all her belongings seized. Worse was to come: Hastings was executed. Jane's best chance of protection was gone. She was now imprisoned and accused, among other things, of sorcery. Prompted by Richard, the Bishop of London made her do penance. She was forced to walk through the streets of London carrying a lighted taper and dressed only in her petticoat.

Jane might have spent the rest of her life in prison, but Thomas Lynom, Richard III's solicitor-general, fell in love with her and offered to marry her. Nothing more is known about Jane for certain, except that she died in poverty. In 1714, Nicholas Rowe wrote a play about her life called *The Tragedy of Jane Shore*.

Anne Neville (1454–85)

Anne was the younger daughter of Richard, Earl of Warwick (the 'Kingmaker') and Anne Beauchamp, who was herself an heiress. When her father decided to switch his loyalty from his cousin, the Yorkist Edward, to the Lancastrian Henry, he needed to secure the position of his daughters as well as of himself. He married his elder daughter Isobel to George, Duke of Clarence, the discontented younger brother of Edward IV and a man given to frequent changes of mind and loyalty. In December 1470 Anne, aged 14, was married to Edward, Henry VI's son. Warwick was demonstrating very firmly that his loyalties lay, not with the Yorkists, but with the Lancastrians.

We don't know what Anne thought of her marriage, but we do know that disaster quickly followed. Her father was killed at the Battle of Barnet in April 1471 (see page 129) and her new husband was killed a month later, at the Battle of Tewkesbury. So, after four months of marriage, Anne became a widow. She was a very eligible widow, holding with her sister a large portion of the Neville family fortune. However, her brother-in-law George, Duke of Clarence, was not keen on all of the Warwick fortunes being divided between the two sisters. He would very much have preferred to see the whole lot go to his wife Isobel. There is a story that, when he realised that his younger brother Richard, Duke of Gloucester, was interested in the widowed Anne, he forced Anne to disguise herself as a kitchen maid and hide in the kitchens with the other staff. Richard, however, found Anne and took her to a place of safety, where he married her.

Anne brought to her marriage to Richard, Duke of Gloucester, the Yorkshire estates of the Nevilles, including Middleham Castle, which Richard made his power base. It was from here that Richard made his successful bid for the throne (see page 130) and was crowned King of England in 1483. But tragedy was to strike. Their only child, a son called Edward, was born frail and died in 1484. Anne and Richard were grief stricken. Anne herself died a year later, from what at the time was described as a 'wasting disease' and was probably tuberculosis.

Question time

1   a   Work out, for each woman, whether they were Lancastrian or Yorkist. Make it clear whether you are certain or are just making a good guess.

b   Did any of the women change allegiance during the Wars of the Roses?

c   Explain, for each woman, why she supported the side that she did.

2   No record of any conversation between any of these women exists. Suppose a meeting had happened, what would they have said to each other? What favours would they have asked? What explanations would they offer? Choose any two women, and write a conversation that they might have had. Remember to keep true to history and true to the period.

3   a   Go back through this chapter and note down everything you can find about Margaret of Anjou, wife to Henry VI. Now write her biography.

b   In what ways is she similar to, and in what ways is she different from, Margaret Beaufort and Elizabeth Woodville?

4   What conclusions can you draw from the lives of these five women about the way women were treated in medieval England?

6 Assessment section

1   a   Use all the information in this chapter to make a timeline of the events of the Wars of the Roses.

b   Which three events do you think were the most important?

c   Compare your three events with those chosen by your partner. Are they the same? If not, why do you disagree?

2   Think carefully about the Yorkists and Lancastrians.

a   Which side do you think had the better claim to the throne at the start of the Wars of the Roses?

b   Did this side keep the better claim all the time?

3   The Wars of the Roses weren't just fought between noble families. Ordinary people took part, too. How do you think these families decided on which side to fight?

4   This verse was found pinned to the door of St Paul's Cathedral in London.

The Cat, the Rat and Lovel our Dog
Rule all England under the Hog.

a   Find out who the 'Cat', 'Rat' and 'Lovel our Dog' were. Who was the 'Hog'? (Hint: something to do with Richard III?)

b   When do you think the verse was written?

c   Why do you think its author, William Collingbourne, was hanged as a result?

Further reading

Cynthia Harnett, *Writing on the Hearth* (Methuen, 1971)

Sharon Penman, *The Sunne in Splendour* (Macmillan, 1983)

The power of the Church

In 1066, above the heads of the invading Norman army several banners waved in the wind. Among them was that belonging to the Pope. What was the significance of this act? It suggests that the Pope supported William the Conqueror's invasion. Why would William have wanted or needed to carry this banner? What does it tell us about the power of the Church in the early Middle Ages?

William had planned his invasion of England with the full backing of the Pope. He had appealed to the Pope for support for his mission. He said that he was aiming to return the wayward English to the true path of Roman godliness. His papal support might gain him credit with the English Church which should remain loyal to the Pope rather than its own monarch. He would want some local support as new monarch. Medieval politicians and rulers, like William, relied on the Church for support but also fought against its power. This chapter will investigate the extent of the Church's power and influence in politics. Were medieval monarchs right to feel so threatened by this powerful religious organisation?

The Church in the Middle Ages

Church with a capital 'C' means the international organisation of the Catholic church. All Christian countries in the Middle Ages formed part of Christendom, almost a huge Christian kingdom. The head of Christendom and the Church was the Pope. Church with a small 'c' usually refers to individual buildings or groups of worshippers, such as a village church or the word 'churchgoers'. The Church was led by different people and organised into different sections, as part of a hierarchy. This organisation still applies to aspects of the Catholic Church and the Church of England today.

Part of Christendom	Led by
Christendom	Pope
Archdiocese	Archbishops of York and Canterbury
Diocese	Bishop based in cathedral
Deanery	Dean
Parish	Priest (some priests looked after more than one parish)

Why was the Church so powerful?

The Church had enormous influence over the laws, land and finances in England. Its power led to conflict with the monarchy and several very tense moments in history.

Digging deeper

The papacy

The papacy is the name for the system of rule by popes. The Pope is the elected head of the Catholic Church and has the official title of the Bishop of Rome. The Pope's home is the Vatican within Vatican City, which is an independent state in Rome. Catholics see the Pope as a spiritual descendant from St Peter and therefore he is the leader of the Roman Catholic Church.

Although the medieval Church was an international one with representatives in all Christian countries, much of the power was held in Italy, the home of the Vatican. Only one Englishman ever became pope. He was called Nicholas Breakspear and became pope in 1154. It was usually Italian clergy who became pope; one wealthy Italian family even produced three popes in a row! At its peak in the thirteenth century, the papacy could appoint emperors, order crusades and carry out investigations against heretics, in addition to making all decisions concerning the organisation and

beliefs of the Christian Church. Popes could also excommunicate anyone who did not deserve to go to heaven, including kings and entire nations (see page 138). You can see that medieval popes had immense political power and rivalled kings for control in many countries. Their representatives in each country – the archbishops, bishops and local clergy – carried out papal commands.

The total power of the papacy did not last. In the fourteenth century the French declared one of their bishops as pope and the papacy moved to Avignon for 60 years. Between 1378 and 1417, there were 'official' popes in Avignon in France and in Rome. This period is called the 'Great Schism' (meaning a division or split). It damaged the reputation of the papacy and led to increasing criticism of the Church (see page 145).

Law, order and punishment

Religion and the Church influenced the punishment of crimes in medieval Britain. In cases where juries could not reach a verdict then the decision was left to God. God's verdict would be shown in the outcome of a test, called 'trial by ordeal' (see page 232). However, it was not only God who had the power to put suspected criminals on trial. The Church and the monarch also ruled over trials to maintain law and order in England.

The medieval Church would send priests to special Church courts if they had committed crimes against the Church's laws, such as letting a woman serve mass (give communion in Church services), or if they had misused Church taxes. It was also the Church that tried the clergy if they had committed any secular (non-religious) crimes. Priests could be found guilty of theft or even murder and be judged by members of the Church rather than the king's court. Sentences in Church courts tended to be less severe; criminals might be asked to do penance of a pilgrimage or public confession rather than face death by hanging. Some criminals would even pretend to be priests in order to escape the usual harsh punishments common at the time in the king's court.

This was one reason for people to resent the power of the Church: clergy seemed to live by different laws and, rather than setting an example to the rest of the world, they seemed to be getting away with murder, quite literally in a few cases. The issue of the Church promoting its own men caused tension with the Crown in the Middle Ages.

The medieval Church had power over ordinary people as well as priests. Archdeacons' Courts of Morality were held for any cases of immorality including adultery or bigamy (having more that one wife or husband). These crimes included breaking major Christian laws and therefore committing serious sins. Examples of such sins included not paying taxes, keeping mistresses and worshipping the occult or the devil. Inspectors would visit parishes and take statements against the accused. Punishments could be as strict as flogging, imprisonment or heavy fines.

These courts gave the Church more power than the king in some cases; not only could the Church punish and protect its clergy, but Courts of Morality could imprison the general public too. Source A shows that clergy were sometimes tried at Courts of Morality alongside the general public.

SOURCE A

The lady of Crawthorne does not come to church as she ought and is bound to do, because she does not contribute to the works of the church or the blessed bread and because she does have her own chapel in which her chaplain does use a bucket as a font.

Elias, a church clerk, keeps a certain Agatha in his house for immoral purposes. He is to be flogged three times around his church.

The vicar of Aldington and Smeeth quarrelled with his parishioners on Sundays and holy days and does not know how to carry on a discussion without flying into a great rage. Also grazes his horses in the churchyard and employs temporary chaplains to do his work for him.

In Wormeswould Juliana, wife of William the Baker, received into her house for three nights a sorcerer, who made a white circle in the house, with many other occult signs.

Entries from visitation rolls from the Courts of Morality, 1292–1328.

The Church not only had the power to try people for crimes, it could also protect people from the law itself. The parish church could provide sanctuary from justice, hiding escaped criminals who could confess and be protected in God's house. If such fugitives (people escaping something) managed to gain sanctuary for 40 days they would be free as long as they left the country and never returned. Monarchs and courts were not always happy with the power that this gave the Church. A politician named Hubert de Burgh was wanted by Henry III in 1232 on charges of corruption. The king's men actually dragged him from the altar of Merton Abbey in Essex, where he was seeking sanctuary, and took him to the Tower of London.

SOURCE B

Hubert de Burgh seeking
sanctuary in Merton
Abbey, Essex, 1232.
Illustration from a
fourteenth-century
manuscript.

One important aspect of the Church's power was the tool of
excommunication. This was the ability to expel a nation, a monarch or an
individual from the Church. This could happen if they had broken Church
laws, done wrong and refused to repent (say sorry), or made an enemy of the
papacy for some reason. Excommunication meant risking the soul's place in
heaven. An excommunicated person could not be involved in the Catholic
Church in any way, so could not attend church, take part in services or go to
confession. All medieval people, including monarchs, were very afraid of the
threat of excommunication. King John was excommunicated in 1215 and this
caused many difficulties for him (see page 89). Excommunication was a
powerful tool, a trump card that the Pope could play, and it meant that often
the Church had the last word in any conflict.

Question time

1   The Church protected its clergy in the Courts
    of Morality. Does Source A agree with this
    statement?

2   What arguments might have been used by a
    medieval monarch when complaining about
    the Church courts?

3   How useful is Source A in telling us about
    the power of the medieval Church?

4   Why might medieval monarchs have been
    unhappy with the power of sanctuary?

5   Can you explain why medieval monarchs
    might also have been unhappy with Church
    courts trying their own clergy?

6   What does the case of Hubert de Burgh (see
    page 137 and Source B) tell us about the
    extent of the Church's power?

Land

It was not only criminals, corrupt clergy or ambitious monarchs upon whom the Church had influence. The Church was the single biggest land owner in England. After the Norman conquest, William the Conqueror gave land to loyal clergy; this meant that one quarter of England was in Church hands by 1086. This made the Church hugely powerful as landowner and employer, as well as wealthy from the payment of rents. The amount of land owned by the Church continued to grow during the Middle Ages. Wealthy benefactors would donate land to the Church in their wills because they saw this as a way to gain entry to heaven; on receipt of gifts of land, priests or monks would pray for the dead souls to go to heaven. The monasteries (see page 170) were major landowners by the end of the Middle Ages and their wealth increased the amount of land held by the Church to one third of the country.

In addition to owning vast lands used for farming, any town where there was an abbey would be under the influence of the abbot. Abbots were feudal lords and would gain money from fees, fines and taxes. In times of local conflict the monarch usually sided with the abbot.

SOURCE C

Before the king's judges at the town of St Edmund, the merchants claim the right to form a guild and to make laws about their town. They agree that the abbot is the lord of the town, but claim that they are free citizens who ought to be able to rule their town. The abbott claimed they had no such right and that they wanted to take away his control. The judges rule in the abbot's favour, award him £200 in damages and send the leading merchants to jail.

The power of the abbot, described in a contemporary chronicle, 1304.

Making a living

The Church had a large income from owning and renting out some of its land. Some plots of land were rented out in order to raise funds for a particular need of a church. In Yorkshire, 'lamplands' were areas of land whose rents were used for the upkeep of the church altar lights.

Alongside the Church's income from rent and the sale of produce from its own worked land (called the glebe), everyone was obliged to pay taxes called tithes. Tithes were one tenth of the produce of the land such as corn, oats and wood, but also the produce of stock or animals such as wool, pigs and milk. One tenth of the profits from all work, called a personal tithe, was also paid. Many parishes had to build a large barn especially to hold the produce received from parishioners. (Tithes weren't actually abolished until 1936. In the 1930s, many farmers took part in marches and rallies to have the law changed.)

Some taxes, like tithes, were paid to the local church; others were paid directly to the local monastery and the bishop, and some were intended for the Pope, e.g. Peter's Pence. The local priest would often be responsible for collecting smaller and more difficult taxes and tithes, so a disorganised or weak priest could also end up being a poor and hungry one.

Below are just a few of the many other taxes collected by the Church in medieval England.

- Easter dues: Church rates paid at Easter

- Godbote: a Church fine for an offence against God

- Hearth penny: a penny paid by free householders on the Thursday before Easter to the minster church

- Mortuary: when a tenant died his second best possession was taken by the Church as compensation for the tithes and other taxes supposedly unpaid by him in his lifetime

- Pit money: a burial fee

- Plough alms: a penny paid by each plough team to the parish priest and collected within a fortnight of Easter

- Soul-scot: a gift made from the estate of a dead person to the parish priest

- Surplice fees: fees paid to the priest at marriages and burials.

Question time

1 Suggest any arguments the merchants might have used against the abbot at the hearing in Source C.

2 Can you suggest reasons why the king's judges might have supported the abbot against the merchants in Source C?

3 Which of the taxes listed above should have been paid by every member of a parish at some point in their life?

4 Discuss with a partner why some of these taxes might not have seemed fair to medieval parishioners.

5 What does the fact that lesser and more complex taxes were left to the local priest to collect tell us about the hierarchy of the medieval Church?

6 What action could a parish priest take in order to collect overdue taxes?

7 From what you have read about the medieval Church so far, make a list of the aspects of people's lives that the Church influenced, and the aspects of people's lives over which it had no control.

Power struggles between Church and monarch

The Church and the monarch had to have close relations in the Middle Ages. Monarchs were believed to have divine rights and to be chosen and supported by God. A papal representative had to carry out the coronation of any new monarch (see Source A). Remember that this relationship between Church and the monarchy still exists here today in some form. Queen Elizabeth II is considered so special that everyone, from the Archbishop of Canterbury to her own children, still bow to her when they meet her.

The Church and William the Conqueror

The coronation of Henry VI at Westminster. Contemporary illustration from an English psalm book, 1470.

Although the monarch needed the blessing of the Church and its support, this did not mean that the Church always had more power. After the Norman invasion of England, William the Conqueror made loyal Norman officials bishops and abbots, whether they had been educated as priests or not. This may not have been the best way to create effective priests but William knew how to create loyal servants. Norman priests would not only be faithful to William, they would also look after the land and run the Church for William at the same time. This meant that from the start of his reign William had a close relationship with the Church. However, he did not have to accept the Pope's laws on every matter and he could be fairly sure that most of the clergy would support him. He continued to appoint and control bishops and met with the Church council to receive financial and military support. William's good reputation with the papacy was due to his support for the Church. He made many appointments in parishes that did not have priests before 1066. He also rebuilt cathedrals and churches.

SOURCE B

The King of England, though he does not always behave as devoutly as we wish, has not destroyed the churches of God: he tries to govern in peace and justice; he has not done anything to hurt the papacy; he is more worthy of honour and approval than other kings.

Pope Gregory, writing in 1081.

Not all medieval monarchs were as fortunate or as powerful as William. Church appointments were usually made by the king, but more often than not in close consultation with the Pope. In reality, archbishops and bishops had so much influence over the laws, courts and land of England, not to mention the beliefs of its people, that they often emerged as rivals to the king's power. As the power of the Church in England fluctuated, so did its ability to challenge the monarchy.

The Church and Henry III

An example of papal power dominating a medieval monarch can be seen in 1220 when the Pope ordered Henry III of England to be crowned for a second time. His original coronation in 1216 had taken place when the country was divided. It was carried out by the Archbishop of Gloucester rather than the Archbishop of Canterbury (the Archbishop of Canterbury had been suspended by the Pope for supporting the Magna Carta. Henry's advisers accepted the Pope's demands for a second coronation.

The Church and Emperor Henry IV

At the end of the twelfth century, Henry IV of Germany, who had the title of Holy Roman Emperor, was furious with Pope Gregory VII. Pope Gregory had banned kings and even the Holy Roman Emperor from appointing their own religious archbishops and bishops. Henry, like most other monarchs, wanted this right as a way of controlling his supporters and getting his own way. With the backing of his German bishops, he dared to criticise Gregory and put pressure on him to step down as Pope. Gregory, in return, promptly excommunicated Henry and anyone who supported him. Nearly a year later, Henry visited the Pope and his excommunication was lifted.

SOURCE C

Iffley Church, Oxford, an example of a twelfth-century Norman church.

Question time

1. What does Source A on page 141 tell us about the relationship between the medieval monarch and the Church?

2. Why was William the Conqueror so careful not to offend the Pope?

3. What does Source B suggest about other kings in Christendom at this time?

4. Make a list of what William and the Church gained from having good relations with each other.

5. What do you think were the benefits to Henry III and the monarchy of having a second coronation? Are these benefits mainly religious or political (to do with power)?

6. Do you think that Henry III could have refused the Pope's demands for a second coronation?

7. Using the examples of King John (see page 89) and Emperor Henry, would you say that the Pope had ultimate power in medieval politics?

8. Draw a summary diagram to show all the different reasons why the Church was important in medieval politics.

Digging deeper

Henry II meets his match

In 1170 the most senior Church man in England was savagely killed in his cathedral by several of the king's knights. The events leading up to this outcome are described below.

Henry II had persuaded the monks of Canterbury Cathedral to elect Thomas Becket as their Archbishop. He did this to try to extend his own power over the Church. Becket was already Henry's Chancellor (chief minister) and friend. Henry expected Becket to take his side in any dispute with the Pope.

Henry wanted clergy to be tried and sentenced in his own courts so that he had control over all the people in England. However, since his promotion to Archbishop of Canterbury, Thomas Becket had become very religious. He had given up his luxurious lifestyle and had become a Gregorian (see page 146). Gregorians were priests who argued about the importance of their role over that of a monarch. They also argued that Church men's priority should be religion rather than politics. Becket therefore argued that clergy should be put on trial in Church courts, and not in those of the king.

Becket turned to Pope Alexander III for backing against the king. Henry was furious. Becket then refused to obey a law passed by Henry ordering that people found guilty in Church courts should also be punished in the king's courts. The argument got so heated that Becket fled to France for six years. While Becket was in France, Henry asked the Archbishop of York to crown his son, Henry III, as the next king, hoping to avoid any problems when he died. Becket thought that this was inappropriate and that Henry was influencing the archbishop's behaviour. The job of crowning monarchs was that of the Archbishop of Canterbury not the Archbishop of York.

Becket returned to England in 1170 to try to resolve the conflict. Henry and Becket met and they reached a compromise. Becket agreed to serve Henry if he could return to his position as Archbishop of Canterbury. As soon as he returned, he punished all the bishops who had taken sides with the king against him, excommunicating the Archbishop of York and his supporters. Henry was outraged that his once close friend was betraying him again. He is said to have shouted the famous words: 'Will no one rid me of this turbulent priest?' Four of his knights took him at his word.

On 29 December 1170, Becket was killed by four different sword blows from the four knights who had hurried to Canterbury. After the murder the knights looted gold and jewels from the church. Henry denied that he had ordered Becket's murder but admitted they had quarrelled. Four years after the murder, Henry went to Canterbury and knelt at Becket's tomb, asking for forgiveness. As a penance he was whipped by monks from the cathedral.

Becket's tomb became one of the most popular sites of pilgrimage in England. He was thought to be a martyr for the Church and was made a Saint in 1173. As for Henry, he and the Pope tried to compromise and work together. The Pope had a lot of influence, but kings and lords still took part in deciding the appointments for senior churchmen.

SOURCE D *A painting from about 1200 showing the murder of Thomas Becket.*

Henry II, King of England, was a man of reddish, freckled complexion with a large round head, grey eyes which glowed fiercely and became bloodshot in anger, a fiery expression and a harsh, cracked voice … He made friends easily and was agreeable, pliant and witty, second to none in politeness, no matter what thoughts he might keep to himself … He was fierce towards those who remained to challenge him, but merciful to the defeated, harsh to his servants, welcoming towards strangers, generous in public, thrifty in private. Those whom he had once hated he never came to love, but those whom he had once loved he scarcely ever called to mind with hatred.

The character and appearance of Henry II, 1133–89. This description of Henry was written by a contemporary, Gerald of Wales, who knew him well.

Greetings to my faithful monks of Winchester: I order you to hold a free election, but I forbid you to elect anyone except Richard, Archdeacon of Poitiers.

A letter from Thomas Becket.

… And straightway the four knights entered the house of prayer with swords sacrilegiously drawn, causing horror to the beholders by their very looks and the clanging of their arms. Inspired by fury the knights called out, 'Where is Thomas Becket, traitor to the king and realm?' At this … he descended from the stair and in a clear voice answered, 'I am here, no traitor to the king, but a priest. Why do ye seek me?' … The murderers followed him; 'Absolve', they cried, 'and restore to communion those whom you have excommunicated …' He answered: 'I will not absolve them.' 'Then you shall die,' they cried, 'and receive what you deserve.' 'I am ready', he replied, 'to die for my Lord, that in my blood the Church may obtain liberty and peace. But in the name of Almighty God, I forbid you to hurt my people whether clerk or lay.'

Then they laid sacrilegious hands on him … At the third blow he fell on his knees and elbows, offering himself a living victim, and saying in a low voice, 'For the Name of Jesus and the protection of the Church I am ready to embrace death.' … The fourth knight prevented any from interfering so that the others might freely perpetrate the murder. As to the fifth, he put his foot on the neck of the holy priest and precious martyr, and, horrible to say, scattered his brains and blood over the pavement, calling out to the others, 'Let us away, knights; he will rise no more.'

An eyewitness description of the murder, written by Edward Grim, one of Becket's priests, between five and seven years after the event.

A casket which contained relics (hair, bones, etc.) of Thomas Becket. It was made in France in c. 1190.

Question time

1. What sort of questions would a historian or journalist want answered if they were investigating the quarrel between Henry and Becket? Make a list of at least six questions.

2. Read Source E and make a list of Henry II's strengths and weaknesses.

3. Having read Source E are you surprised at the contents of Source F? Explain your answer.

4. How helpful are Sources E to H in our investigation of the Becket story? For each source describe the questions it helps us to answer and state how useful it is.

5. In groups discuss which you think is:
   a. the most interesting source
   b. the most unreliable source
   c. the most reliable source
   d. the most useful source.

   Be prepared to justify your decisions to the rest of the class.

6. Research information on Thomas Becket in order to write his biography. Find details about:
   - his background
   - his work experience
   - his work for Henry II
   - his actions in the quarrel with the king
   - his reputation after his death.

Criticism of the Church

By the end of the Middle Ages the monarchy had won the long-term power struggle with the Church. In 1135 Pope Martin V said about England: 'It is not the Pope but the King of England who governs the Church in his dominions.' The Church was also losing the battle for people's unquestioning support. Corrupt priests, friars, monks, bishops and archbishops had begun to damage the reputation of the Church. There were reports of laziness, gluttony, drinking and breaking vows of chastity. Even nuns were not free from such criticisms.

It was not only in England that the Church was facing criticism: in both eastern and western Europe, the Church was under attack. It was also divided within itself, and criticisms that started in the medieval period developed in later centuries to change European Christianity permanently. The events changed the face of European politics as well as religion.

e low bont bien li grieu a guile de cozziers
Chauces de fer chauces · z font as efcuers
O euant pozter les armes z mener les deftriers

This painting of nuns going back to their monastery after a night of fun is taken from a medieval manuscript.

Not only was the monarchy's influence expanding at the expense of the Church, the Church also faced damning criticisms of hypocrisy and corruption which had serious long-term effects. Many criticisms actually came from within the Church itself: for example, from the Gregorians, named after Pope Gregory VII (Pope, 1073–85). Their main argument was that the soul was the most important thing to humans and therefore that priests were more important than monarchs. Gregorians accused many priests of pampering laymen (men who were not from the Church) and political leaders, at the expense of people's spiritual welfare.

Digging deeper

The Orthodox Church

The Catholic Church had split into East and West, each having its own Emperor and then Pope. The Catholic Church in the East was based in the then Byzantine Empire with Constantinople at its centre. It is also known as the Orthodox Church. Orthodox Christians had similar beliefs to those in the Western Church. In the Middle Ages, pilgrimages to the Holy Land were popular among the rich. Orthodox Christians also put a lot of faith in religious icons (pictures). Critics believed that Orthodox Christians put more faith in the religious icons than they did in Jesus and God. The religious and organisational split between east and west Europe created a division that resulted in wars for centuries to come.

Arguing over Church appointments

The argument that priests were more important than monarchs caused trouble over the issue of Church appointments. Nearly 100 years before Becket was murdered in Canterbury Cathedral, William Rufus quarrelled with his Archbishop of Canterbury, Anselm Bec (see page 50). Like Becket, Anselm was in an awkward position. He felt split between two masters: the Pope, and the man who had appointed him – the king. In an argument with William Rufus, Anselm agreed with the Gregorians by saying that the Pope was the true authority for Church men, not the king. William forced Anselm to leave the country, but he was invited back by William's successor, his brother Henry I, in 1100. Henry too argued with Anselm because his time away from England had led him to hold even stronger beliefs about the respective roles of Church and monarch. Anselm argued that all Church appointments should be made by the Church. This threatened the monarch because the Church owned considerable amounts of land in England as well as receiving tithes. Henry I was worried that the Church might pose a serious challenge to his power and the loyalty shown to him. Henry and Anselm reached a compromise: the king did not have automatic appointment of Church men but kept some influence. The argument continued with subsequent monarchs and was encouraged by other groups of reformers.

Digging deeper

Wyclif and the Lollards – heretics or modernists?

The Lollards were a group of people who followed the ideas of John Wyclif. The word Lollard was a European name for a religious critic. Wyclif and the Lollards posed another challenge to the Church's power in England.

John Wyclif (1320–84) was a priest and lecturer from Oxford. He studied philosophy and religion at the University and became Master of Balliol College. Wyclif developed new ideas about Christianity and the Church which challenged the existing doctrine (core beliefs). He believed that God had a plan for the world, and that some members of the Church, even the Pope, may not necessarily be part of God's plan. What was most important about religion, according to Wyclif, was each individual's direct relationship with God. He argued that the papacy was a creation of man, not from the Bible. This meant that there was no need for a Pope, as Christ was the true Head of the Church. Wyclif questioned why priests should have the power to absolve people from their sins, decide on a suitable

penance and even excommunicate someone. Also, the Bible was believed by Wyclif to be the whole truth for Christians. This meant that it was vital that it was translated into English or the vernacular (spoken) language in every country, so that it was accessible to everyone. In 1397 Wyclif commissioned a readable version of the Bible in the vernacular. He also sent out bands of preachers to share his ideas with the public.

Lollards were academics, knights, noblemen and craftsmen. They questioned:

- the morality of spending money on pilgrimages rather than helping the poor

- the emphasis on Latin which could not be understood by most people

- any form of luxury or corruption of bishops and monks, such as wealth and wives

- why women should have a lower status than men in the Church and in society.

Lollards were popular in the late fourteenth century, but after 1401, when an order to burn heretics was issued, they were banned and persecuted. Anyone suspected of having sympathies with Lollard ideas was questioned by the Church and, if found guilty of heresy, imprisoned or executed.

The Lollards represented a reaction to corruption felt to be a problem in some parts of the Church. They also represented a challenge to the Church and its ideas. Wyclif died peacefully: unlike his followers he was not persecuted. He managed to have the English translation of the Bible completed, and the ideas of the Lollards spread in differing forms across Europe.

Portrait of John Wyclif, an engraving c. 1550.

 Question time

1. In Source C, which Lollard argument helps to explain the hostile reaction of the Church to the movement?

2. The Lollards failed to change any of the doctrines or habits of the Church, so why were they significant in medieval England?

Enemies of the Church

The immense power of the Church was used against a range of religious and political enemies. It was not only a few rebel monarchs and the Lollards who dared to challenge the Church. Although the power of the Church was used against individuals for political reasons, any groups of people who were thought to have slightly different beliefs (called heretics) were often persecuted. The monarch also chose to persecute enemies of the Church, especially if they posed a threat to law, order and the traditional hierarchy, as did the Lollards in the fourteenth century (see page 147).

Girolamo Savonarola

SOURCE E

Savonarola burning at the stake in Florence. A contemporary illustration.

One famous medieval heretic was Girolamo Savonarola, a Dominican friar from Italy. He was famous for his criticisms of political and religious corruption. His passionate sermons and writings made him popular with the people of his home of Florence, but very unpopular with the Church, in particular Pope Alexander VI, whom he criticised. Savonarola even supported an invasion of Italy (by the French), arguing that the invaders were cleansing a corrupt country on God's behalf. Savonarola also opposed the new influences of the Renaissance that were spreading across Europe. In Florence, Savonarola became so powerful that he led a successful revolt to expel the leading family, the Medicis. He actually ruled the Republic of Florence in 1494–8. In 1497 the Pope had had enough of this challenge to his authority and excommunicated Savonarola. However, Savonarola refused to stop preaching and was arrested, accused of heresy, tortured, hanged and then burned at the stake in the main square in Florence.

Question time

1   Do you think that the Church's harsh treatment of heretics shows that it was still very powerful, or that it was under threat?

Money lenders and scapegoats: the treatment of Jewish people in England

The Church did not only exert power over Christian people in Britain. Jewish people had come to Britain shortly after the Norman conquest, and during the medieval period the extent of their freedom was in the hands of the Catholic Church and the monarch. It was the Church and the monarch who were responsible for the harsh treatment of the Jews in England and their subsequent expulsion. Christians were often scared of the Jewish people because they did not understand their different customs and religion.

The practice of money lending

The hostility of Christians towards the Jews meant that Jewish people were not able to become craftsmen because they were excluded from trade guilds (to which all tradesmen had to belong). The main job left open to Jews in the Middle Ages was one which the Catholic Church had banned: that of money lending. Christianity taught that it was a sin to charge interest on loans of money. Jewish people were not restricted by their religion and could charge interest on money they lent out, and so make a living. They were legally allowed to do this from 1215.

Within Christendom Jews were often tolerated. Norman landowners and leading Church men often relied on loans from Jewish money lenders when finances were tight. Norman barons even encouraged Jewish financiers to move to England. The Jews were usually protected by the rule of the monarch, but they had to pay for this protection through very high rates of tax. Although protected to some extent, Jewish people were not treated equally, and from 1215 they had to wear spiked hats as a symbol of their differences, or strips of yellow material on their clothing. They were also made to fast, just like Christians, during the period of Lent, and were not allowed to have Christians as their servants. Sometimes Christians attacked Jews out of fear and suspicion, so Jews tended to live in main towns near the protection of a royal castle. As a result, Jewish families were forced to live in a certain part of a town called a ghetto, the Jewish Quarter or Jewery.

The scapegoat when things go wrong

Hostility towards the Jewish people was made worse by the Crusades (see Chapter 9) and especially after 1187 when Jerusalem was lost to the Muslims. The loss of this symbolic city led to riots where Jews were often the victims. The Jewish people were also blamed for the Black Death (see page 237); they became scapegoats for many crimes and seemingly inexplicable events.

The treatment of the Jews depended on the monarch ruling at the time and national feeling. In 1275 Queen Eleanor ordered the removal of the Jews from and to certain towns: from Gloucester to Bristol, from Worcester to Hereford, and from Cambridge to Norwich. The sudden influx of hundreds of Jewish people into a thriving medieval town may have caused added tension. In 1290, Edward I expelled the Jews from England completely. This expulsion lasted until 1655.

Jewish communities had also been established in France, Germany, Holland and some parts of Spain and southern Italy. As in England, Jews were at first protected by the Church, monarchs and local rulers. However, a similar hostile reaction gradually developed. Jews all over Europe were driven out of their homes and fled to Poland, Lithuania and Turkey for safety.

Digging deeper

Resentment and prejudice against Jews

Jewish money lenders often became wealthier than many Christians. Aaron of Lincoln, for example, was so wealthy that he owned a fine house in the heart of the city. Jewish women as well as men often became rich and influential in their local area. The wealth and power of many Jewish people caused much jealousy and resulted in them being seen as a threat to Christians.

Rumours in Norwich

In 1144 rumours flew around the city of Norwich that the local Jews had sacrificed a 12-year-old boy in a religious ceremony. The young boy, called William, had been seen entering a house in the Jewish Quarter of Norwich. He disappeared and his body was later found in the woods. This information came from a man called Theobald who was a Jewish convert to Christianity living in the town of Cambridge at the time of the supposed sacrifice. Following the discovery of the body, the citizens of Norwich rioted and the Jewish people were forced to hide in the castle for safety. Theobald may have made up the accusation because Jewish people were often accused of child murders. The children were usually declared martyrs (someone who has died for their faith), as was William.

Persecution in York

In 1190 the Jews in York gathered together at Clifford's Tower for protection from the local people. The tower stood on a motte, surrounded by a moat and bailey. The locals set fire to the tower, demanding that the Jews convert to Christianity. The Jewish men cut the throats of their wives and children to save them from being murdered by the mob which surrounded them. The remaining Jews were enticed out of the castle by the mob and promptly murdered. A huge bonfire of the loan papers given by Jewish money lenders was built outside the castle.

 ## Question time

1   What is it about Theobald which makes him more or less likely to be a reliable witness of the supposed sacrifice in Norwich?

2   Why do you think that Jewish people were often blamed for mystery crimes in medieval towns?

3   What motives did the Christians of York have for attacking the local Jewish community?

 ## Question time

1   What does the story of the Jews tell us about the Church and the monarch in medieval England?

Assessment section

1   Create a diagram that sums up the relationship between the Church and the monarch in the Middle Ages.

    You can include examples from earlier chapters if they are relevant. Your diagram could be split into two:

    ● events and factors that caused a monarch's power to increase

    ● events and factors that caused the Church's power to decrease.

2   'The Church influenced England's political affairs only when the monarch was particularly weak.'

    Do you agree with this statement? The statement is a hypothesis – it provides a starting point for reasoned discussion and argument. Steps a–c will help you to find examples from earlier in the book to both support and challenge the above hypothesis.

    a   Create a timeline to cover the period 1066–1485. On the timeline, make notes to indicate:

        ● when the Church interfered in political events and affairs

        ● which monarchs were in power, and whether they were strong or weak.

    b   Make a list of the Church's influences which were consistent over time – those not affected by any changes in monarchy.

    c   Write a conclusion to sum up your research. Try to write a few paragraphs.

3   'Who was the most powerful influence in the Middle Ages – the Church or the monarchy?'

    Write an essay to answer the above question. You will need to decide whether you think that the Church or the monarchy was more powerful, or whether you think that both institutions relied on each other for their power. Be careful to provide historical evidence to support your argument.

Further reading

T.S. Eliot, *Murder in the Cathedral* (Macmillan Education, 1988)

Geraldine McCaughrean, *The Canterbury Tales* (retold) (Oxford University Press, 1984)

Religion and the people

The medieval period is often known as the 'Age of Faith'. You may have heard of the popularity of monasteries and pilgrimages. Did you know that people believed that bones of important religious people had special holy powers and could even heal you? You will investigate these beliefs in more detail in this chapter. This age was certainly a very religious and very superstitious period and it was the Christian Church which, to a large extent, controlled people's beliefs.

The Church was a powerful political influence, and its power over people was far reaching. The Church was a major landowner, employer and source of wealth, and also affected everyone's daily life. Across Christendom the Church and the Christian religion influenced people's work, rest and play. The few people who dared to question its truth were dealt with harshly.

The religious beliefs of medieval people

Christians in Europe in the early Middle Ages went to church regularly and attended special services called masses. They listened to sermons given in English by the parish priest, and tried to act upon his advice. The rest of the mass was spoken and sung in Latin and prayer books were written in Latin. This meant that parishioners recognised the different parts of the services that they heard every week but did not necessarily understand the words being used. Most religious teaching was carried out through stories in stained-glass windows, wall painting and plays.

The Church's moral code

People were taught to follow the Ten Commandments, which were sometimes painted on the walls of the church. The Ten Commandments were the laws given to Moses and written about in the Old Testament of the Bible; they still give Christians their moral code of behaviour today. People also believed that there were seven deadly sins that they had to take special care to avoid. These sins had been written about in the fourth century by Church men and were: anger, greed, lust, envy, sloth (laziness), pride and gluttony (eating and drinking too much). If anyone broke any of the Ten Commandments or gave in to these vices they were committing a sin.

Across Europe it was the Church that controlled all aspects of education. All schools and universities were under the control of the Church; so in effect the Pope, archbishops and bishops directed all aspects of learning. Bishops issued licences to teachers and made sure that they taught ideas which fitted in with the Church. Local schools were even held in the porch of the parish church. The Church directed what people believed at all levels, from the parishioners listening to their weekly sermon, to lawyers, teachers and politicians.

Medieval Christians had the same basic beliefs as modern Christians. However, their beliefs were more literal. This means that they had vivid images of God, the devil, heaven and hell in their minds. Medieval people were terrified of the possibility of facing eternal torture if they went to hell. The Church gave them hope of the paradise of life after death in heaven. It was their link to Jesus, God and any hope of going to heaven. As long as they were good Christians, following the Church's laws on earth, then they would not burn in hell when they died. For people who had such a short life expectancy in comparison to modern standards (they lived until about 45 years old) and could easily die from the flu or an accident at work, then this was vital reassurance. Christians across Europe believed that their route to heaven was through the Church. Parish priests taught people the consequences of leading a sinful life, but also about how to make amends.

Doom paintings were a type of painting showing vivid images of heaven and hell and what would happen when a person was judged by God and met their doom (or fate). Doom paintings were made in manuscripts and on the walls of medieval churches. Some still exist today.

SOURCE B

The side to our left was dreadful with burning flames, while the opposite side was equally horrible with raging hail and bitter snow blowing in all directions. Both sides were filled with men's souls, which seemed to be hurled from one side to the other by the fury of the tempest. For when the wretches could no longer bear the terrible heat they leapt into the heart of the terrible cold. My guide said 'This is not Hell as you imagine'. He led me to a terrible scene. I saw a group of wicked spirits dragging with them five human souls howling and wailing into the depths of darkness while the devils laughed.

This description of hell is taken from The History of the English Church and People *by the Venerable Bede in 731.*

Digging deeper

Dante: a medieval poet and politician

Dante was an Italian poet who wrote in Italian as well as traditional Latin. He is famous for writing an epic poem called *The Divine Comedy*. In this poem Dante describes a journey between hell, purgatory and heaven. The journey is also supposed to represent his individual spiritual journey as a Christian. Dante believed that his life after death depended on leading a good life on earth.

Dante lived in Florence, but was forced to leave when the city was run by a rival political group to his own. They accused him of financial corruption and he was given the death sentence. Dante escaped to live in northern Italy for the rest of his life.

SOURCE C

'They sank their fangs in that poor wretch who hid,
They ripped him open piece by piece, and then
Ran off with mouthfuls of his wretched limbs ...
Soon after leaving him I saw two souls
Frozen together in a single hole,
So that one head used the other for a cap.
As a man with hungry teeth tears into bread,
The soul with capping head had sunk his teeth
Into the other's neck just below the skull.'

'I saw light that was a slowing stream,
Blazing in splendid sparks between two banks
Painted like rubies set in rings of gold.'

'I saw her face flame with so much light,
Her eyes so bright with holy happiness,
That I shall have to leave it undescribed.'

Extracts from The Divine Comedy, *written by Dante between 1307 and 1321.*

SOURCE D

The frontispiece (opening illustration) of Dante's Inferno, *part of* The Divine Comedy *written in the fourteenth century. In this painting you can see the town of Florence where Dante lived and worked, and also the paths to heaven and hell.*

Question time

1　Do you think that each of the extracts from Dante's poem (Source C) refer to hell, purgatory or heaven? Give reasons for your answer.

2　Describe what you can see in heaven and hell as shown in Source D.

3　How similar is Dante's description of heaven and hell (Source C) to that shown in the medieval doom painting (Source A)? Explain the differences between the sources as well as the similarities.

4　'Dante was a poet, not a historian or a priest, and so he cannot be relied on for information about medieval religion.' Do you agree with this statement?

How to get to heaven in the Middle Ages

As well as attending church and trying to be a good person, medieval Christians needed the parish priest to help them to get into heaven when they died. They not only needed him for funeral rites and a blessing on their death but as a constant link to God during their lifetime. Medieval Christians believed that God had given priests authority, through the Pope and archbishops, to teach them in religious matters and also to forgive their sins. People would confess any sins they had committed to the priest who would give them a penance (some form of act to make amends for their sins). A penance could be in the form of a fine or some special prayers. Once a penance was completed then the person would be forgiven by the priest on behalf of God, and so their slate would be clean.

A Christian would be baptised by the priest as soon as possible. Marriages also had to be carried out by a priest, and funerals involved many different processes, not just a few prayers and a blessing. The wealthy left money to make sure their souls had every chance of gaining eternal freedom

Good deeds

There were other acts that a person could do to show what a good Christian they were. It was usual practice for people to leave money to the Church in their wills. Donations could pay for new furniture or paintings in the parish church, and for prayers to be said on their death. People could sometimes buy 'pardons' from pardoners, who were actually selling forgiveness on behalf of the Church and the Pope. Many people regularly gave money to the poor or to help run hospitals. Another important act would be to go on a pilgrimage to a holy shrine (a common activity in the Middle Ages investigated later in this chapter). Another way of gaining forgiveness and getting to heaven was to punish yourself to show how sorry you were. People would sometimes whip themselves or wear an uncomfortable hair shirt to show their dedication.

Holy relics

An ornately decorated gold case or jar, filled with the bones of a human finger; a nail; some small splinters of wood; some loose teeth, finger nails or pieces of hair; a fragment of ancient material. This list is not the ingredients of a magical spell but objects called relics, which were highly prized in Christendom. The objects, bones, teeth or hair were believed to be from the body of a saint (see Source H on page 144). Nails were believed to be from the cross on which Christ was crucified; material from his shroud or the Virgin Mary's veil. At one point there were two different heads of John the Baptist travelling around Europe in a shrine. One monk explained this strange phenomenon by saying that one was his head as a young man, the other in old age!

Owning or visiting relics could ease your path to heaven. Relics were believed to have special powers to perform miracles such as healing. Relics were just another small part of the religious practices which allowed people to show what devoted Christians they were.

The power of saints

St Catherine. This portrait is by Giovanni Battista c. 1487.

Saints were another important way of showing piety or being a good Christian. Many saints had suffered and died for Christianity and they had all led holy lives. They set a good example so medieval Christians would learn about them and try to copy their actions. Books were written about them for the few wealthy people who were literate. For the majority of the population they learned about the saints from stories and from stained-glass windows in church. Each saint had his or her own symbol and area that they could influence. St James, St Catherine and St Mary were the most popular saints in England during the Middle Ages. St Catherine was a mystic who had visions, meditated and also cared for the sick in fifteenth-century Italy. Miracles were also explained as the work of saints. St Foy de Conques was believed to be able to cure blindness; a book of his healing miracles was compiled in eleventh-century France. Each saint also had a special day in the Church calendar when feasts and celebrations remembering their life were held.

Religion and the people

Each parish had a church for worship but some also had smaller shrines, built to honour a particular saint. Saints were worshipped in their own right, and were seen as God's servants and messengers. People offered gifts as well as prayers at these shrines and believed that by doing this miracles could occur, for example they would be cured of a disease or their crops could be saved from flooding.

Pilgrims would flock to a shrine if a saint's body was present. The saint's shrine was thought to be particularly holy if the body was intact. Such a shrine attracted many pilgrims and this added to the income of the abbey or place of pilgrimage.

SOURCE B

First, I leave my soul to Almighty God, the Blessed Mary, the Blessed Margaret and all the saints, my body to be buried in the parish church of St Margaret, Paston, between the south door of the same church and the tomb of Beatrice, late my wife.

I leave to the vicar of the said church for my tithes and other things if they be not paid 3s 4d. To the light of the Blessed Margaret in the chancel of the said church 7 pounds of wax. To the repairing and improvement of the said church and its ornaments 3s. 4d … To the prior and convent of Bromholm 6s 8d … The residue of all my good I give to my sister and my son. What remains they shall spend in works of charity and piety for my soul and the souls of Beatrice and all my ancestors …

Extract from the will of Clement Paston, Lord of Paston, 1419.

SOURCE C

His body to be buried in the churchyard of the parish church of Caddington (no dedication or gift given); to the high altar for tithes forgotten 2s; to the light before the great crucifix 4d … land to sons Robert and Thomas; to wife best horse, to son next best horse, wife to choose third horse and best cow, next best cow to son Robert …

Extract from the will of John Crowche of Caddington, 1500.

Question time

1. a Explain why medieval Christians believed that they had to go to the parish priest in order to confess their sins.

   b What else could medieval Christians do to try to earn their way to eternal happiness in heaven?

2. It was a tradition in wills to leave the second best animal to the Church or the parish priest. What might this tell us about John Crowche in Source C?

3. Compare Sources B and C. What do they tell us about the influence of medieval religion?

4. a Can you find out how many saints are officially accepted by the Catholic Church or the Church of England today?

   b Can you think of any modern people who might one day become saints?

5. Find out about some more medieval saints. Find out what they did that led to their canonisation.

Religious rituals

Already we can see the hold that the Church had over Christians across Christendom. The Church, through its parish priests and religious practices, ensured that good Christians had hope of getting to heaven. Much of the Church's control was in the form of a wide range of religious rituals or actions that were a regular part of Church life. These rituals, many still part of Catholic and Church of England worship today, included the many parts of each Church service, mass and holy communion. Rituals ranged from the clothes that the priest wore to acts of devotion based on the story of the crucifixion. Below are four examples of religious ritual that are still practised in many Christian churches today.

The Stations of the Cross

These are 14 different pictures or carvings placed on the walls of a church, each showing a stage on Christ's journey towards his crucifixion. The first station is where Christ is condemned to death, the last is where his body is laid in its tomb. Although the 14 different stages were not formalised until the eighteenth century, medieval worshippers would visit pictures in their chronological sequence for an act of devotion, meditation or prayer.

Priest's vestments

The parish priest would wear robes, or vestments, with a colour associated with the relevant stage in the Christian calendar. His clothes would be put on in a particular order, accompanied by a special prayer.

The use of incense

Holy parts of the church would be wafted with incense during mass. This included the Bible and the altar, as well as the congregation itself. Special holders for the incense were called censers and were often made from beautifully crafted gold or silver. The smoke from the burning incense was considered to be symbolic of prayer.

Observing feast days

The Church's influence could be seen over people's working life as well as their behaviour. Corrupt carpenters or farmers who profited from selling poor-quality goods would have to go to mass and make confession. The Church also directed men when they could make a living and actually go to work. In addition to Sundays there were more than 100 holy days on the calendar when people were not allowed to work. The phrase 'holy days' became 'holidays' and they were usually celebrated with village feasts as well as Church services. Everyone was expected to observe holy days. To do otherwise, and go to work as usual, was to show disrespect for the particular saint or holy person. One man was drowned by the Church for working on a holy day. A painter from the eleventh century who continued in his work on the holy day of Erkenwald, preventing local people from offering their candles and gifts inside the church, was reported to have fallen from his scaffolding and taken ill, before having a dramatic vision where he was visited by a dead clergyman and chastised (told off) for his neglect of the holy day.

Question time

The road to heaven.

1 a Copy the picture of the road to heaven. Add extra details to it to help you to remember the information in this section.

   b Also add descriptions of what medieval people might expect to find in heaven or hell when they arrived there.

Digging deeper

The parish church – a medieval community centre

Medieval churches were not just religious buildings. Marriages, funerals, baptisms, daily services and weekly masses were the core of the Church's work in each parish but they were much more than just places for parishioners to receive spiritual guidance and comfort. They were more like a medieval community centre. On entering a church, parishioners would be able to smell the strong sweet incense, burnt in ornately decorated censers during mass. Young and old people alike would be terrified by wall paintings showing poor souls suffering in hell; and cheered by pictures of Christ and the angels in heaven. They could sit during a Church service and look at the coloured glass windows that told a story of a saint's battle against evil, or one of Jesus' miracles.

Medieval churches were also busy bustling places most days of the week. They were open to the public and had few pews or seats that are seen today in many parish churches. The medieval parish church would be a place to give and receive information and notices. School lessons could be held by the priest in the porch. Churches also acted as theatres, providing entertainment in the form of religious mystery or morality plays telling tales of Good versus Evil. On holy days feasts would be held in the church including music, theatre and sport such as wrestling. Churches were often small markets for local produce and also the place that poor people could receive charity in the form of alms (donations of money or gifts).

The importance of the parish priest

We have seen that the parish priest was the everyday link between medieval people and the huge organisation of the Church. In the early medieval period priests were often from peasant families in the village, but by 1400 they were more likely to be educated men from wealthier families.

No one argued with the parish priest. As God's representative on Earth, priests were respected and influential men. This made it harder for people to make any form of criticism when priests occasionally did not keep to their vows. The priest was very important within a parish and had much influence. It was a powerful job but priests had to co-operate with the local lord because he was the person responsible for choosing potential priests for the parish. The priest might have to check that feudal taxes were being paid to the lord, in addition to the tithes.

There were many tasks for the priest to do. Priests were carers, charity workers, accountants, will makers, readers, tax collectors and teachers: all these in addition to holding services and offering spiritual advice to the parishioners. By the thirteenth century it was rare to find a priest who was married. They were dedicated to the Church and far too busy to have a family. Some had secret mistresses and this caused problems for the Church's reputation in later years.

Latin was the language of the Church so priests needed to be educated to read Latin and be able to write. They had access to scriptures and religious teachings that were a mystery to everyone else in medieval society. There was an element of mystery to the Latin Church services that put priests above their parishioners. At least their sermons were in English so that villagers and townsfolk could get advice. With the education required for the job came additional responsibilities such as the writing of charters for local landowners or wills for ageing parishioners. One quarter of the tithes collected in a parish would be used as food and income for the priest; three quarters would go to the local bishop. The parish priest also charged a fee for baptisms, marriages and funerals, and he received any profits from crops grown on the glebe (land given over to the Church). The priest did not get paid by the diocese but this security of income from services, tithes and traditions, combined with the respect that the priest usually gained from his parishioners, meant that a priest's life was a relatively comfortable one in the Middle Ages.

You must teach your people when they come to church to stop their chatter, gossip and jokes, and say their prayers instead. Don't let them stand about or lean against the pillars or the walls, but make them kneel to pray for grace and mercy. They shall stand up to hear the gospel read and bless themselves. Then when they hear the bell for the consecration, they must all kneel down, young and old, and hold up their hands and say gently and softly 'Jesus, Lord, thou art welcome, in the form of bread that I can see. Jesus shield me today from sin, and forgive me my sins before I leave this church. May I not die in sin.'

Extract from a fifteenth-century book giving advice to parish priests.

The priest should ask the peasants whether they have cheated by not paying their full tithes to the Church; whether they have been obedient to their lord; whether they have broken into a neighbour's land with their plough or animal. They must be told that it is a sin to work hard only when their lord is present and to be idle when he is absent, and they must not grumble when he corrects them.

Extract from a handbook for medieval clergy, 1380.

Question time

1 Why were medieval peasants likely to own up to any crimes they might have committed to the parish priest?

2 Some people in the Middle Ages complained about having to pay tithes to the Church. Some farmers in Devon even staged a protest about it, pouring 10 per cent of their milk on the ground in the church yard in front of their parish priest. Does Source C suggest that tithes were unpopular in medieval England?

3 Some historians have suggested that the Church was a stabiliser in medieval society, i.e. it kept society ordered and stable. Can you find any evidence to suggest that the parish priest and parish church fit this description?

Building houses for God

Perhaps the most obvious reminder of the power of the medieval Church is the many parish churches scattered over the British landscape. Over 9000 parish churches and 17 cathedrals from this period survive. These buildings were built to last, and are a permanent reminder of the power of the Church. Parishioners could not forget the influence of the Church with a tall tower looming in the distance and church bells pealing to call them to mass. The position of the church in the village was also significant: it was often at the highest point or in the centre, implying its dominance and focal point for activity.

Modern photograph of the village of Flitton, Bedfordshire, showing the dominant position of the parish church.

We know from written builders' contracts that the new churches and extensions were built from stone. Stone was a permanent feature on the landscape, unlike the wood and thatch of other village buildings. Local landowners would often pay to have churches built or extended in the latest fashion. Many older, wooden churches were pulled down to make way for a new building in the latest architectural style. Some church buildings were erected so quickly that, like the church in Hadstock in Essex, they soon fell down.

By the thirteenth century, churches in England were being built to a Norman design. Norman influences had made churches larger, with thinner walls and bigger windows than the small, Saxon-style buildings. The amount of light, space and height available in parish churches increased as time passed.

Digging deeper

Architectural styles of religious buildings in the Middle Ages

All across Europe huge cathedrals, built in the medieval period, loom over the landscape (see Source B). In France, Italy and the rest of Christendom increased wealth led to a building boom mirrored in England. Kings, princes and local landowners funded major building works and local traders often sponsored parts of a new church or cathedral. Trade guilds often paid for the design and building of stained-glass windows. In addition to costly glass windows, many other aspects of a church required funding for highly skilled craftsmen who created paintings or frescoes, ironwork and stone carvings and woven textiles – all depicting Biblical stories. Most European cathedrals followed the main architectural styles but there were some regional variations. Church men in Spain, for example, often took Moorish or Islamic designs and incorporated them into their Christian buildings.

$\triangleright\triangleright\triangleright$

SOURCE B

A Romanesque church. The picture shows the west front of Ely Cathedral in Cambridgeshire, completed c. 1189.

Church architecture can be divided into two main types: Romanesque and Gothic. Romanesque churches in England are called 'Norman'; they date from the eleventh and twelfth centuries. Key words for this style are bold, round, simple, thick, heavy. Gothic architecture from the thirteenth century is called 'Early English'; fourteenth- and fifteenth-century Gothic is called 'Decorated'. Key words here are pointed, thin, tall, elaborate.

Question time

1   Why is it difficult to work out by looking at a photograph of a church or cathedral which architectural style it belongs in?

2   What are the similarities and differences between the cathedrals in Sources B and C?

3   Medieval cathedrals were show pieces for the towns and cities in which they were built. What type of buildings in the twenty-first century can be described in the same way?

SOURCE C

A Gothic church. The picture shows the west front of Wells Cathedral in Somerset, completed in the thirteenth century.

BUILDING

- Pulleys and cranes, carts and scaffolding.
- No safety measures.

GLASS

- Stained glass coloured by adding chemicals to the molten glass, painted to show more detail and held together by strips of lead.
- Furnaces on the work site to melt lead and make glass.

STONEWORK

- Master masons and masons of different grades according to experience.
- Detailed plans drawn on huge slabs of plaster or wood.

ARTISTS

- Most of the skilled craftsmen were artists in their own right.

WORKERS

- Each aspect of church building relied on an army of workers, from travelling stone masons to locally hired labourers such as craftsmen, carpenters, metalworkers, painters, glaziers, masons, paviers, wallers, marblers, image makers, tool carriers and hod bearers.
- Master masons had to monitor the work of all the other workers.
- Each type of job would be paid a different wage.

Medieval technologies and craft workers

Many different technologies were needed to create the splendid churches, monasteries and cathedrals of the medieval period. As the architecture became more complex, increased skill was required to make sure that these buildings stayed standing.

Question time

1. Which type of worker do you think would be paid most highly for their work on a religious building site?

2. Discuss in pairs the different skills needed to build a Gothic cathedral or church compared to those needed to build a building from an earlier period.

Pilgrims and pilgrimages

Another important part of medieval Christianity was the visiting of holy places or shrines, where prayers could be offered to a saint or special religious person. Pilgrims tended to be wealthy people who could afford to spend time away from work and fund the journey, although records show that some working people occasionally went on pilgrimage. Lower down the social scale they were a popular way to show virtue. The less well off could make a pilgrimage to a shrine in England such as Walsingham or Canterbury. At Walsingham in Norfolk a pilgrim might get to see the holy jar holding what was believed to be the Virgin Mary's breast milk – that would be a very special relic indeed.

Fewer women than men went on pilgrimage. Women had to ask permission from their husbands, fathers or abbot before they could make a pilgrimage. Also, they could not travel alone or in small groups; they would need to travel with men for protection. Women were not encouraged to go on pilgrimage. Perhaps men and the Church felt that women might be corrupted by the experience, or might prove a temptation to men on the journey! Women, however, were keen to visit shrines, and making a pilgrimage in their own country became more acceptable.

Many people who went on pilgrimage were carrying out a penance to make up for a sin that they had confessed to their priest. Most pilgrims believed that they would be rewarded in heaven for the dedication shown in making a pilgrimage. Some hoped for a reduced period in purgatory. Other pilgrims hoped for a miracle to be performed at a holy site. The religious incentive of visiting holy shrines of saints was great, but there was also a certain holiday feel to the journey. Before leaving, pilgrims would take a vow and be blessed by a bishop or priest. Pilgrims were also supposed to wear a special robe to indicate that they had given up worldly clothes. Many rich people did not keep to this custom, because the robes were often uncomfortable and impractical.

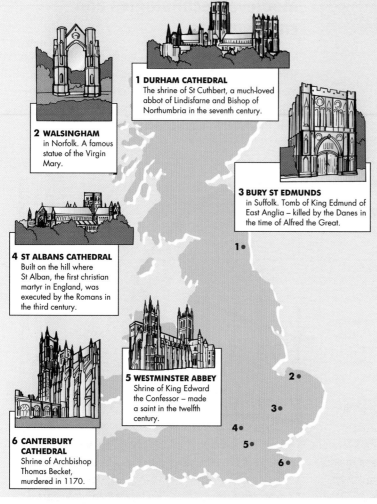

1 DURHAM CATHEDRAL
The shrine of St Cuthbert, a much-loved abbot of Lindisfarne and Bishop of Northumbria in the seventh century.

2 WALSINGHAM
in Norfolk. A famous statue of the Virgin Mary.

3 BURY ST EDMUNDS
in Suffolk. Tomb of King Edmund of East Anglia – killed by the Danes in the time of Alfred the Great.

4 ST ALBANS CATHEDRAL
Built on the hill where St Alban, the first christian martyr in England, was executed by the Romans in the third century.

5 WESTMINSTER ABBEY
Shrine of King Edward the Confessor – made a saint in the twelfth century.

6 CANTERBURY CATHEDRAL
Shrine of Archbishop Thomas Becket, murdered in 1170.

The main sites of pilgrimage and why they are significant.

A contemporary illustration of people on a pilgrimage in the Middle Ages.

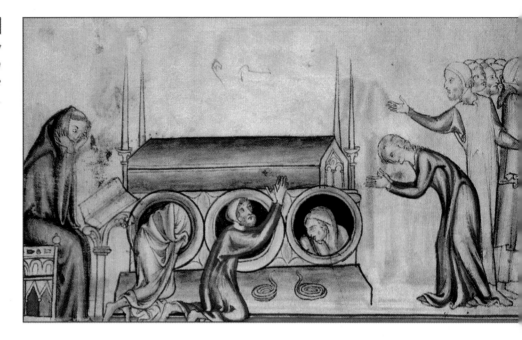

Digging deeper

Chaucer's famous pilgrims

Geoffrey Chaucer was born in the early 1340s. He worked as a page and then as a messenger for the king's court. Taking secret messages to important people across Europe meant that Chaucer travelled to Flanders, France and Italy. On his travels he had the chance to read widely and was inspired by several poets of his age, including Boccaccio (see page 179). He began writing, and his poems include a collection of linked poems called *The Canterbury Tales*.

Chaucer's tales are based on a fictional pilgrimage of people to Canterbury where each pilgrim tells the others a story about their lives; Chaucer narrates, adding further description of his characters. Some of Chaucer's pilgrims are pious, good people; others are corrupt and have rude tales to tell. The stories are interesting because, through the mouths of these imaginary people, we can learn many things about attitudes of different people in medieval England.

SOURCE B

When the sweet showers of April have pierced the dryness of March to its root ... when people long to go on pilgrimages, and pious wanderers to visit strange lands and far-off shrines in different countries. In England especially they come from every shire's end to Canterbury to seek out the holy blessed martyr St Thomas a Becket, who helped them when they were sick.

It happened one day at this time of year, while I was lodging at the Tabard in Southwark, ready and eager to go on my pilgrimage to Canterbury, a company of twenty-nine people arrived in the hostelry at nightfall. They were of various sorts, accidentally brought together in companionship, all pilgrims wishing to ride to Canterbury. The rooms and stables were commodious [roomy] and we were very well looked after. In short, by the time the sun had gone down I had talked with every one of them and soon become one of their company. We agreed to rise early to set out on the journey I am going to tell you about.

Extract from a modern English version of The Canterbury Tales *by Chaucer c. 1387.*

▷▷▷ Who were Chaucer's pilgrims?

- a ploughman
- a summoner (summons people accused of immorality to Church courts)
- a knight
- a monk
- a merchant
- a parish priest or parson

- a miller
- a friar
- a married lady from Bath
- a squire
- a pardoner (sells pardons for people's souls)
- a clerk
- a knight's son
- a prioress

- a reeve (farm manager)
- a yeoman (small farmer)
- a lawyer
- a shipman
- a nun's priest
- a physician (medical man)
- a cook
- a nun

Prioress – wears fine clothes and jewellery, and spoils her pet dogs with meat and milk.

Ploughman – works hard, often for no wages, and pays his tithes fully. Rides a humble mare.

Parish priest – spends his time preaching and giving money to the poor, visiting the sick and teaching local people.

Some of Chaucer's pilgrims.

Monk – a fat, greedy gambler. He owns fine horses and clothes, dislikes studying, and neglects the rule of the monasteries.

Wife of Bath – a professional pilgrim who had already been on three visits to Jerusalem. Also an expert in love, having had five husbands.

Question time

1 a What different levels of society are represented on Chaucer's fictional pilgrimage? Draw them in a form of hierarchy, and group similar people together, for example all religious men can be grouped together.

   b On your diagram add key words to describe those characters mentioned in the summary above.

2 Find out more about Chaucer's pilgrims. Add key words from your research on to your diagram.

3 What do we need to remember about Chaucer's poems when using *The Canterbury Tales* as evidence about medieval England? Explain your answer including at least two different points.

The pilgrims' journey

In England there is a 120-mile long track leading from Winchester to Canterbury called the Pilgrims' Way. In medieval times pilgrims would travel this way by foot or on horse, or on a litter (carriage carried by servants) if wealthy. Pilgrims travelling abroad would hire a passage on a boat to take them to Jerusalem or wherever they were going.

Pilgrims would stay in hostels or in the guest houses of monasteries along the journey, but would need to carry basic provisions with them. The pilgrim is famous for carrying a bourdon (staff) and a scrip (bag for food) but they would also have needed a water bottle and basic baggage. Journeys were hazardous; men, and most certainly women, could not travel alone for fear of attack. Pilgrims could be robbed or shipwrecked or suffer from a disease or injury. Crossing mountains, like the Alps, or any sea voyage were potentially the most dangerous aspects of a pilgrimage. Terrible weather conditions plus the possibility of animals going lame from the strain of the journey were problematic.

Instruction manuals were written advising pilgrims on all matters associated with their journey, including what equipment to take with them. One such manual advises pilgrims to choose a high berth on the lower deck of a boat to avoid the unpleasant waste and the heat of the lower areas. These sea journeys were obviously not any form of luxury. Another medieval record advises pilgrims to spend several hours a day killing fleas and lice on their beds if they are to get any sleep at all on the journey.

Pilgrims would be given advice about which shrines to visit en route to places such as Rome, Santiago de Compostella or Jerusalem. In Jerusalem pilgrims were even given guided tours. The Church of the Holy Sepulchre, the site of Christ's tomb, was open only twice a year so it would be a rich and lucky pilgrim who gained access to this holy shrine. Access to other sites in Jerusalem was tightly controlled by Muslim officials because the city was in Islamic hands. Throughout their pilgrimage groups had to be accompanied by a priest who could verify that they had carried out their pilgrimage and therefore fulfilled the terms of their penance.

Once at the religious site, pilgrims would pay to buy a special badge made of lead, which they could wear on their cloak or hat. The badges resembled a symbol of the appropriate holy shrine: at Compostella pilgrims received a badge of a shell, the symbol of St James; in Rome their badge was of a napkin; from Jerusalem they brought back a palm branch. Pilgrims' badges or symbols would tell everyone how devout (strictly religious) they were.

Pilgrimages were not considered to be essential in gaining salvation, but they were certainly a way of demonstrating piety. Some Church men began to criticise the popularity of pilgrimages arguing that they had become too commercial, almost like a modern-day tourist trade and that they led to immorality. Other Christian thinkers believed that pilgrimages went against the universal nature of Christianity by placing so much importance on shrines and places rather than an omnipresent (present everywhere) God.

Isolation from the corruption of the world – vows, veils and centres of learning

Monasteries

In such a religious period as the Middle Ages there was a large increase in the number of men and women who chose to isolate themselves from society and dedicate their lives to God. Monasteries and convents existed before the medieval period but not in great numbers. Like the Church itself, monasteries experienced a boom in popularity and also became tremendous influences, both in their local communities and England as a whole.

The idea of monasticism within Christianity had come from the Roman period when individual men went to desert areas in Egypt to lead a solitary life of meditation and fasting. Some men went in groups to set up communities of people who wanted to escape the world and focus on their religion. This idea gradually spread to western Europe and monks there followed the rules established by St Benedict of Nursia who lived from 480 to 547. Some monasteries were established next to cathedrals in large towns, others were built in wild, remote areas where the harsh landscape would mean that the monks had to work hard to become self-sufficient. These monks believed in isolation from the corrupt world, and total poverty, humility and obedience became central beliefs. Monks would leave society for work and study; there would be no time for entertainment or selfish actions. A peaceful, almost silent life would enable them to focus on serving God.

In the early Middle Ages, boys were sometimes given to monasteries at a young age, as a gesture of a family's faith. By the twelfth century joining a monastery was voluntary and, although boys as young as ten years old sometimes joined a monastery, they could leave before they took their holy vows if they did not want to stay. Boys aged 15 years or older, with a religious calling, would become trainee monks, called novices. They would help the other monks, sing in choir and study, being taught to read and write by older monks (Source B). They would be supervised by the Master of the Novices for at least a year. The master had to check that the novices were suitable for monastic life. Taking their vows would mean that they pledged themselves to a life of poverty, obedience and humility, including chastity and a commitment to monastic life. They could not leave the monastery without the permission of the Abbott. When they took their vows, monks would be given a tonsure – their hair would be cut and shaved leaving only a circle, to represent Christ's crown of thorns. Young monks would then train to become fully-fledged choir monks and would follow the rules of the monastery closely. Training young monks was not always easy (see Source B).

At the night services, and indeed at all the hours, if the boys make any mistake in singing psalms or chant, or fall asleep, or transgress [break the rules] in other ways like that, let them be stripped immediately of frock and cowl and beaten in their shirt, either by the prior or their own master, with smooth and supple osier rods [willow branches] kept for that special purpose ...

A master sleeps between each pair of boys in the dormitory and sits between them in the rere-dorter [lavatory], and at night all the candles of the lanterns are fixed on the spikes on the top of the lanterns, so that the boys can clearly be seen in all that they do. When they are in bed, let a master always stand among them with his rod and, if it be night, with his candle in one hand and his rod in the other. If one happens to linger after the others he is promptly given a smart touch of the rod; for children should ever have punishment with care, and care with punishment. And note that this is the only corporal punishment they receive, to be beaten with rods or pulled smartly by the hair; they are never disciplined with kicks or the fists or palm of the hand or any other way ...

One boy must report another if he knows anything against him, or, if he is found to have concealed anything on purpose, he is beaten as well as the offender.

Extract from the Written Collection of Customs and Laws of the Norman abbey of Bec, *giving the Cluniac (Benedictine) rules about monasteries.*

Question time

1   Why did monks want to live outside the world rather than within existing communities? Explain your answer carefully.

2   Rewrite the advice (Source B) for dealing with novice monks in your own words, explaining the reason behind each method.

Digging deeper

St Benedict's Rule

St Benedict's Rule gave all medieval monasteries their basic code of behaviour. It was popular in the medieval period because it was not as strict as rules of earlier monasticism. It tried to lay down fair rules to enable all monks to agree and focus on their faith rather than argue over how to behave. The Rule included laws on all aspects of a monk's life:

- clothing
- giving up personal possessions
- sleeping arrangements in dormitories
- vegetarian diet with descriptions of portions and types of food allowed
- the treatment of guests in guest houses
- the importance of caring for the sick in specially built infirmaries and silence in the monastery.

Idleness is the enemy of the soul. Therefore, at given times the brethren ought to be occupied in manual labour, and again at other times in prayerful reading ... A mattress, woollen blanket and pillow is enough for bedding. All monks should take it in turns to wait on each other so that no one is excused kitchen work.

Extract from St Benedict's Rule.

St Benedict also wrote down the suggested structure of each day. The work of the monastery was to reflect its priorities. The monks' day started at about 3 am with a service called Prime, the first of the new day. Each of the main Church services has a special name:

- Prime: service at dawn, or 6 am in summer.
- Wash in the cloister wash basins, then breakfast unless fasting.
- Terce: 9 am service including mass.
- Meeting in the chapter house or meeting room, to give out daily tasks, hear confession, issue punishments.
- Work (copying, in the kitchen, gardening, teaching, caring for the ill, in the guesthouse or on the farm).
- Sext: midday service including mass.
- Dinner then private reading, then work.
- None: 3 pm service followed by a short rest.
- Vespers: 4.30 pm service.
- Wash for supper.
- Compline: dusk/6 pm service.
- Bed until midnight.

- Matins/Lauds: midnight service.
- Sleep again until Prime.

SOURCE D

From Easter until 1 October, the morning – from after Prime until about the fourth hour – should be spent doing whatever work has to be done. From the fourth hour until Sext, they should devote themselves to reading. But after Sext, when they have risen from table, they may rest on their beds in complete silence; or anyone who wants to read by himself may do so, but without disturbing the others. None should be said slightly early, halfway through the eighth hour; then again they should do whatever work needs to be done until Vespers. Should local conditions or their poverty make it necessary for them to do the harvesting themselves, they must not be disgruntled; because then they are genuinely monks, when they live by the work of their hands, like our fathers and the apostles. Yet everything should be done with moderation, on account of the faint-hearted.

Extract from St Benedict's Rule.

Question time

1 At which point in the Church year do the monks carry out most reading and prayer?

2 Is there any evidence that St Benedict's Rule was not that harsh and included some compromise or flexibility in its interpretation?

3 Make a list of other evidence that Source D gives us about the life and priorities of a medieval monk.

The spread of monasticism

As monastic life became more popular in the religious age of the Middle Ages, the size, wealth and power of monasteries also grew. The original type of monastery in England was the Benedictine order, which included several independent abbeys. Some monasteries differed in their interpretation of St Benedict's Rule and new orders (types) of monastery were established. Many of these new orders wanted to reform monasticism because they felt that it had relaxed and moved away from its original austerity (strictness).

The first new order to challenge the Benedictine order was that of the Cluniacs, from Cluny in Burgundy, France. Monasticism spread in England in the tenth and eleventh centuries, and several other orders had developed by the thirteenth century, including the Cistercians, Carthusians, Franciscans and Dominicans (see table below). So many different orders existed that by 1215 the Pope resorted to banning any new orders; new monasteries had to adopt one of the existing orders.

Monastic orders.

Order	Foundation	Aims	Details
Cluniac	Cluny, France	To lead a strict life and be more centralised in their organisation	Became large and wealthy; criticised by the Cistercians for their elaborate buildings and rituals; had 38 monasteries in England by the sixteenth century
Cistercian	Citeaux, France	To lead a more holy life	Included choir monks and lay brothers who were not educated but took vows and worked as labourers; undyed woollen habits gave them name of 'White Monks'; became the most popular order in England
Franciscan	St Francis of Assisi	To live in poverty	Became the 'Friars'; they travelled the world preaching and begging for their food, totally rejecting any worldly possessions and wealth
Dominicans	Spanish priest called Dominic de Guzman	To live in total poverty but as highly educated men	Called 'Blackfriars' in England because of their black woollen habits (robes)
Carthusian	St Bruno of Grenoble	To live a solitary life keeping strictly to vows	Lived in individual cells and spent most time there praying and studying; most strict of all the orders, almost constant fasting and harsh living conditions, few in number

Question time

1. Design a notice board that would be posted in the cloisters of every busy monastery. It might include the daily routine, important messages and common rules that monks should not forget.

2. Find out about the different types of monk. Describe their daily routines in a monastery. You will need to organise your description into sections which could be based around different parts of the day, or different types of monk. You will also need to sum up the common ingredients of monastic life for all monks, whether they are a librarian or a lay brother.

Digging deeper

Fountains Abbey – a fine medieval monastery

Fountains Abbey is near Ripon in North Yorkshire. It was the most powerful Cistercian monastery in the North of England, once owning land all over Yorkshire. The monastery is set in the Skell valley for protection from the weather and is surrounded by fertile farming land, the river Skell and various streams coming down from the hillside. It was founded in 1132 by a group of monks who had left St Mary's Benedictine Abbey in York, intending to set up a more austere monastery and join the new Cistercian order. When they first arrived in the valley they probably lived in wooden huts and built a wooden church. After a few years a huge abbey was built from stone.

Fountains Abbey, like most monasteries, gradually added new buildings over the centuries. It grew most quickly during the twelfth century, and at its peak the abbey possibly had as many as 200 lay brothers and 50 choir monks. The lay brothers usually lived outside the centre of the monastery, closer to the outside world. They worshipped in the same church as the choir monks but had their own entrances, exits and seating areas. The lay brothers slept in a huge dormitory, above the cellarium, which was the store house as well as the place for several workshops.

St Benedict's Rule stated that monks should not have the luxury of heat and that fires should only be lit at certain times of the year. There were few fireplaces and chimneys in the abbey – in the guest house, the abbot's lodgings and the warming house, where sick monks might go after being treated. The fires in the warming house would be lit only from November to March. The only other fires would be used for cooking and baking.

Like most abbeys, Fountains Abbey was often granted land in people's wills. The monks gradually extended the land that they owned and successfully farmed sheep as well as running small granges (or farms). By the fourteenth century the abbey was renting out a lot of its land and so making a profit from rents as well as from the sale of any produce from its own land.

SOURCE E

The ruins of Fountains Abbey.

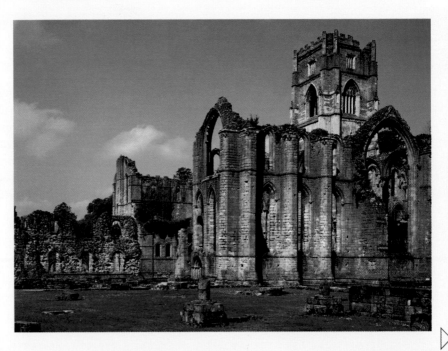

The monastery had a large impact on local society at the time. Some of its impacts are described below:

- The plan of the abbey (see below) shows that there were various opportunities for the monks to help people from the local area in addition to accepting guests in the guest houses. Such visitors could be important Church men or merchants or pilgrims on the way to the nearest shrine.

- Surrounding the abbey lay fields of farm land. Sheep fleeces and other farm products would be sold at the local market.

- As the monastery gained wealth from gifts and the successful farm businesses, it became more powerful.

Key
a Church
b Cloister
c Simple refectory (or dining hall) with storerooms and dormitory above
d Kitchen
e Main refectory with the abbot's high table, plus stools and trestle tables for monks. A monk would read aloud during meals from a pulpit in one wall of the hall
f Monks' day rooms, with dormitory above
g Parlour, a small room where the monks were allowed to talk (from the French verb *parler*, meaning 'to talk')
h Assembly hall, called Chapter House, where the abbot held meetings of the whole monastic community
i Infirmary (hospital) for monks
j Infirmary for local people
k Guest houses for travellers and pilgrims

River Skell

Plan of Fountains Abbey showing links to outside world.

- Compared with the rest of medieval society, the monastery was a very hygienic place. It was built to maximise local water supplies and developed clever engineering systems for water, drainage and sewage.

- Health care was also important. Monks cared for the sick, following the example set by Jesus. They would care for the sick using herbal remedies as well as providing an opportunity for rest and food.

- Education was very important for the monastery. Not only did the monks translate and copy ancient manuscripts and so maintain the level of learning from earlier periods, but they also sometimes taught in local schools.

Question time

1 Make a list of what you have learnt about Fountains Abbey. Choose the two most important things that the information tells us about medieval monasticism and explain them in writing.

2 Using the plan of Fountains Abbey, create your own summary chart of the various ways that monasteries influenced medieval society. You could have different headers on your chart such as education, health and hygiene. Add more of your own headers and fill each column or section with ways in which monasteries led the way or provided a service to the community. If possible add extra points from your own research.

Women in holy orders

Just as there were different orders of monasteries, there were different convents (where nuns lived) ruled by slightly different religious codes. There was a significant increase in the number of convents, from 20 to 100, in the early medieval period, and by 1200 there were over 3000 nuns in England. Nuns were very similar to monks in that they had the same aims and simple lifestyle. Nuns took similar vows and had to wear veils to cover their hair and head, in addition to the plain robes like those worn by monks. Nuns differed, however, in the type of work that they did and their reasons for seeking holy orders.

Why would women want to give up their lives and become nuns? Many women felt that they had a religious calling to take holy orders, adopt the veil and become a nun. Some women wanted to prove themselves and achieve something in a role other than wife or mother: to study and learn, to take on a position of responsibility, even to become an abbess and run a convent. For many women joining a convent was as much a method of escape from a future marriage or a routine life as a religious vocation. Many women had to pay to be supported in the nunnery or convent and so most nuns were from wealthy noble families. Some nuns lived in total isolation from society, with no guests or personal possessions and giving any spare food that they had to the poor. They usually ate only vegetables and very little fat, and so made their life as simple as possible to focus on devotion to God. Not every young women was happy in her role as a nun. In 1318, one prospective nun – Joanna, from Clemthorpe nunnery – staged her own mock-funeral to try to escape from the nunnery.

Convents were mainly separate communities from monasteries in order to avoid any distractions from the opposite sex. They were, however, often reliant on monasteries and abbeys for political and financial support. They were, rather more informal places, like living in a private family household. They were not as large or wealthy as many monasteries, and were usually only given tithes, small amounts of land or buildings by local abbots and archbishops, and small bequests. Convents would often include a guest house and sometimes take in retired women or young

children from the local community. Some women who became abbesses had a lot of respect and power in the local area.

Nuns would spend much of each day working in the garden growing vegetables and herbs or in the kitchens preparing food for themselves and any guests. They were often taught to embroider delicate cloths. They would decorate altar cloths and priests' vestments in fine silk threads and even gold. This work was acceptable as long as it did not interfere with their dedication to God.

Question time

1   What does Source F tell us about the abbess and the role of nuns in medieval Christianity?

2   Find out more about the daily life and routine of a nun. Make notes in the form of a diagram or chart using bullet points or short phrases rather than full sentences.

3   Write a comparison of the life of a nun and a monk in an average-sized convent or monastery in the early Middle Ages.

Accusations of corruption in the Church

Visitations to monasteries by inspectors in the fifteenth century found adultery, drinking and gambling taking place. At Bardney in 1438 the monks were found to play dice, own possessions and visit the local pubs. Although these scandals are remembered more than the many devout monasteries, they helped to introduce a mood of anticlericalism, which means a lack of support for men of the Church.

Corruption occurred not only in monasteries, but in all aspects of Church life, from archbishops to parish priests and nuns. The Church expanded in size and wealth during the Middle Ages, and monks and parish priests became more powerful and in some cases more removed from the people. We can see in records of the Church courts that priests were not beyond corruption; morality courts included cases of priests quarrelling, having affairs, ignoring their duties and even grazing horses in the graveyard.

SOURCE A

A medieval monk helps himself to the beer.
An illustration from a thirteenth-century manuscript.

The public would not support a large, wealthy organisation which was seen to be spending its profits on its own luxury and living a life contradictory to its vows and beliefs.

SOURCE B

In Westwell the vicar is blind and incompetent and no one is serving the church except one chaplain. The tithe lambs are grazed in the churchyard in the spring. The vicar is instructed that this is not to be done in future.

The vicar of Deal does not visit the sick, but when anyone comes to ask him to visit sick persons, he says bad words to them. The chaplain comes and denies the charges.

At Adisham, the roof of the church is out of repair, one of the censers [incense holders] requires new chains and there is no processional book. The rector received 30 sheep by the will of Master Richard his predecessor to maintain a lamp in the chancel to burn by day and night. Two prayer books are badly bound and of little value. A tree in the churchyard is in a dangerous state and the parishioners fear that it may do damage to the church. The clerk neglects his school and does not serve in the church either on Sundays or on weekdays.

Extracts from visitation rolls at Canterbury, 1292–1328.

SOURCE C

We are gravely displeased to learn from reliable witnesses that certain vicars and other ministers of our cathedral church ... to the offence of God, the notable hindrance of divine services, their own damnation and the scandal of our cathedral church ... are not afraid to indulge in irreverent and damnable disorders, laughings, gigglings, and other breaches of discipline during the services ... To specify some out of many cases: those who stand in the upper stalls of the choir, with lights in reach at matins [morning service], deliberately pour the drippings of the candles upon the heads or hair of those standing in the lower stalls ...

The Bishop Grandisson of Exeter wrote this in his register in 1330.

Question time

1   Do you think that visitations were a fair way of gaining evidence against local criminals and corrupt clergy (see Source B)?

2   What reasons does Source C give for the Bishop being disgusted at the pranks played by some clerks in his cathedral?

3   Do you think that this sort of behaviour was common during Church services?

4   Look at Sources A to C. Which is the most useful source for the investigation of medieval clergy?

5   Why is it difficult to find out whether the clergy were really as corrupt as has been suggested?

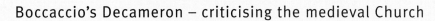

Digging deeper

Boccaccio's Decameron – criticising the medieval Church

The Italian poet and writer Giovanni Boccaccio wrote a collection of tales called the *Decameron*. In the *Decameron*, ten people are forced to spend ten days together fleeing from the plague that has hit Florence. They tell each other stories as entertainment. The collection was written between 1345 and 1353 and became a highly respected and influential piece of literature.

One of Boccaccio's storytellers describes scandalous monks and abbots with secret mistresses, and friars who only accuse rich men of heresy so that they can keep the huge fines for themselves. Another story involves a friar who proudly gives alms (gifts of charity) to the poor. The gifts that he gives are vegetable peelings and slops that would be fit only for pigs rather than humans.

Boccaccio's stories expose some criticisms of the Church and show that people were concerned about its corruption all over Europe. We can see how the *Decameron* influenced Chaucer's *Canterbury Tales*, where different characters on a pilgrimage each tell four stories (see page 167).

 Question time

1   Return to the section on Chaucer's pilgrims on page 167. How can you tell that Chaucer might have been influenced by the work of Boccaccio? Try to find at least two different reasons in your answer to this question.

Mystical, mythical and unorthodox beliefs

Although almost all of the people of England would call themselves Christian during the Middle Ages, there was a variety of beliefs in existence. Priests sometimes neglected to teach their congregations and the people turned to a combination of magic, superstition and traditional Christian beliefs.

Within the Christian Church there were individual people who wanted to worship or express their religion in an unorthodox way. Mysticism is an approach to religion which involves direct communication with the divine being, or God. There were several mystics in medieval Europe who did not worship God in the same way as the Church, and many of these people were women. Mysticism often involves visions, trances and meditation. The Church did not always feel comfortable with mystics because they were seen as a challenge to traditional worship and order.

Whilst anybody expressing strong opinions about alternative beliefs would be condemned and punished as a heretic, folklore and superstition were accepted. Religious practices, like most things medieval, were often home-grown in their nature. Examples of this include prayers from the early thirteenth century, written to Mother Earth and praising the power of herbs. Even monarchs and the Church sometimes incorporated a mythical element into their beliefs, such as the fable of Caladrius (see Source A), a bird who could predict the fate of sick kings by turning his head towards or away from them. Many of these superstitious beliefs and myths were adapted to take on Christian aspects, and in this way became more accepted by the Church.

Caladrius predicts the fate of a sick king. Illustration from an English manuscript c. 1200.

Digging deeper

Margery Kempe – fourteenth-century mystic

Margery Kempe was the daughter of a mayor from King's Lynn in Norfolk, then called Bishop's Lynn or just Lynn. She ran her own brewing business and had a large family of 14 children. At the age of 30, Margery decided that she wanted to dedicate her life to God, but she did not want to join a convent. She started having crying fits and also visions during which she received messages from God. At first she did not change her daily life, but chose to wear a hair shirt underneath her usual clothes as a sign of her dedication. Margery spent several hours a day in meditation and prayers. She also wanted to become celibate but it took her several years to persuade her husband that this was a good idea. Margery's husband was actually very sympathetic. He travelled all over the country with Margery and looked after her when she had her crying fits. They visited important Church men and told them the messages that Margery received in her visions, but the Church men were unimpressed. Margery made several pilgrimages, including one to Jerusalem, where the group she was travelling with left her because her crying and constant talk of God annoyed them so much. She was also interrogated by the Mayor of Lincoln and Archbishop of York who both decided that her visions were genuine and sent her away. It seemed that Margery was treated like a mad but non-threatening old woman. She was an example of someone who gave up most of her family and a successful business to focus on Christianity, in her own way, outside the usual rituals and practices of the Church.

By the end of the Middle Ages religion still had a huge influence on people's minds and was still part of everyday life. However, different forms of Christianity were spreading across Europe and critics from inside and outside the Church began to question its control.

Question time

1 Some people interpreted Caladrius as a symbol of Christ, turning his face towards sinners who were to be saved. What does this suggest to you about medieval religious beliefs?

2 How would wearing a rough hair shirt and becoming celibate help Margery Kempe in her religion?

3 Why do you think that Margery was interrogated by the Mayor of Lincoln and the Archbishop of York?

8 Assessment section

1 The medieval period is often referred to as the 'Age of Faith'. Make a list of all the evidence from this chapter and your knowledge that agrees with this interpretation.

2 How did the Church have so much power over people's minds? Plan your answer to this question before you answer it in full. You can use different headings to structure your work such as:

- learning
- the village priest
- rituals
- fear.

3 What problems do historians face when researching religion and belief in the Middle Ages?

Further reading

Geoffrey Chaucer, *The Canterbury Tales*

Geraldine McCaughrean, *The Canterbury Tales* (retold) (Oxford University Press, 1984)

Rosemary Sutcliff, *Witch's Brat* (Red Fox, 1988)

9 Crusading spirit

This chapter will investigate the thousands of Christians who left their homes to become crusaders between the eleventh and thirteenth centuries.

A dictionary will tell you that a crusade is a campaign against something that is believed to be bad. The French word for crusade is 'croisade' based on the Latin 'crux' which shows you that the campaign was usually against enemies of the cross, or Christianity. In the medieval period this word took its meaning from a series of military expeditions made by European Christians to fight against Muslims in what we refer to as the Middle East. The aim of most of the Crusades was to protect the right to safe pilgrimage to the Holy City of Jerusalem and to attempt to gain the Holy Land from Muslim control. Crusades were also held against the Muslims in Spain, a Christian sect called the Cathars in southern France and pagans in eastern Europe. The Crusades were focused around the 'Holy Land ' but also directed at Egypt and as far east as Constantinople. There was no constant fighting but a series of planned campaigns, varying in size and success. The fought-after crusading area of the Holy Land remains hotly disputed by Muslims, Jews and Christians to this day.

The Crusades

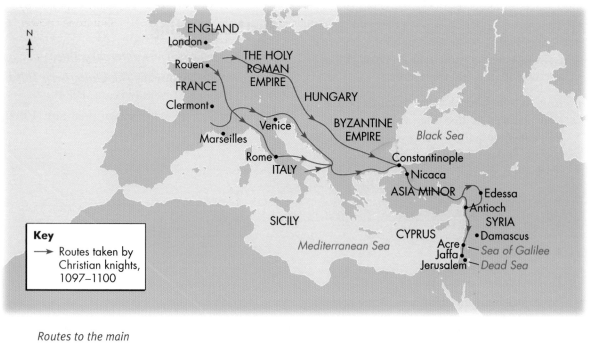

Routes to the main crusading areas.

The main events of the Crusades

There were seven official Crusades, but there were many other smaller crusades and holy wars during the twelfth and thirteenth centuries as shown in the timeline below.

638	Jerusalem is taken over by Muslims.
1079	The Seljuk Turks take over Jerusalem.
1095	The Byzantine Emperor appeals to the Pope for help against the Seljuk Turks. Pope Urban calls Christians to crusade to ensure safe pilgrimage to the Holy Land.
1095	The People's Crusade, led by an elderly hermit called 'Little Peter' from Amiens in France, ends in disaster.
1096	The First Crusade. Fighting takes place in the Holy Land for several months before the first crusader state of Edessa is created. Further victories against divided Muslims lead to the creation of other crusader states including Jerusalem and Tripoli.
1145–9	The Second Crusade. 50,000 men, under Louis VII of France, go to defend the new Christian crusader states against Muslims. The Christians fail to keep Damascus and Edessa from the Muslim Turks.
1187	Battle of Hattin. The Muslim leader Saladin takes Jerusalem and expands Muslim control in the crusader states.
1189–92	The Third Crusade. King Richard I of England and King Philip of France lead this crusade to try to regain land for Christendom. Richard I captures Cyprus and Acre, but is forced to make a truce with Muslim leader Saladin and agrees to leave Jerusalem.
1198	The Fourth Crusade. Constantinople is sacked (taken over) and a Latin Empire is created by the Italians. The crusaders are criticised as being selfish because it seems that trade, power and private deals are the incentive for this crusade rather than religion.
1212	The Children's Crusade. Up to 10,000 people, some in their teens, leave their homes in France and Germany. Many young people die on the journey to Alexandria, and those who get there are sold into slavery.
1217–22	The Fifth Crusade. Led by Andrew of Hungary and Leopold of Austria against the Muslims in Egypt. They take Damietta but fail to take Egypt.
1228–9	The Sixth Crusade. Led by the Holy Roman Emperor, Frederick II, who makes a treaty with the Sultan of Egypt to peacefully regain Jerusalem.
1244	Jerusalem is lost again to the Muslims.
1291	Acre is lost to the Christians. The crusaders leave the Holy Land.
1453	Constantinople is retaken by the Ottoman Turks and the Pope fails in his attempt to raise another crusade.

In the fifteenth and sixteenth centuries other crusades or religious wars were fought all over Europe, including North Africa, Spain, Mexico and the Balkans.

Who went on crusade, and why?

In the eleventh century, an elderly hermit called 'Little Peter' from Amiens in France led a group of approximately 15,000 eager recruits from northern France and the Rhineland on crusade. They were ordinary folk, disorganised and unprepared for the journey and battles that lay ahead of them. As a result, many of them perished, returned home or were sold as slaves. This disastrous crusade is known as the People's Crusade.

After the eleventh century, crusaders tended to be professional knights making up an army rather than a motley crew of ordinary folk. The knights were called to a crusade by the Pope, for only he had the authority to call Christian knights and soldiers from all over Christendom to fight for their religion in a Holy War. The crusaders always travelled abroad to fight against enemies of Christianity. They were often known as Franks because many of them came from the land of the Frankish people (France and Germany). Most of the Crusades were fought in the Holy Land against Muslims, particularly the Turks, who were known by crusaders as 'Saracens'. This was an ancient Greek word for an Arab but came to be used in the Middle Ages for any Muslim person. In Spain the word used was 'Moor'.

Question time

1   The word 'crusade' or 'crusader' is still used today – and not just about the religious crusades of the medieval period. Here are two examples:

   a   A newspaper headline: 'Government minister in moral crusade'. What do you think this phrase means?

   b   The British built a tank called the 'Crusader' in the 1940s. Why do you think that was thought to be a good name for an armoured vehicle?

2   Which countries in the modern world make up the area which was the focus for most of the Crusades? You will need a modern map or atlas as well as the map on page 182 to answer this question.

3   Working in groups, produce a large map of the area in which the Crusades were fought. Research different aspects of the Crusades (e.g. dates, places, leaders, outcomes) and add these to your map. You may need to put the information around the edge with strings leading to the right places.

The First Crusade, 1096

The battle for Jerusalem

Jerusalem is a sacred city for a number of different faiths: Muslims, Christians and Jews. It contains important shrines and is the site of historic events central to each of these main religions. Within the city of Jerusalem there is the Wailing Wall (or Western Wall), the remaining part of King Herod's temple and a site of prayer and pilgrimage for Jews.

There is the Dome of the Rock mosque where the Muslim prophet Muhammad is said to have ascended to heaven. Jerusalem also holds the Church of the Holy Sepulchre, supposedly built on the site of Christ's tomb. In the Middle Ages, each religious group wanted safe and uninterrupted access to its shrines.

Who ruled Jerusalem?

Jerusalem was taken over by Caliph Umar (a Muslim leader) in 638, and he gave Christians and Jews freedom to worship. Umar respected other religions and thought that tolerance would increase support for the Muslims. Caliphs who ruled after Umar were not as tolerant as the early Muslim leaders. In 1009 the Church of the Holy Sepulchre was destroyed by the Caliph of Egypt, and religious freedom was removed for Christians and Jews. Later that century the Seljuk Turks (also Muslims) drove the Egyptian Muslims out of Jerusalem. They wanted total control of the region as part of their expanding empire and posed a significant threat to Christianity. The unstable position of Jews and Christians in the Holy Land meant that travel to Jerusalem was dangerous. Pilgrims needed protection, and slowly Christians began to take action against this new enemy.

Pope Urban's speech

Not only had the Christians lost control of Jerusalem, they were also rapidly losing control of Asia Minor to the invading Turkish armies. In 1095 Pope Urban II was asked by Emperor Alexius, the Byzantine Emperor, to send men to help defeat the Turkish Muslims. The Byzantine Emperor was the leader of the Roman Church in the East, and therefore a rival to the Pope, but many people in the West thought that the Eastern and Western Empires should be united again, as they had been under early Roman rule. Whether his motives were religious or political, Pope Urban would certainly not have wanted the Muslims to gain additional land in the East, and in 1095 he gave a speech calling for a religious war against the Muslims. This speech marked the start of the First Crusade.

SOURCE A

There is an urgent task which belongs both to you and God, in which you must show your good will. For you must hasten to carry aid to your brothers dwelling in the East ... For the Turks have attacked them and have advanced far into Roman territory ... They have seized more and more of the lands of the Christians and have already defeated them seven times in many battles, killed or captured many people, destroyed churches and have devastated the Kingdom of God.

If those who go lose their lives on the journey or in fighting, their sins will be absolved immediately. I grant this by the power God has given me ... Let those who have fought wrongfully against others now rightfully fight the infidel, let those who have been robbers become soldiers of Christ, let those who were hirelings for a few pieces of silver now win eternal rewards ...

Extract from Pope Urban II's speech, 1095, as recorded by the chaplain to Count Stephen of Blois, who was to become a major military commander of the crusaders.

The First Crusade was successful because it reclaimed Jerusalem and established the 'Frankish' or crusader kingdoms in the Holy Land. However, with this victory came an enormous amount of unjustified slaughter as Christians killed Muslims and Jews within Jerusalem. The Christian victory and settlement was not permanent, and slowly the Muslims regained land.

Question time

1 Why is the Middle East known as the 'Holy Land' by Christians and Jews?

2 Why do Muslims think of Jerusalem as sacred?

3 Find out the meaning of the following words or phrases from Source A (look them up in a dictionary to find a modern English alternative but try to work them out first by looking at how they make sense within each sentence):

- pagans
- absolved
- the infidel
- hirelings
- eternal rewards.

4 Read through Source A and note down examples of the following:

- the likely rewards for willing crusaders
- the crimes the Muslims were accused of
- possible warnings or dangers of crusading
- words or phrases used that would help persuade the listener to join a crusade.

5 Explain what Pope Urban's political and religious motives for calling a crusade might have been.

6 What are the advantages and disadvantages for the historian of the written version of the Pope's speech, as recorded by a chaplain in Source A?

Digging deeper

The siege of Jerusalem

Military victories for the First Crusade only came after two years of hard fighting in the land between Constantinople and Jerusalem. The crusaders had managed to take the cities of Nicaea in 1097 and Antioch in 1098 before moving to Jerusalem in 1099. Having created a crusader state in Edessa and won the city of Antioch, the crusaders gained confidence in military action. However, only 1500 knights remained, less than half those who had set out on the crusade. Their victories were made easier by the disunited Muslim enemy.

The Christian army used successful methods of siege warfare to capture Jerusalem (see Source B), but on arrival at the city their chances had not looked great. Also, although they started their attack as soon as they arrived on the outskirts of Jerusalem, it took three weeks before their seige equipment arrived and they could make a serious challenge on the city. In addition to this, the defending Turks had stored away food so the crusaders could find little to survive on. The Muslims were also rumoured to have poisoned the wells outside the city walls.

Attack!

The Christian archers fired arrows, and steel hooks attached to long ropes were catapulted onto the city walls in order shake them down. Huge battering rams with iron-capped heads attached to mobile towers called siege engines were used to break down the city defences. Moats were filled with boulders to enable the crusaders to cross them. The aim of siege warfare was to starve out the enemy and reduce its supplies as well as its ammunition. Breaking through defences would then be met with less opposition. The surrounding crusaders nearly exhausted their own supplies and relied on Italian trading ships to dock with reinforcements.

Defence!

The Turks defended the city as best they could. They used bales of straw to try to withstand the shock of the powerful battering rams. These were often a failure because they could easily be set alight by the enemy. They hauled up dead bodies of crusaders on to the city walls in order to steal their weapons and armour. They also threw pots of 'Greek fire' over the walls; these were almost like bombs, containing sulphur, resins and oils which exploded on impact with the ground.

SOURCE B

A picture from a fourteenth-century French manuscript showing crusaders attacking the walls of Jerusalem.

SOURCE C

Among those carrying soil to the city ditch to build an earthwork for the assault, was a certain woman who was working hard and diligently to further the task. Without stopping she went tirelessly to and fro, encouraging others ... this woman was hurrying to put down her load when a Turk, lying in ambush, struck her a fatal blow with a javelin. She fell to the ground and lay writhing in agony.

Extract about the events of 1187–91 from Chronicle of the Journey of King Richard I, *written in the early thirteenth century.*

SOURCE D

The bravest of the Turkish soldiers entered Syria and by forced marches day and night made haste to enter the royal city of Antioch before us. When they heard this, the whole army of God gave thanks and praise to the Almighty and hurrying towards Antioch laid siege to it. Many a battle have we had there with the Turks, and seven times, with fierce courage and under Christ's leadership, we fought the people of Antioch and the countless hosts who came to their aid. We won all those battles but in those same battles many of our fellows were killed and their souls borne to Paradise.

While my Chaplain was hurriedly writing this letter on Easter Day, some of our men reconnoitering the Turks fought a ferocious battle against them, capturing 60 horsemen, whose heads they brought back to camp.

A letter from a crusader, Count Stephen of Blois, to his wife Ada, daughter of William the Conqueror, 1098.

SOURCE E

A siege machine throwing heads into the town of Nicea. Illustration from a contemporary manuscript.

It took a month for the crusaders to get into Jerusalem and once they did they ran riot, murdering 70,000 Muslims and Jews. Buildings were burnt to the ground, and looting was common place, including candelabras from the Dome of the Rock temple. At the siege of Jerusalem the crusaders had with them the 'holy lance', believed to be the spear that had cut Christ's side at the crucifixion. Such holy relics inspired the army and encouraged it to fight for its religion and for salvation. The particularly bloody violence in Jerusalem, however, badly damaged the reputation of the crusader armies.

The Christians celebrated this initial victory in the First Crusade and it came to represent the successful start of the Crusades. The newly created Kingdom of Jerusalem was ruled by Godfrey of Bouillon and his brother.

When Godfrey of Bouillon died in 1100, the Christians had to send in reinforcements to try to maintain hold of Jerusalem and were under pressure from attack for most of the twelfth century. Jerusalem was finally recaptured by the Muslims under Saladin, Sultan of Egypt, in 1187, so the joy for the Christians of capturing Jerusalem was relatively short lived.

 Question time

1. Identify the weapons that are being used in Source B and say how they should be used in a siege.

2. Is there anything within Source C to suggest that the Chronicle is biased towards the Christian crusaders?

3. Why do you think it might be easier to be an attacker than a defender in a medieval siege?

4. What do Sources D and E tell us about the tactic of siege warfare in the Crusades?

5. Why do you think that the letter in Source D might have remained intact as historical evidence when so many medieval sources have been lost or destroyed?

Protecting the crusader kingdoms

After the success in Jerusalem, the First Crusade swept though the Holy Land taking the Muslim Turks by surprise. Christian kingdoms and states were created from captured land and some crusaders stayed behind in these kingdoms to secure the area for Christianity.

The crusaders who remained in the Holy Land wanted to live in safety and peace. They often strengthened existing Muslim fortresses, adding layers of walls and towers. They liked their crusader castles to be surrounded on three sides by high rocks, a cliff face or water in order to enhance protection. One example is Saone Castle near Antioch. It stands on a high, rocky ridge with clear views over the surrounding countryside.

Knights of the holy orders

In order to protect the Christians who settled in the new crusader states, as well as those making pilgrimage to Jerusalem, two holy orders of knights were founded. These holy orders were a combination of monasticism and militarism; they were based on religious principles but ultimately became a fighting force. The Knights Hospitallers of Saint John of Jerusalem had originally cared for sick pilgrims and established a hospital in Jerusalem. They then became a fighting force and were eventually pushed back to Rhodes and then to Malta, which they held for Christianity. The Knights Templars were established as protection for pilgrims once their safety in the Holy Land was no longer guaranteed. Named after Solomon's Temple where they had their headquarters, they became an elite fighting force. They were based in crusader castles and provided soldiers for the Crusades.

The crusader states.

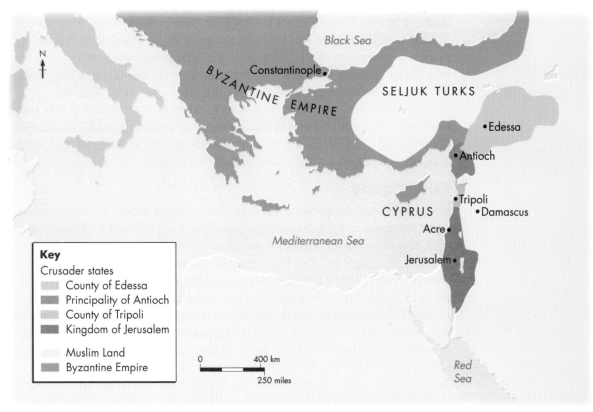

A crusader with the cross symbol on his tunic.

The power and success of the monastic knights soon brought their downfall. They were accused of secrecy, corruption and even heresy. The Templars and Hospitallers certainly seemed to profit from bequests left to them and the secrecy of their orders made people suspicious. Rulers were also jealous that they had power from the Pope to be obedient to no government, they ruled themselves. The Knights Templars were disbanded by the Pope in 1312.

Going on crusade

The early crusaders were a combination of knights, lords and labourers, who became more like specialist soldiers as the Crusades progressed. These professional crusaders were encouraged to carry out their crusade for a variety of reasons; the most obvious of these was religious motivation. The Christian faith was believed to be in danger from pagan invaders in the Holy Land, and Christians all over the world had a duty to protect their religion. However, as with most things, many crusaders were also influenced by a number of other factors: political, personal and financial. Some were attracted by the chance of a new life in the East: labourers could escape the poverty of their feudal lands and start afresh abroad: traders could see potential markets and there was certainly land up for grabs as the battles raged. There were other benefits from going on a crusade; a lord's property would be protected by the Church until he returned from a crusade; any legal actions being taken against any crusading knight or soldier would be suspended. Some men may have been attracted by the apparent glamour and excitement that the Crusades had to offer. Indeed, some western Christians remained in the East and tried to make a new life for themselves once fighting had finished.

'Taking the cross'

Soldiers leaving for war in the twenty-first century are trained, armed and at least partly prepared for what lies ahead of them. The Crusades were more a combination of a pilgrimage and a war; preparations for a pilgrimage included getting a blessing from a priest and taking a holy vow. Knights and professional soldiers 'took the cross', which became the crusaders' symbol, and cloth crosses were worn on their tunics. It was only the Pope who could call on Christian knights to go on a crusade. Adequate financing was also necessary for potential crusaders. Some lords paid high taxes or mortgaged out their land to fund the journey.

Raising money

Medieval monarchs and also the Pope turned to the public to borrow money and raise taxes to fund crusading campaigns. King Richard I, for example, sold land, titles, town charters and offices to raise money for the Third Crusade (see page 56). The Pope granted crusaders who took vows and travelled to the Holy Land automatic absolution (forgiveness of sins) and a place in heaven. It is not surprising that ordinary people wanted a chance to fight for the religion that they believed in so passionately. Those people who could not go to fight in the Holy War could contribute to the Crusades through taxes. They would feel involved and would also be granted full absolution of their sins by the Pope. One tax in England was called the Saladin Tithe, after Salah al Deen, the dreaded Muslim sultan who fought Richard I in the Third Crusade (Source B).

Excommunication has already been pronounced by the archbishops, bishops and rural deans in every single parish against anyone who does not legitimately pay this tithe [10 per cent tax] ... This money is to be collected in each parish in the presence of the parish priest.

Extract from the Chronicle of Roger of Howden, *a priest in Yorkshire, dated 1198.*

It would not be easy for Christian lords and landowners to leave their families and their estates for years at a time. You have read about the impact that the Crusades had on the reign of England's crusading monarch, Richard I (see page 56). For knights, absence from home often meant selling up land or other possessions in order to pay for the trip. Wives and families would usually be left behind and marriages were tested as couples wondered what their partners got up to in their absence. Some couples swore oaths to be faithful on holy relics, others made do with romantic love letters sent home from the East. A few crusaders took their wives with them to make a new life in a crusader state.

Getting there

Crusaders travelled by carriage, horse or foot across France and Spain and then by hired boat to the Holy Land. As on a pilgrimage, monks and priests would travel with the crusaders, preaching to them along the journey. They would encounter many problems: bandits were a common threat, for example. Naïve travellers could be attacked and robbed anywhere on their journey and in the Holy Land too. Christians, Muslims and even some opportunist crusaders made a living from stealing from likely victims. Other dangers included becoming sick from a disease such as dysentery or cholera and also being shipwrecked. The journey east took a long time, and fighting along the route was common, especially after the crusade had left Europe. It took the First Crusade three years to reach Jerusalem, and many crusaders gave in to the difficulties and returned home.

Crusaders also had to adapt to the very different climate and the cultural differences in the Middle East. Marching on foot or by horse for months at a time weakened many crusaders. Heat and lack of water were particular problems. Crusader knights wore white tunics with red crosses on top of their armour to reflect the rays of the sun (see Source A). However, hot dry weather was not the only problem for the crusaders; the winter months brought freezing cold hail which would easily rust the armour of soldiers.

Life in the crusader states

New kingdoms or states such as Antoich, Edessa, Jerusalem and Tripoli were created during the early crusades (see page 189) and named after the cities they surrounded. Some of these states lasted for two centuries. Christians called the new settlements 'Outremer', which meant 'beyond the sea'.

Before the period of the Crusades, Christians had lived in the region for many years along with Jews and different Muslim groups. During the time of the early crusades the Christains were able to take advantage of the unstable Muslim governments to take control of different provinces. The crusaders turned some mosques into churches and built their own buildings in the European style. Crusader states and cities such as Acre would have had many aspects of European culture. The cultural 'exchange' worked both ways. Local goods such as sugar and fruit were traded in markets and also taken to other parts of Christendom by Italian traders. Some Franks began to adopt Muslim customs, such as an Egyptian diet, although an Islamic writer admitted that these crusaders were in the minority.

Whenever I visited Jerusalem I always entered the Aqsa Mosque, beside which stood a small mosque which the Franks had converted into a church. When I used to enter the Aqsa Mosque, which was occupied by the Templars, who were my friends, the Templars would evacuate the little adjoining mosque so that I might pray in it. One day I entered this mosque, repeated the first formula, Allah is great, and stood up in the act of praying. Upon this one of the Franks rushed on me, got hold of me and turned my face eastward. 'This is the way thou shouldst pray!' he said.

A group of Templars hastened to him, seized him, and repelled him from me. I resumed my prayer. The same man, while the others were otherwise busy, rushed once more on me and turned my face eastward. 'This is the way thou shouldst pray!' he said.

The Templars again came in to him and expelled him. They apologised to me: 'This is a stranger who has only recently arrived from the land of the Franks and he has never before seen anyone praying except eastward.'

Thereupon I said to myself, 'I have had enough prayer.' So I went out and have ever been surprised at the conduct of this devil of a man, at the change in the colour of his face, his trembling and his sentiment at the sight of one praying towards the Qiblah [to Mecca].

Muslim view of the crusader settlers, 1133–45, from the memoirs of Usama Ibn Mundqidh, an Arab aristocrat who lived in Damascus.

A game of Persian *shah (chess)* between a crusader and a Muslim. Contemporary illustration.

It is not true to say that Christians and Muslims lived side by side in total harmony and equality in the new kingdoms. In settler towns the Christians would often occupy the central districts whilst the Muslims would be forced to live further out. Few crusader settlers farmed the surrounding area, preferring to rely on local villagers to grow produce for them. The crusader rulers demanded taxes from the local Muslims which increased the level of resentment between the two groups.

Question time

1 What are the similarities and differences between a pilgrimage and a crusade?

2 What do Sources C and D suggest to us about the relations between Muslims and Christians in the crusader kingdoms?

3 Why do you think that the people living in the region of the Holy Land in the time of the First Crusade were so tolerant of each other?

4 Do you think that Usama Ibn Mundqidh is a reliable witness of relations between Muslims and Christians (see Source C)? Weigh up the arguments for and against him before you make a final decision.

The Battle of Hattin, 1187

In the years following the capture of Jerusalem, the defeated Muslim forces regrouped and became more united in their opposition to the Christian invaders. At the Battle of Hattin in 1187 the crusaders suffered a massive defeat by Salah al Deen's (Saladin's) Turkish armies. Many historians consider the Battle of Hattin to be the turning point in the Crusades. The defeat led to the Muslim recapture of 50 crusader castles by 1189 and of the holy city of Jerusalem. It also prompted the organisation of the Third Crusade.

Digging deeper

Salah al Deen

Salah al Deen was called Saladin by the crusaders. He was the Sultan (leader) of Egypt and leader of the Muslim armies from 1176. He helped to regain Muslim lands including the Holy Land, and pushed out the Christians from the Middle East. Saladin fought against rival Muslim groups too; he captured all of Egypt and Syria and was a highly respected military leader.

After the Battle of Hattin and during the Third Crusade, Saladin ordered the murder of any Templars and Hospitallers caught by Muslim enemies. However, when he recaptured Jerusalem in 1187 he did not murder the Christians in the city, preferring to ransom them or sell them as slaves. He was criticised by some Muslims for this, but others argued that he was a wise and tactical leader, removing the elite force that threatened the Muslim armies but maintaining support by demonstrating his mercy (especially after the crusaders had murdered Muslims and Jews when they had taken Jerusalem). In order to take as many crusader lands as he could, Saladin offered good conditions for any town which surrendered. He also allowed many Christians to pay a tax for their freedom, therefore gaining financially as well as politically.

Famous as a man of honour and capable of cruelty, Salah al Deen is sometimes compared to Richard I, the Lionheart, because they were great military rivals. During the Third Crusade when Salah al Deen heard that Richard had a fever he sent him fruit as a delicacy and ice from the mountain tops to cool him down.

Salah al Deen was not just famous in the Middle East; Saladin was also made a hero in the West. Christians in England at the time were asked by King Richard I to pay a tax to fund the Third Crusade. They called this tax the Saladin Tithe (a 10 per cent tax on goods and money).

Salah al Deen respected the determination of the crusaders but thought that they would have to be wiped out. He died of yellow fever in 1193, some 100 years before the final Muslim victory in the Crusades, but he had certainly helped to regain Muslim control of the area.

Question time

1 Why do you think that Salah al Deen was so popular in the West as well as the East?

2 Write an epitaph for Salah al Deen which could have been read out at the court of King Richard I back in England. (An epitaph is a short statement that recalls the life and achievements of a person following their death.)

The Third Crusade, 1189–92

We have seen that Richard I raised large sums of money for this crusade. The boxes below contain statements which provide a summary of the Third Crusade. Your task is to sort out all the information in order to describe the crusade for yourself. Start your summary with its aims, then move on to describe the events and finally the outcomes. You may want to carry out some of your own research to make your summary more complete.

Some Christians were determined to avenge defeat and regain Jerusalem, which had been taken by Saladin four months after his victory at the Battle of Hattin.

Jerusalem was kept by the Muslims but people of all religions were guaranteed the right to safe pilgrimage.

The end result was in effect a draw. Although Richard I's army was highly trained and disciplined it was limited in how far it could move inland away from coastal supplies. Saladin's army could not be beaten. Richard and Saladin came to a truce over Jerusalem.

During the siege of Acre, and in a harsh winter, many crusaders starved. They fought over bread, gnawed at old animal bones dug up from the ground and even killed prize chargers (horses) in order to eat the horseflesh.

The siege of Acre was prolonged by the double-dealing of Conrad of Montferrat who wanted to become King of Jerusalem so secretly passed supplies to the Muslims inside the walls.

The crusaders won back Acre and Jaffa but not the city of Jerusalem.

The most famous siege of the Third Crusade was that of the city of Acre. It was one of the longest sieges in the Middle Ages, lasting over two years. The Christian army, led by King Richard I of England and King Augustus of France, eventually got through the Muslim defences.

After the Third Crusade, crusading became less popular. The crusader states had not proved a long-term success and traders were frustrated over the disruption to trade caused by the wars.

One important effect of the Third Crusade was to show the Muslim leaders that, although there were only a few crusaders remaining in former crusader states, the Holy Land was so important to Christianity that a huge crusade would be gathered if necessary.

Of the three crusader leaders, only one, Richard I of England, continued fighting after the siege of Acre. Frederick of Germany died before reaching the Holy Land and Philip of France returned home after victory in 1191.

Question time

1 Why do you think that the Third Crusade is the most well known of all the Crusades?

2 Who gained most from the truce of the Third Crusade?

The Fourth Crusade, 1198

The aim of the Fourth Crusade was to capture Jerusalem because it had not been captured in the Third Crusade. However, by this time many crusader armies had lost their original focus and the wars were fought against a wider range of enemies. Constantinople, the centre of the Christian Empire in the East, had been captured by the Greeks (who were rivals to Alexius, the Byzantine Emperor). Alexius promised support for the Crusades if the army first helped him to regain his position of control in Constantinople.

The crusaders went to free the city of Constantinople. They removed the rival Greek Christians from the city but did not receive a welcome or any of the promised help from the Byzantines. In the attack on the city, Emperor Alexius was murdered and chaos followed. The crusader armies attacked and held the city and surrounding land for themselves rather than return it to Byzantine rule, and an eastern Latin Empire was created.

Holding Constantinople weakened the force of future crusades. Forces had to be kept in Constantinople to maintain it for the Christian Western Empire and crusader forces were therefore weakened by their division. The ruthlessness and greed of the crusaders damaged their reputation for the future.

The effects of the Crusades

Although the first 50 years of the Crusades saw gains of land for the crusaders, after that time the Muslim warriors gradually pushed the Christians out of the Middle East. Acre was the last town to be held by the Christians. It fell in 1291. Acre had been held for 100 years but Christians were eventually outnumbered 5 to 1 by the Muslims. The loss of this city marked the end of the Crusades in the Holy Land but they continued elsewhere in different forms.

The Crusades in the Holy Land had lasted for over 200 years. They saw large armies travel over thousands of kilometres to fight in an unfamiliar land. Christians, Muslims and Jews were all killed in the fighting. Christian knights won land from the Muslims in battles and sieges, and they extended Muslim forts and built crusader castles still in existence today. They settled to form a small crusader empire and brought European customs and building styles to the Middle East.

Europe was also influenced by land that had been taken over by the expanding Muslim Empire. Southern Spain and Sicily, for example, still contain evidence of considerable Islamic influences, most obvious in the design of buildings but also present in food and art and other forms of culture.

SOURCE A

A European building in the Middle East. The picture shows Krak des Chevaliers in Syria, built c. 1142.

SOURCE B

An Islamic building in Europe. The picture shows the Court of Lions at the Alhambra in Spain, built in the fourteenth century.

Below is a summary of many of the effects of the Crusades on European culture:

- trade was stimulated between Asia Minor and Europe
- sugar
- using pigeons for messages (pigeon post)
- astrolabes (equipment to measure the distance from the stars to Earth)
- lemons
- silks
- the magnifying glass
- astronomy
- styles of decoration and art
- the lute (musical instrument)
- apricots
- learning was encouraged in Islam unlike Christianity in the Middle Ages; Arabic scholars had ancient knowledge unheard of by many in the West
- travel to the East developed by experience including new navigational techniques and safe trade routes
- soap
- the trebuchet (a large catapult for firing missiles)
- surgical methods and tools for specific operations
- lenses
- mathematical skills including Arabic figures which are easier to use than Roman numerals
- spices
- mirrors
- cotton
- castle building with round towers joined by a long wall – rather than square keep which is easier to break through.

Question time

1   Using the list on this page, create your own summary chart of influences on Europe from the Crusades. The ideas will need sorting into different themes for columns on your chart. One example might be 'technology'.

Assessment section

1. Draw a diagram for three different crusades to show their impact. You could use a flow diagram and have different arrows for short-term and long-term effects.

2. Why do you think that historians cannot agree over how many crusades actually took place?

3. Historians have argued that it was the first four crusades that were the most important ones in history. Do you agree? Prepare to explain your answer to the rest of the class in a short presentation and then write up your ideas in an extended answer.

   It would be useful to plan your argument before you start to write – either in a diagram or list format. You will get marks for the argument that you give but also the level of detail. This will include any additional research that you have carried out.

   You might choose to argue that a certain crusade was more important than all the others, or that it was less important.

4. In March 2000 Pope John Paul II apologised to the world for various examples of Christian violence, including the Crusades, and prayed for peace across the world. What does this message tell us about the importance of the Crusades in today's world?

5. Do you think that students in schools today should learn about the Crusades? Have they got anything important to teach us about the past – and the present?

Further reading

Wendy Cooling (Ed), *Centuries of Stories* (Collins, 1999)

Christopher Gravett, *The World of the Medieval Knight* (Hodder Wayland, 1996)

Cynthia Harnett, *The Woolpack* (Methuen, 1951)

Jill Paton-Walsh, *The Emperor's Winding Sheet* (Macmillan, 1974)

Sheila Sancha, *Walter Dragon's Town: Medieval People at Work* (Collins, 1987)

Henry Treece, *The Children's Crusade* (Puffin, 1958)

R. Welch, *Knight Crusader* (Oxford University Press, 1962)

Society's order

Would you have coped living in the Middle Ages? You might expect medieval life to be miserable. Consider the prospect of working hard on the land all day and then going home to a bowl of tasteless vegetable soup and a straw bed on the floor. However, as you will discover, Britain in the Middle Ages was not simply the backward society of its stereotype. The strict hierarchy of the feudal system can certainly be seen in the lifestyle and conditions of medieval people, but times changed. Over the period, the population rapidly increased, then decreased in size. Although remaining a largely rural country, Britain's towns grew, as did trade and wealth. People had new challenges to face. You can judge for yourself whether medieval life was as grim as the stereotype.

Who's who in medieval England?

The 'upper crust'

At the top of the feudal system (see page 25), the monarch and his barons and knights lived in castles and manors, and owned large areas of land. The lesser lords, who looked after the land in the country, lived in manor houses. Lords were responsible for many or several villages, which were collectively called a manor. Some villages had a manor house, and its size made the lord's presence more obvious, but all villagers felt his influence in many ways. Using the feudal system, the rich controlled the daily lives of the majority of the population. The 'upper crust' of feudal society had many privileges of status.

The phrase 'the upper crust' comes from how bread was cooked in medieval times. Loaves of bread baked in wood burning ovens would have solid, burnt and charcoal-stained bases. The rich, of course, would eat only the top part of the loaf, or the upper crust, hence the nickname for wealthy folk.

The labourers

The majority of the population in the Middle Ages were, of course, peasants (see page 26). Technically they were not slaves, but they were not really free either. Within 100 years of the Norman conquest it was no longer possible to buy slaves at a market in England as it had been at the time of the Domesday Book in 1087. This is because, as the population rose, more people wanted to work the land and it became more efficient for lords to rent out their land, in return for labour, than to buy slaves to do their work. Serfs and villeins (see page 26) are examples of peasants who were in effect servants of the lord but received their own houses and land in return for work.

The growing number of towns in the country also meant an increase in merchants, traders and craftsmen, the emergence of a new group of people who weren't answerable to the lord of the manor.

Where people lived

Medieval living was communal; shared living and lack of privacy was usual for rich as well as poor. Only the lord and lady, and possibly their children, had their own rooms. We shall now consider the lives of the rich.

Castles were designed and built largely for defensive purposes (see page 28), but, as medieval England became a more peaceful place, castle living was replaced by more manor houses. In a manor house, as in castles, lords and ladies had small private apartments high up in a tower or wing, reached by a staircases. A great hall was the focal point of the house, and in addition to the main bedroom there was sometimes an upstairs room called a solar, which was the lord's private room. Within the lord's bedroom the four-poster bed was protected from the cold by thick curtains, and in times of danger a guard remained on duty inside the room.

The great hall was the most important and public of rooms where lord, family and guests spent most of their time. Most people did not have their own bedrooms but slept in the same hall that they had met, eaten and danced in during the day. In larger manors, the lady of the manor had her own room, possibly with a window, by which she could sew and embroider. The kitchen, pantry and buttery were the other important places in a manor house or castle, but these were territory only for the servants.

The space and privacy for anyone in a castle or manor house was little. The lord and his lady could always retreat to their solar for their meal or some peace if they had no guests and wanted privacy. Even going to the toilet was usually a group event: the garde-robe or 'privie' contained more than one seat which dropped its contents into an open sewer or river far below (see diagram on page 201). Extra rooms for guests were often added during the medieval period, so it is quite hard to tell the original manor house in the buildings still standing today.

Dark and gloomy surroundings

Gas and electricity were not available in the medieval world. All work had to be done in daylight, or by candlelight. In order to make the most of daylight hours people would get up at about 5 am and be in bed at night by 8 pm. The winter months could be fairly miserable.

Beeswax or the cheaper tallow (animal fat) were used to make candles, though only the relatively rich could afford candles of any kind; rush light was commonest in peasant houses. Torches would be set in holders around the walls of every room. Glass to let in natural light was very costly indeed, so much so that it would be removed from any windows in a house if the lord was absent. With only very small windows for security, warmth and expense, medieval homes were very dark. Fireplaces were an important innovation and made a great difference to living arrangements.

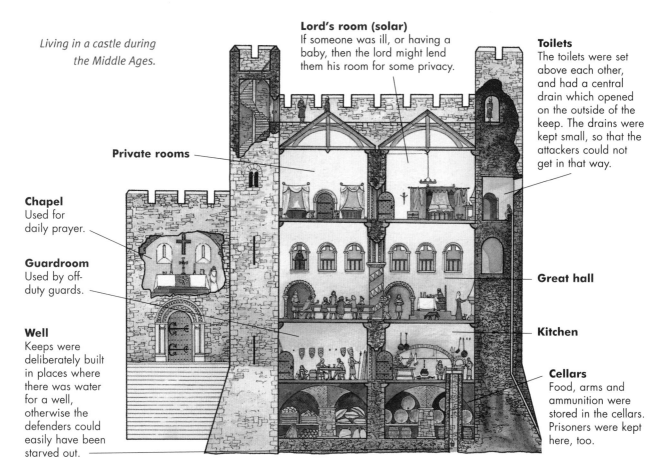

Living in a castle during the Middle Ages.

Lord's room (solar)
If someone was ill, or having a baby, then the lord might lend them his room for some privacy.

Toilets
The toilets were set above each other, and had a central drain which opened on the outside of the keep. The drains were kept small, so that the attackers could not get in that way.

Private rooms

Chapel
Used for daily prayer.

Guardroom
Used by off-duty guards.

Well
Keeps were deliberately built in places where there was water for a well, otherwise the defenders could easily have been starved out.

Great hall

Kitchen

Cellars
Food, arms and ammunition were stored in the cellars. Prisoners were kept here, too.

Medieval houses were also much colder, damper and smellier than today. Floors were generally made from beaten mud or wood, and the floor of the great hall was covered in rushes or rush matting. The walls of homes for the rich, however, were sometimes decorated in rich colours and fine tapestries, or covered in painted wooden panelling. In towns, wooden houses were cramped together and represented a fire risk with their timber frames and thatched roofs. Houses had ladders outside them and a hooked pole to pull down any thatch that might have caught fire. Roads were sometimes made from gravel or cobbles but usually were just mud.

Question time

1   Make a list of all the differences you can think of between life for the rich in the Middle Ages and life for the wealthy today. What do wealthy people have in their houses today?

2   How many similarities between their lives can you find so far? Make a second list and discuss these in pairs.

3   Write down three hypotheses – theories that you will test against facts – about life in medieval England. You will test each hypothesis during the study of this chapter. Your hypotheses could be about the role of some of the following: women, trade, hygiene, medicine, peasants, farming, the lord, the feudal system. For example, one hypothesis is: 'The feudal system was unfair for peasants: they got nothing in return for their loyalty.'

Eating in the Middle Ages

Most meals were eaten with fingers. The only cutlery – if any – was a knife-like tool called a thwitel, or whittle, which was used to hold or slice chunks of meat or vegetables. Drinking cups were made from earthenware or metal. Only the very rich ate from tableware, with plates made from wood, pewter or silver. Most people ate from the thick bottom crust of a loaf of bread, which was sliced off and used as a plate. This was called a trencher and was often shared between two people. Used trenchers were given to the poor, and were a welcome gift. You might expect that medieval table manners were very poor indeed; however, it was considered very rude to dip your fingers into your trencher or wipe your hands on the tablecloth.

All meals, for both rich and poor, were prepared and cooked in the manor kitchen or in the one room of the long house that a peasant family would share with their animals. Every household, from manor house to small cottage, would grow most of their own produce, and extras or luxuries would be bought from the local market.

Daily diet

Your daily diet depended on the amount of money you had. For the rich, meat was cooked on spits, which resembled a very simple, giant barbecue. It was the job of the spit boy to turn the rotisserie handle to ensure that the pig, sheep or cow was cooking evenly – a very hot and tiring job. During Lent and on Fridays, when no meat could be eaten, the rich ate plenty of fish. However, the poor could only afford meat when their animals had just been slaughtered. They would eat mainly pottage and rye bread. Pottage was a type of soup, usually made from beans and peas and flavoured with herbs and spices. Their diet was actually healthier than the meat-based meals eaten at the manor house! However, the diet of most peasants was also fairly repetitive – bread and pottage every day. Also, in some years, bad harvests brought famine and malnutrition to the countryside: because they were dependent on a staple diet, peasants were particularly vulnerable to crop failures.

Any meat eaten by rich or poor was not necessarily fresh so plenty of spices were used to mask flavours of smoked, or even rotten food. Spices were also used by the poor to disguise the taste of the pottage, even though the vegetables it contained did vary with the seasons. Peasants looked forward to harvest time, believing that the lord of the manor would then put on a fine feast for his villagers. Ale for the poor and wine for the wealthy were the only forms of drink because water was not suitable for drinking. There was no tea or coffee so the only hot drink was mulled wine.

Digging deeper

Feasting in the great hall

What is your ideal meal? What foods would you expect to see at a modern-day feast? Just like today, no expense was spared for special meals or feasts in the medieval court, in castles and manor houses. Menu and recipe books show the tastes of the rich in medieval England. Each feast consisted of several courses, and each course often included a mixture of sweet and savoury foods. At the wedding of King Henry III's daughter to the King of Scotland in 1251, the bill for the bread alone came to £7000.

Feasts were eaten in the great hall of the manor or castle. Trestle bases were placed around the walls of the hall in a large 'L' shape. The servants would bring in the food already placed on a trestle top which would then make up the tables. After the feast the trestles could be removed to make way for dancing, acrobats and other entertainment, and then later the room was used as a sleeping place for the less important guests.

For meals, the lord sat on a platform called a dais and was the only person to sit on a chair with a back; even his family sat on benches (this is where the word 'chairman' comes from). The lord's family and most important guests sat closest to the lord. Before the introduction of fireplaces the great hall itself was kept warm by a huge fire on a trolley which was moved around.

SOURCE A

Contemporary illustration of a medieval banquet and trestle table.

SOURCE B

A fashionable yeoman who came from a great banquet has told us about the feast … Without bread and wine and ale, no one at a feast will be at ease, but the choicest of all three were provided there … the course which they had first: the head of a boar, larded, with the snout well garlanded, and enough for the whole household of venison fattened during the closed season. And then there were a great variety of cranes, peacocks, and swans, kids, pigs, and hens. Then they had rabbits in gravy, all covered with sugar, red and white wine in great plenty; and then quite a different multitude of roasts, each of them set next to another: pheasants, woodcocks, and partridges, fieldfares, larks, and roasted plovers, blackbirds, woodcocks, and song-thrushes, and other birds I cannot name; and fried meat, crisps, and fritters, with sugar mixed with rose-water. And when the table was taken away, sweet spice powder, maces, and enough spicerie, and plenty of wafers.

A menu for a thirteenth-century feast. It was written in French with an English explanation. From the Treatise of Walter of Bibbesworth.

Question time

1. What are the main differences between the diet and meals of the rich and the poor in medieval England? Why did these differences occur?

2. Look at Source B. Why would the thirteenth-century menu have been written in French but used in England?

3. What can't we tell about a medieval feast from the menu in Source B?

4. What are the similarities with and differences between the meal that is described in Source B and an expensive meal that we might have today, for example at a wedding?

Entertainment for rich and poor

Games, sports and music were popular in the medieval world as they are today but they were mainly enjoyed by the rich. This is because the rich had far more time and resources to enjoy games involving complex rules or equipment. Medieval sources tell us of a wide variety of pastimes: chess, wrestling, dancing, jousting, archery, leaping, javelin, tug-of-war, apple bobbing, piggy-back fighting, dice, acrobatics, watching boar or bear bating, and cock or bull fighting were all common activities. By the late fourteenth century cards also became popular, and are believed to have been introduced by the crusaders or Spanish traders from the Islamic Empire.

At court, tournaments were a highly popular but risky sport. Tournaments were practice for knights and they would sometimes engage in a mock battle called a mêlée. You may have heard this word still used today for a confused fight or struggle. In a mêlée two groups of about 50 knights fought each other using blunt weapons. Jousting was also popular. This was where two knights charged towards each other, each with a flat tipped lance. Points were scored for the different hits they could make, including knocking the opponent from his horse. There was often a designated jousting fortnight at court each year, held during the summer months. Another sport that was popular with the rich was real tennis, a complex form of tennis with many different rules. Its only similarity with modern-day tennis is that it involved hitting a ball over a rope in a courtyard. Monarchs and lords also paid for entertainment from minstrels who performed plays, songs and stories, and enjoyed puppet shows, trumpeters, drummers and acrobats. One performer, Matilda Makejob, was famous in medieval England for her naked somersaults!

Hunting was a frequent pastime and it wasn't just enjoyed by men: rich ladies also participated. Hawking in particular was popular with wealthy men and women. Hawks or falcons were used to hunt small animals and birds, and ferrets were used to hunt rabbits. Deer and large game were hunted using bows and arrows; bears were hunted with spears. Certain animals such as deer and rabbits were the prerogative of royalty and nobility. This meant that it was a crime for anyone else to hunt them. As you can imagine, poaching was common but carried severe penalties: cutting off a hand, or even execution, could result from poaching from the king's land.

Making your own fun

For the poor there was much less time to engage in entertainment and it was certainly not provided for them. Physical games like wrestling and football were popular. Medieval football was more like modern-day rugby but with fewer rules and more violence. The ball was made from a pig's bladder, inflated or stuffed with beans or peas. In the fourteenth century, Edward III actually banned football and other physical sports because he was concerned that the country was losing the valuable skills of archery needed for war.

Women of the village danced and sang at feasts and if a villager was very lucky they might see a wandering entertainer like a minstrel once a year, possibly at the annual local fair. The most popular seasons for such games were during the Twelve Days of Christmas and also at carnival time on Shrove Tuesday just before the start of Lent. Large-scale festivals and feasts were largely determined by the Church's calendar.

SOURCE B

After the ambassador had spoken with the King and Queen he was escorted … to the Queen's rooms where they were playing bowls and ninepins and dancing. In the morning, … after breakfast the young Prince was carried in by his tutor to greet the ambassador and then they set out to hunt. The King gave Gruthus a royal crossbow with silken strings, in a velvet case embossed with the royal arms. The heads of the bolts were gilded. In the hunting they killed six bucks which the King gave to the ambassador … In the evening the Queen held a great banquet, inviting all the most important people at court to meet Gruthus. At nine o'clock they went to the chambers of pleasure, all hung with white silk and linen, the floors carpeted. The bed was of down, the sheets from Rennes, the counterpane cloth of gold, edged with ermine, the hangings of white satin. There was a beautiful bathroom, and when the ambassador had been undressed by the Lord Chamberlain they both went to bathe, alongside other great lords. Afterwards they ate green ginger and drank syrups, ate sweets and sipped spiced wine. A few days later the King made him Earl of Winchester.

A description of how King Edward IV entertained an ambassador from Charles, Duke of Burgundy in 1472. The ambassador, Louis de Gruthus, had helped Edward when he had been an exile, and the king wanted to reward and thank him.

Some five hundred hired entertainers were invited to dance at the opening of a new courtyard at a new house. They leapt about so much that the brick wall of the house and then the roof collapsed and fell. About fifty of them were crushed and killed instantly. The rest, in complete panic, escaped death, though a hundred were seriously wounded or suffered grave internal injury.

A description of an unfortunate housewarming party, from The Annals of Ghent, *written in the fourteenth century.*

SOURCE D

It behoves the young and virtuous woman ... to behave with far more modesty than the man. The movement of her body should be humble and meek ... Nor should her gaze be haughty or roaming, she should keep for the most part her eyes on the ground ...

Someone dancing in a long garment should dance with solemnity, all his gestures should be grave and as refined as his attire requires ... because the long robe would not work with too much moving here and there ...

Extracts from a treatise written by Guglielmo Ebreo of Pesaro in the fifteenth century, On the Practice or Art of Dancing.

SOURCE E

This picture shows the inside of a wealthy town house in the fourteenth century. Its cellars are well stocked with wine for the drinking party. One of the guests has had too much to drink and is being sick. Illustration from a late-fourteenth-century manuscript.

Question time

1   Why do you think that there was a wider range of games and entertainment for the rich than the poor?

2   What gifts does King Edward give to the Burgundian ambassador in Source B?

3   Read Source D. What does the advice on dancing suggest to us about:

   a   the popularity of dancing as a form of entertainment

   b   how the wealthy danced

   c   how men and women were expected to dance?

4   Look at Source E. Why do you think that a medieval artist would paint a picture of men getting drunk and being sick? Use your knowledge of the ideas and values of the period to answer this question.

5   Does Source E suggest that getting drunk must have been a common pastime in the Middle Ages?

Medieval clothing – what to wear?

Loose woollen tunics were worn by both men and women in the early Middle Ages:

- Those worn by women were floor length. By the late fourteenth century they had become slightly tighter fitting. Richer ladies wore jewellery and decorated hair pieces.

- Men's tunics were originally floor length, but their length and shape changed during the medieval period, becoming shorter. By the late fourteenth century, men's tunics were worn with hose (like thick stockings). The length of men's tunics then reflected their social status: those of the poor were floor length; those of the clergy or professionals like lawyers were ankle length; and those of merchants were calf length.

Cloaks were worn by everyone as a coat, or outer layer. Hoods lined with fur were essential for rich men and women, as were undershirts or tunics made from silk or satin, becuase these were a symbol of their wealth. Footwear was generally flat shoes made from leather. Long pointed toes were fashionable and stuffed with moss to help them keep their shape – but they were not for peasants working in the muddy fields all day!

Vegetable and herbal dyes were used to colour clothing. Madder root, for example, gave a red colour which is still used in products today, but the shades available were certainly not as bright or varied as those we are familiar with.

Question time

1 Look through all the visual sources in this book which contain figures of men and women. Make a list of what the men and women are wearing, whether they are rich or poor, and whether the source comes from the early or late medieval period.

What conclusions do you make as to the most common forms of clothing worn by men and women in the Middle Ages? What were the main differences between the clothes of the rich and those of the poor?

Growing up in the Middle Ages

Most women had several children during the Middle Ages: at least ten babies were born to each peasant family, many of whom would die before they were two or three years old. Looking after young children was not a full-time job for rich or poor. Poor women often relied on their older children to care for younger brothers or sisters; or they would strap the baby on their back in a sling or a basket and take them into the fields with them. Richer women employed wet nurses. These were women who had just had a child themselves and so were able to breastfeed another infant too. The rich chose to wrap up their babies in tight sheets called swaddling because this was thought to help their bones to grow straight and strong. It also helped to keep them quiet and out of trouble!

Young children were taught to keep busy and to copy adults although they did have toys to play with. Rich parents could buy dolls, tops and toy soldiers; the poor had to make objects themselves. Parents let their children have a little fun but they also beat them for any wrongdoing.

Sent away at an early age

Children of the rich had slightly longer to adjust to the adult world than those from peasant families. Sons of lords were often sent away at the age of 15 to another household as a page, and then as a squire.

- A page worked for a lord, helping him to dress and cleaning his armour.

- The page then became a squire, which was essentially a trainee knight. A squire in a lord's household was taught to fight, wrestle, hunt, ride and behave as a knight should. He was also expected to carry and care for a knight's weapons in battle.

- At 17 or 18 squires were fully trained and ready to fight as knights for the monarch if necessary. Squires went through a religious ceremony and plenty of feasting on becoming a knight, because it was considered a great honour.

Daughters from wealthy families were sent to live with relatives or friends, in order to learn how to become a lady in a household. One foreign observer of English life commented that the English could not really like their children because they sent them to live with other people. However, it was believed that it was easier to discipline someone else's child.

Off to work, age seven

As we have seen the children of peasant families had a very different lifestyle. They worked with their fathers and mothers in the fields from the age of seven or eight – as soon as they could start work. Younger children helped to sow seeds, scare birds away from crops, or card wool (separate the different strands). Children in peasant families grew up relying on each other as much as their parents. By the age of 14 they were trained as adults and expected to work as hard as their parents.

Village children received no formal education unless they had a very committed village priest to give them free lessons. And, of course, this was only if their parents could spare them from helping on the land or from looking after younger brothers and sisters. In addition to this, the lord had to be seen to give permission for a child of a peasant to be educated. In general, this made education for the poor very unlikely.

Children of townsfolk were often trained in their family's workshop or business from a young age. Boys were sent off at the age of 11 or 12 to become an apprentice in a trade; girls sometimes became apprentice seamstresses or worked as servants in larger households. Education, as we think of it, in terms of literacy, numeracy and a wide range of lessons, was a privilege reserved only for those who could afford it; it was not a basic right.

The apprentice system

In order to become skilled in a trade and set up business in the long term, young boys had to go through many years of hard training. Their parents paid for them to become apprentices to a master who owned his own workshop or business. Apprentices usually slept in the workshop and their payment, if any, was more like pocket money. Apprentices were closely monitored by their masters: they could not visit inns or gamble or get married. If they were lucky they had the company of another apprentice at the same workshop, with whom to play football or other games.

It took seven years as an apprentice to become a journeyman, which meant that you could leave your original master and earn a living in another workshop. This way you could further your skills and experience, before finally becoming a master in your own right. However, this only happened with a lot of savings and the permission of the town guild (see page 213), who could refuse on the grounds of there being too many cobblers or smiths in town already. In order to become a master, a journeyman also had to produce a piece of work of the finest quality. This 'masterpiece' was inspected by members of the guild to check the quality.

SOURCE A

This painting, made in 1482, shows a guild master judging the work of a carpenter and stonemason who want to become masters.

A privileged education

Literacy skills were rare in the early Middle Ages. Monarchs had to sign their name, but a simple cross shape was sufficient for a signature. Rather, it was the duty of the monarch's clerks, or the clergy, to do the real writing and reading. In the early medieval period it was not only the poor who were taught about Christianity from pictures in Bibles. However, gradually clerks, monks and priests shared their knowledge, and wealthy families began to receive an education.

The education of wealthy children improved during the Middle Ages. Sons were taught to speak English, French and some Latin. Up to the age of 11, they were trained at home in music, dance and arithmetic by tutors. Then, unless they were very wealthy, boys were sent to early grammar schools where their studies broadened to include some science and law, and the scriptures as well as Latin and maths.

Girls from wealthy families received some education in reading and writing. They were taught a little Latin from the psalter (the Bible, prayer and psalm book). Letter writing and some basic arithmetic were also considered important to their education. Girls were taught to do fine embroidery and weaving, and to prepare themselves to manage a household on marriage.

A girl's education was given by her mother, or possibly a local priest; it was the education of sons that cost families money – for tutors and formal education. Girls, however, needed financial investment from their fathers in the form of a dowry, to be given to the family they would marry into.

For continued academic education there were two choices for men: taking holy orders and becoming a monk or a priest, or going to Oxford, founded in 1167, or Cambridge, founded in 1209. The universities of Oxford and Cambridge were the only two in the country. A university course could take as long as nine years to complete, although many men attended only for two or three years. After nine years of study, men were fully trained in medicine, law or religion. Women did not go to university in the Middle Ages.

Question time

1   Draw two spider diagrams containing information about the childhood and education of medieval children. Draw one for the rich and one for the poor.

2   Are the differences between the childhood of rich and poor children greater in the Middle Ages than they are today? Discuss this question in groups, or as a class.

3   Create a manual for a young, rich mother from the Middle Ages who is unsure about how to bring up her children. Include some additional research if you can.

Wedding bells

The average age for a wealthy girl to be married was 17, although a few marriages were arranged by eager families for 13 or 14 year olds. Landed families sought to arrange a suitable marriage for their son or daughter because land and money would change hands once a marriage proposal was agreed. They wanted to make sure that a son or daughter bettered themselves by marriage.

A betrothal of marriage, what we today call engagement, was as legally binding as the actual marriage vows. Daughters often tried to change their parents' minds about a choice of husband, or made secret promises to their sweethearts. Margery Paston, daughter of a wealthy landowner from Norfolk, upset her family by becoming betrothed to the bailiff on her father's estate. Margery kept their betrothal a secret until after her father's death, fearing his outrage. On finding out, her mother Margaret Paston (see page 222), wanted to throw Margery out of the household, and forbade her daughter from seeing her beloved. However, Margery and her sweetheart were eventually married, though Margery was disowned by most of her family.

Daughters of peasant families often had to leave home and work as a servant in order to save for a dowry of their own. If they could afford it, the lord of the manor might arrange for an early marriage between different peasant families because this would bring more workers to his manor in the long term. In many marriage arrangements the husband was rather richer and older than his bride.

Marriage ceremonies were often held in a public place outside the church, so that the exchange of vows could be heard by many people. Marriage was considered a special ceremony blessed by God, so divorce was seen as unacceptable. The only grounds for a man to divorce his wife would be if they were actually blood relations, though proving this in court was a costly experience. Some men did make up false ancestries to get rid of their wives, but divorce itself was very rare. You will investigate the problem that a royal divorce settlement brought to England under the Tudors (see Chapter 2 in the second book in the Headstart in History series, *Reformation and Rebellion*).

Towns and town life

The emergence of medieval towns

Towns of England with more than 2500 inhabitants by 1300.

Between 5 and 10 per cent of the population lived in towns in the medieval period. In 1066 there were only five main towns in England; after the Norman conquest (by the time of the Domesday Book) this number had risen to 100. During the Middle Ages, the number of towns continued to increase; each town contained a population of between 2000 and 5000. New towns like Liverpool and Portsmouth developed near the coast as ports; others developed inland at a crossing point of a river or two roads, or near a castle or abbey. Some towns grew up as religious or academic centres. Between 1100 and 1300, 140 new towns emerged, including Leeds and Hull. Ancient towns such as York and London grew bigger.

Medieval towns attracted people to set up shops and businesses. They sold services to local lords and businessmen who, in turn, encouraged more business. Those working in a town included bakers, butchers, fishmongers, brewers, cook, weavers, tailors, robemakers, washerwomen and shoemakers, to name but a few. Some towns had different areas, or quarters, allocated to specific trades. The famous 'Shambles' in York was the quarter of the slaughterhouses and butchers' shops.

Most towns were well protected, with high walls and several different gates, or a moat. At the gates there were guards to collect tolls – an entry charge for traders. Typically, different amounts were charged depending on the size of loads. It would also cost much more to bring a cartload of goods than, for example, a horse. Sometimes these tolls were used to fund street paving and repairs – so heavy carts had to pay more.

SOURCE A

A medieval street with shops and market stalls, from a French manuscript painted in 1460.

Gaining a charter for freedom

Once a town was large and established, it could petition the lord for a charter to become independent. Towns often had to pay the monarch for a charter to give it town status. For example, during the reign of King John (1199–1216), many towns were granted royal charters because the king needed extra income. A charter enabled towns to govern themselves, by electing a council and a mayor. They could then fix their own taxes as long as they sent some to the lord or the king, of course.

Rights and responsibilities

Unlike villages, towns were not subject to the strict code of the feudal system. Citizens could always vote for a different mayor if they were unhappy with the existing one. Any peasants who managed to escape from their manor and had not been caught by their lord for a year and a day could have their freedom. That is not to say that towns did not have their own hierarchy. People from peasant families rarely rose to any position of importance in a town. Townsfolk also had responsibilities. In addition to payment of taxes, many townspeople took turns to carry out watch duty (see page 230) and also to maintain the standard of the road outside their home or shop.

Buying and selling

Goods that could not be grown easily on homestead plots or in village fields were bought at local markets. Finer and more rare produce, such as ribbons, knives and some spices, were bought at the market, as well as a range of everyday produce. However, the rich might have to travel to London for luxuries such as ginger, pepper, treacle or rice.

As well as buying produce from local weekly markets, shops in towns did a thriving trade. Most food shopping in town was done daily from the variety of shops available; there were no refrigerators or freezers to keep produce fresh. Often the shops occupied the whole of the ground floor of a house with the living quarters above. Craft shops were more like workshops, with the craftsmen working on the item that you required. In addition to weekly markets and shops in town, some towns had permission to hold fairs, usually on an annual basis. Fairs were held on feast days, often near to sites of pilgrimage or outside a large town. They were like a giant market with a wide variety of entertainers and stalls.

No escape from taxes

Traders were subject to tolls and taxes in the towns where they sold their produce. These often favoured local traders and, just as taxes or 'protection' in the twenty-first century can disadvantage certain industries or countries, in the Middle Ages they could also cause resentment. In the late twelfth century, for example, the London merchants boycotted the thriving market town of Bury St Edmunds in Suffolk in protest at the taxes they were expected to pay. Traders were also monitored by assize courts, which had the right to measure and tax produce. Any lords or abbots who held markets or fairs on their land also profited from the dues as well as income from any fines received from dishonest traders. Traders tried to regulate their own standards and maintain quality as well as a good reputation. This was a function of town guilds.

Digging deeper

Town guilds

Town guilds (clubs or societies) were established as social and charitable organisations for different trades but they served many other functions. They can be compared to modern trades unions in some respects.

- Guilds restricted their membership to people who were of a certain level of craftsmanship and therefore kept the reputation of each trade high.

- Only members of a guild could set up a business in town.

- Guilds set wages, prices and conditions of work. Working by candlelight in dark cellars was forbidden, for example, because the poor light meant that quality of work would suffer.

- Guilds monitored the quality of goods made because some traders tried to cheat their customers. Silversmiths might mix lead with silver, and alemen might use measuring cups which held less beer than they should. Traders caught defrauding (cheating) the public brought the guild into bad repute, so guild members ensured that cheats were taken to the mayor's court.

Social support

In addition to monitoring business, some guilds had a social role. They collected funds and supported families with any problems – in effect, they gave out limited forms of sick pay and widows' pensions. Guilds sometimes built almshouses for people in their guild who could not afford to maintain rent payments on their homes. They were also often responsible for maintaining a certain part of the parish church: for example, a side chapel or the candles used in services. Some guilds funded the embroidery of altar cloths or palls to cover coffins during a funeral.

Entertainment

Another role of the town guilds was to provide entertainment. Early guilds were known as 'Mysteries' and from them came the 'Mystery Plays'. Each guild performed a play based on a Bible story related to their craft: the carpenters performed a play about Noah's Ark; the goldsmiths performed a play about the gifts given to the infant Jesus. The plays were part of the celebrations held at Corpus Christi, a Church feast. Of course, the guilds also held their own private feasts – including an annual celebration of their hard work and success.

Guilds met at the guildhall in a town. There is likely to be a guildhall in any town near you if the town existed during the Middle Ages.

Maintaining standards

One of the main functions of a medieval town's guild was the regulation (the restriction) of trade. Merchants were only allowed to sell according to the rules of the market, which would be decided by the guilds; any attempts to do more profitable deals on the side were punished. Quality of goods too, was maintained by assize courts and by-laws; butchers especially were regularly prosecuted for displaying 'measled' meat for sale.

SOURCE B

- William le Cook and John Hereward are fined for sharing carcasses of oxen and selling them at different stalls as if each one of them sold the meat entire.

- Walter atte Walle, a butcher, sells measled meat to foreigners from a market outside the Borough, against the ancient custom of Colchester.

- This is an indenture of apprenticeship for eight years, between William Mate of Colchester, tanner of shoes, and John son of John de Leyre. A bond for £10 is placed by the master with Robert, rector of Frayling in case of the death of either master or apprentice.

- Thomas Snok's wife and John Packard's wife sell their beer without having their signs exhibited and unlawfully use cups which deceive people.

- John Pedder, Robert Cook and Cecily Davy collect the offal of fish and flesh from their shops and throw it in the street by night, which is abominable.

Extracts from the court rolls of the Borough of Colchester, 1310–52.

Question time

1   Study Source B carefully and answer these questions:

   a   What sort of things are traders doing in order to cheat the public?

   b   Give examples of action taken by the court to maintain standards.

   c   Why would the court be concerned that a trader was selling bad meat to people outside the town of Colchester?

   d   Is this borough court only concerned with standards of trade? Explain your answer carefully.

2 Have a conversation with a partner in which one of you is master and one of you is an apprentice in your local medieval town. The apprentice has dared to question the value of joining the guild and the master needs to explain clearly all the aspects of the guild's importance.

3 Find out about the role of modern trades unions and find similarities and differences between them and medieval guilds. This will involve you talking to some adults or carrying out research in your school library. You can discuss the similarities and differences as a group.

4 Which other organisations, if any, carry out the roles in the twenty-first century that the guilds used to perform in medieval England?

5 Divide into groups. Each group consists of town councillors who need to draw up a list of rules for the traders and townsfolk of the medieval town that you were elected to represent. Your rules can cover any aspects of town life but avoid including twenty-first century knowledge and anachronisms. (An anachronism is something which doesn't belong in a particular time period – a motor car in the medieval period, for example.)

Trade links – at home and in Europe

A network of roads linked towns with other trading towns. Carts and packhorses would travel along these, to fairs and markets and also to the ports. Thirty-five packhorses were needed to carry the same amount as a 5-ton lorry, and they only travelled at one or two miles per hour. The roads themselves were not good and bad weather often made them impassable. However, a network of towns supported each other with all the necessary goods. Many goods not available in this country were imported from Europe. These imports included important foodstuffs like salt, spices and wine, and luxuries like glass and silks. English goods such as wool, cloth and tin were exported abroad to foreign markets.

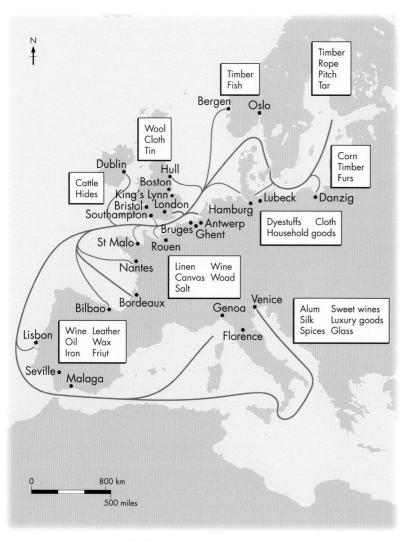

Medieval trade between Britain and Europe in the 1450s.

Question time

1. Look back to the map on page 8 and then at the map on page 211. Where in the country was the greatest distribution of towns in 1086? Had the distribution changed by the late fourteenth century?

2. a. Which medieval town was nearest to where you now live?

   b. Find out if there are any medieval buildings still standing. What were they used for?

3. Study Source A on page 212 carefully. Discuss in pairs what you can see going on. What is for sale? What else do people have to pay money for in this town?

4. Using your knowledge of this period, or with the help of an encyclopaedia, give the main reasons for the development of one of these medieval towns: Canterbury, Bury St Edmunds, Oxford, Bristol.

The medieval village

The medieval village usually consisted of about 25 houses or homesteads, a manor house and a church. Many families also lived in hamlets. These were small clusters of homesteads built away from the larger village. During medieval times more people came to live and work together, and villages as well as towns grew in size. Drastic changes in population during the Middle Ages (see Chapter 11) also left many villages deserted by the late fourteenth century. However, it is the life of the people in a medieval village that we'll be looking at in this section.

Who's who in the village?

The most important person in a village, whether he lived nearby or not, was the lord. Second to him was the priest or his curate. If his lands were extensive, the lord would employ a bailiff or steward to supervise rent collection, the farming of his land, and to manage the accounts. Bailiffs would also judge crimes at the manorial court, along with senior villagers and the lord.

Villagers were chosen to act in positions of responsibility to help to organise the farming system:

- The reeve acted as a foreman, checking that peasants arrived on time to carry out required work on the lord's demesne (his land). Reeves organised the building and maintenance of barns and checked that planting was done at the right time of year.

- The hayward was, as his name suggests, responsible for the harvest.

- The constable carried out any necessary arrests and organised for offenders to be brought before the manor court. Wages for constables were very low so many had to take other part-time work.

Most positions of responsibility within the village were unpaid, although some villages gave an additional strip of land to the man who took on the job.

How many people do you know with the surname Smith, Cooper, Reeve or Heywood? These names were also types of work in medieval England. In larger villages, tradesmen like cobblers and carpenters were needed. They probably led more comfortable lives than the peasants, who were out in the fields in all weather.

Village homes

Medieval houses were dark, damp and smoky places. The small 'long houses' of peasants were made up of one large room, and probably no windows. There was a fire in the middle of the room, but no chimney to release smoke. The floor was made of beaten earth and there were only a few items of furniture: a table, possibly a stool and a mattress for everyone to sleep on.

The inside of a medieval peasant home.

Question time

1   Draw a diagram to represent the approximate hierarchy of people and positions within a medieval village.

2   In pairs, look at the reconstruction of a long house and talk about what you notice about the living conditions. Look for furniture, comfort, heat, light, space, privacy, dangers and health risks. Draw up a list of conclusions about living in a medieval peasants' home.

3   'Reconstructions like the one above are drawn by modern artists and cannot tell us anything useful about medieval life.' Do you agree with this statement?

Digging deeper

At the bottom of the feudal system

Not only did the lord expect the peasants to work in return for their homes on his manor, he also received goods as taxes and even had an influence over family life. Peasants did not only have to work for the lord a few days a week (called boon work); they also paid rent, usually given in the form of livestock and taxes on special occasions such as when a couple got married. This was all in addition to the tithes they owed to the Church. Families also had to use their lord's water mill to grind their corn, and of course pay for the privilege of doing so.

Lords had influence over the family life of tenants, arranging marriages and remarriages and organising for the care of any children made orphans. Young orphaned boys were often made wards of the local lord, which meant that he took responsibility for them and placed them in an apprenticeship or with a new family.

Peasants could not leave the manor without permission from the lord. There was, however, little reason for them to do this. The most any peasant could expect in their lifetime was a couple of visits to a fair or market. Any peasants who tried to escape from their manor could be chased and punished on capture. This was in the lord's interests because a loss of workers meant less income for him.

How much freedom?

Peasants did, however, have a few basic rights. They were protected by common law and could pass land on to their sons with the payment of a duty upon their death. Richer peasants could also choose to pay a fine rather than ask the lord's permission to leave the manor or marry someone from outside. But, as peasants who moved to the towns also found, it was possible, though very unlikely, for a peasant to become a man of importance. The only real way to gain a higher position was within the Church, via its education and own hierarchy: for example, the

Bishop of Lincoln in the thirteenth century, Robert Grosseteste, was the son of a villein.

Villages sited around monasteries had slightly less interference from the lord, but taxes were still collected and tithes had to be paid. There was little doubt that life was hard at the bottom of the feudal system. Lords, however, would argue that their responsibilities to their tenants and workers were significant and that they had to maintain an income to be able to afford to fight and work for the monarch.

SOURCE A

Richard Est holds one messuage [homestead] and half a virgate of land [a virgate is about 14 acres]. He pays one half-penny by Martinmas for salt. And at Michaelmas one quarter of unadulterated wheat for sowing, one peck of wheat and four bushels of oats and three hens. And at Christmas one cock and two hens and two pennies-worth of bread or two pence. And he will plough and harrow at his own expense a quarter of one acre of land. And he will work throughout the whole year a second day, either carrying or mowing or reaping, or doing carting service or whatever other work shall afterwards be imposed upon him by the lord or his bailiff, except on Saturdays and on feast days. And he will find at harvest-time two men to reap for two days for the customary boon work [for the lord] at his own expense ... neither will he marry his son nor his daughter nor sell his oxen and calves, nor his colts and fillies, and neither will he fell the oaks nor the ash-trees without licence of the lord.

A villein of Cuxham, 1298, describing some of the tasks a peasant had to carry out for the lord. This is an entry in a survey of the tenants of the village of Cuxham in Oxfordshire, made by Merton College, Oxford, which owned the manor, in 1298. There were 11 other villeins in Cuxham, doing similar service for the lord.

SOURCE B

Simon Godith surrenders his tenement to his son in return for a room, a garden, a bakehouse, 5 butts of land in one croft and 4.5 butts in Pertons Field. Simon's son will also pay him 8d a year and a cartload of sea-coal.

Simon Palmer surrenders his tenement in favour of his son William, who is to pay him annually 3.5 ells of woollen cloth, one piece of linen cloth and a pair of stockings, as well as a livery of 2 strikes of wheat every fortnight.

Wealthier peasants might be able to retire and even organise a pension from their son. This example is from the court rolls of Stoke Prior in 1296.

SOURCE C

I have no pennies to buy pullets,
Nor geese nor pigs, but I have two green cheeses,
A few curds of cream, a cake of oatmeal,
Two loaves of beans and bran, baked for my children,
But I have parsley and pot herbs and plenty of cabbages,
And a cow and a calf.
This is the little we must live on till the Lammas season.
Poor folk in hovels,
Charged with children and overcharged by landlords,
What they may save by spinning they spend on rent,
On milk, or on meal to make porridge.

An extract from the poem Piers Plowman *by William Langland, written in the fourteenth century. Lammas was the time for celebrating harvest festival, traditionally the first day of August.*

Question time

1 Read Source A. Make a list of the work and taxes owed by the villein in Cuxham to his landlord.

2 What have the peasants in Source B done to ensure their own happy retirement?

3 Read Source C. Pick out two words or phrases that William Langland uses to make his sympathy more obvious to the reader.

4 What does William Langland describe as desirable items but impossible luxuries for the peasant in the poem?

Crops, livestock and working together

Village settlements were surrounded by three or four large open fields, mostly divided into smaller strips, in addition to plots owned by the lord and the parish priest.

- One of the open fields would be kept fallow each year: left for animals to graze on and also for the soil to recover from growing crops. There was the added benefit that grazing animals would add home-made fertiliser while the field was resting.

- A second field was often left by the lord as common land, on which the peasants kept livestock and from where they collected wood.

- Peasants owned several different strips of land in the two remaining fields, and these were farmed. However, the strips that each peasant owned were not in the same part of the field, for reasons of fairness. The strips might be divided by twigs, stone or earth banks to act as markers: there was not enough cultivated land to waste leaving a large gap between each strip. Although the peasants worked together and agreed on the main crop to be grown, when it should be harvested and so on, there were often disagreements over the relative size of plots and accusations of moving the markers.

- Peasants could, however, grow whatever they liked and keep a close eye on their own plots of land surrounding their houses. These personal plots were called tofts. On their tofts peasants grew vegetables and herbs, and kept bees and various livestock, including cattle, sheep, pigs and poultry.

The open field system meant that the peasants were forced to work together as a unit. It was in everyone's interest in the village to work hard and produce the greatest yield possible at harvest time. This field system caused many peasants to move away from distant hamlets and live within the village, closer to their strips of land and the common. The main crops grown in the fields were wheat, oats and barley, although this varied across different regions. Highland areas, such as Scotland and the North of England, favoured oats, barley and cattle farming. Lowland areas grew more wheat and grazed more sheep.

Not only did they need to agree on the best crop to grow on the main fields, they also had to ensure that their animals did not escape and ruin the land. Most villages had enclosures called pounds where stray animals were kept; their owner had to pay a fine for their release. Many rural villages still have their pounds or streets named after them today.

A short and miserable life?

Remember that peasants would have little time for themselves or for entertainment, other than at feast time or some small relaxation after church on a Sunday. Livestock had to be fed every day of the week, so there was never any complete rest. Work took priority for most of the daylight hours, especially in autumn and winter.

Remember too that life expectancy was significantly lower in the Middle Ages than in the twenty-first century. To live to about 40 years old was considered a very good age. Poor hygiene, poor diet and lack of medical knowledge were causes of high mortality rates, as were accidents – safety wasn't a priority at work or at home.

Question time

1. What does Source D tell us about working in the fields in medieval England?

2. What would be the gains and the losses of having strips of land in different places across a large field, rather than located all together in one area?

3. What resources would a peasant be able to get from keeping cattle, sheep, pigs and livestock?

4. Research further to find out details about housing and agriculture. Use some of these key words to help you in your search: wattle and daub, cruck, byre, fallow, three field system, bailiff, common.

5. Why is it unhistorical to say that medieval peasants led a miserable life? What conclusions can we draw about their lifestyle?

6. Using the basic outline provided below copy and add detail to make a labelled plan of a medieval village. Work individually or in groups to produce a giant version for the classroom wall. Add details of the crops grown, jobs carried out, people at work, features of homes and tofts, and anything else you can think of. Different groups could label their plans to represent different times in the calendar.

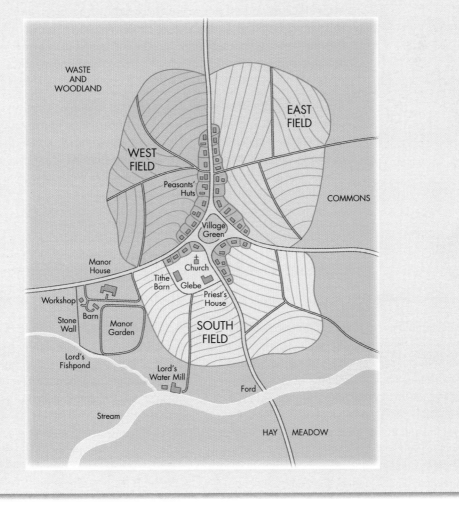

Medieval women

One of the main differences in the experience of medieval women, compared to the experiences of women in the twenty-first century, is that women were generally considered to be part of the chattels (or possessions) of men. Fathers and husbands answered for their wives and daughters in court and were responsible for their chastisement (punishment); even the Church ruled that women should be servants to their husbands. Women were thought to be inferior to men in physical, emotional and moral strength. However, some women were able to demonstrate their capability and their role in society was often more than that of being a mother and a homemaker. Some women did work as craft workers, a few became surgeons, and a widow would sometimes run her husband's business.

Wealthy women

Rich women experienced a little formal education (see page 209) and certainly some time for leisure activities, such as dancing and music, but they also helped to run their family households. As manor houses had to be self sufficient and all houses of the wealthy had a constant stream of guests, this was a demanding managerial role. Wealthy widows inherited land and fortune from their husbands, but the local lord usually arranged for a suitable remarriage to be made. The new husband would take over the responsibility of the widow's land and remaining wealth.

In towns, women could become business managers, but usually only if they took over their husband's business on his death. For example, Margery Kempe was a successful brewer in the town of Lynn (see page 180). Wives of gentry could sometimes represent their husbands in business if they were busy elsewhere. In such ways, some women were able to show their talents whilst acting as their husband's deputy.

Digging deeper

Margaret Paston – more than just the wife of a landowner

The Paston family from Norfolk is famous for its letter writing. Between 1425 and 1499 the family wrote and kept regular letters to each other and these offer us a rare insight into medieval life. Margaret Paston married into the family in 1440. She married John Paston who was training to be a lawyer in London. He spent most of his time there while she lived with her in-laws and then later ran his estates herself. Although her marriage was arranged, and in her letters she addresses her husband formally as 'Right worshipful husband', they seem to have a good and loving relationship.

John certainly trusted his wife to manage his estates in his absence. Margaret had to take care of all aspects of estate management. She had to calculate and monitor tax collection, rents and sales of produce; supervise the harvest; purchase all provisions for the estate and manor household; and negotiate with local farmers, agents and tenants on her husband's behalf.

SOURCE A

There be divers of your tenantries at Mautby that had great need for to be repaired, and the tenants be so poor that they are not a power to repair them; wherefore if it like you I would that the tenants might have rushes to repair their houses with. And also there is windfall wood at the manor that is of no great value that might help them towards reparation.

Letter to John Paston from Margaret, April 1465.

Margaret could be a compassionate lady of the manor but she took bold action when required. In one letter she describes how she has sent men to take cattle from a tenant farmer in lieu of outstanding rent. Source B concerns the serious problems Margaret had to deal with whilst John was away in London. The Pastons' letters date from the time of the Wars of the Roses (see Chapter 6), and violent attacks were more common during these years of civil war.

SOURCE B

Right worshipful husband, I recommend myself to you and ask you to get some crossbows and arrows. For this house has so few of them that none of our men can shoot out, although we have never had so much need ...

In this letter to her husband, Margaret expresses her concern for her safety.

Managing a family

In addition to managing the local political problems of the family, and the day-to-day running of their estate, Margaret also had about seven children to look after. Margaret's eldest son John gained a reputation at Court as a flirt and reveller and caused his parents concern in his reluctance to work or take life seriously, and also in his ability to spend money unnecessarily.

Margaret and her husband sent John, aged 30, to live in an estate on the Norfolk coast to prevent him damaging his reputation further and wasting more money. Margaret also had to deal with the marriages of her two daughters, one of which caused her further problems (see page 210). The Paston family letters give us a rare insight into medieval life, and especially into the daily life and routines of women because these were not normally recorded in such detail.

 ## Question time

1   You learned about the role of medieval women earlier in this chapter. Do you think that Margaret Paston was a typical medieval woman? Did she take on tasks or responsibilities which may have been unusual for a medieval woman? Make a chart to list and categorise all the different activities that Margaret is involved with.

2   How would you describe Margaret's personality?

3   Carry out additional research into either the Paston women or the role of wealthy women in medieval society. Make notes of your findings in a diagram, using your own subheadings such as education, daily life, problems, children.

4   Use the Internet or your school library to help you write a manual for a woman in medieval England who is newly married into a wealthy family. Include advice on husbands, children, running a household and dealing with the neighbours.

Village women

Women who lived in villages worked at seeding, weeding and spinning. Their main jobs were to make cloth and deal with the production and preservation of all food – as well as care for very young children. Like most jobs, spinning was a lengthy process, even after the introduction of the spinning wheel in the fourteenth century, but was seen as luxury after working in the fields. Staying at home to look after the farm was also a luxury that few families could afford for their women or their children. Medieval pictures show women carrying their spinning with them on their way to fetch water – they were obviously doing more than one job at a time! Today, unmarried women are sometimes still referred to as spinsters – the name comes from this central aspect of a medieval woman's work.

A poor woman's lack of freedom did not prevent many women from showing independent streaks. Medieval court rolls tell us of women who married without permission or who were flogged for marrying their cousins or blood relations; and of fathers who were fined for the recklessness of their daughters.

Richard de Putewey gives the lord half a mark for license to marry Agnes, daughter of Edric Trappe and take her inheritance.

Thomas Colling paid 6d for an inquiry as to whether he should have the chief chattels of his wife's parents, as she was their eldest daughter. He specifically mentions a mare, a brass pot and a large vat. The court says that all the sisters must be treated as one heir and share alike. So that Thomas's late wife would have had a half-share of the mare.

The sheriff of Shropshire held an inquest on the 26th June 1276 into complaints of the tenants of Hales, which found that if any of them married their daughters out of the manor they were to pay the lord 2s for merchet, and if within the manor 12s.

Ralf de Attewood has five daughters. The third, Alice, has married without the lord's license, for which he is fined 2s. If this happens again his goods and chattels are to be confiscated.

Lucy Edrich complains against John Edrich and Edith his wife, that they are keeping her out of a reasonable part of her father's lands. John says that their father gave the land to Edith, but the jury say that Lucy should have her share.

Records detailing the cases of independent women in the village of Halesowen, 1270–1307, taken from the court rolls.

1 Read Source D. In pairs, find evidence in these court rolls of:

   a the feudal system in operation

   b women showing independence.

2 What doesn't Source D tell us about these independent women?

3 Discuss why there are so few famous women from medieval England or why we know so little about the lives of women in medieval England.

Health and hygiene

Despite all generalisations to the contrary, medieval people did have baths, though standards of personal hygiene in medieval times were not the same as ours. Public communal baths, called 'stews', actually existed in some villages. King John was said to have had a bath every three weeks.

Dealing with dirt

Public hygiene in medieval towns was particularly poor. Roads were made from gravel or cobbles but were usually just dirt tracks. Sewage and waste was emptied into open drainage ditches or gutters in the middle of streets. These often became blocked and were not emptied very often. Townsfolk would usually just wait for a severe rainstorm to carry all the waste into the nearest river. Many toilets in towns like London emptied straight into the river. The same river would also be used for washing and cooking.

SOURCE A

A modern reproduction of a medieval water closet from Suigleton Open Air Museum, West Sussex.

The men who had the unpleasant job of occasionally emptying drainage ditches and privies (toilets) were called rakeries, or rykeries, and they were paid by the ton for the waste that they removed! This was, however, a fairly well paid job. The poor would share privies but even a private privy was really just a seat on top of a cesspit (a pit for the disposal of waste matter). In the country the manor houses would have garderobes and privies, which emptied out into a cesspit. The peasants would also have primitive chamber pots and the waste would be emptied straight onto the land. Of course the fields themselves were convenient toilets, although local laws often insisted that you went a good distance from the nearest house! The only people who were able to organise toilets where the waste was automatically washed away were monks. Monasteries were deliberately built over rivers and channels of water diverted to act as a constant flushing sewer.

It may be hard to believe but most local councils did not take action to prevent the poor conditions and hygiene in medieval towns. However, some mayors passed by-laws to prosecute people who dumped rubbish in the streets, or butchers who sold 'measly' (infected and rotting) meat (see page 214). During the Middle Ages, people did not know the scientific connection between dirt and disease, but townsfolk did not want the smell of rubbish and human and animal waste outside their front door. Local by-laws helped to prevent large-scale outbreaks of disease (epidemics).

SOURCE B

The dung that is found in the streets shall be taken out of the city in carts; or put into the dung boats.

No one of the brewers, or other persons who rent the fountains and the great upper pipe of the Great Conduit in Cheapside, shall from henceforth draw any water from the pipes that run below the Great Conduit.

No one shall throw water from the windows, but shall carry it into the streets.

Each person shall make clear of filth the front of his house under penalty of half a mark.

Such pigsties as are in the streets shall be removed; and if any swine be found in the streets, let them be forfeited.

Extracts from the regulations of the city of London concerning sanitation.

Itchy living conditions

People also suffered from inflictions caused by unhygienic living conditions. Lice and fleas were commonplace and people often had worms living in their digestive system. There was little that could be done about these irritations, other than washing and improvement in public health facilities. The crusaders sometimes took a flea picker with them to the Holy Land. This was actually a person with the job of killing fleas living on the knights themselves!

Question time

1 What does Source A tell us about health and hygiene in medieval towns?
2 Read Source B. How did the regulations in London try to combat the problem of dirty streets?

Cures and knowledge of disease

Medical experts knew very little about the human body and disease in the Middle Ages. What they did know was based on the knowledge of doctors like Hippocrates from Ancient Greece and Galen from Ancient Rome. Their research into different diseases, and their natural explanations of disease and the structure of the human body, had been recorded and passed from century to century. After the fall of the Roman Empire much of their knowledge was lost to the Western world. Arabic doctors continued to study their findings and translated them into Arabic from Greek and Latin.

In Christendom only monasteries had the skill and knowledge to study these great collections. During the medieval period, medicine was studied at a medical school in Salerno in Italy; universities did not start teaching medicine until the late twelfth century. Another reason that medieval doctors knew so little was that they did not research for themselves. Dissection (cutting up bodies to examine them) was not accepted by the Church and any form of enquiry into natural explanations was often considered heresy.

These are some of the ideas held by medieval medical experts:

- Disease is the will of God and is caused by sin.

- The human body is influenced by the movement of the planets (created by God).

- Bad air or atmosphere causes illness.

- The human body (created by God) is made up of four balanced humours. When these humours are out of balance, disease follows.

Spiritual and superstitious healing

Another popular approach to healing was for the patient to pray, offer gifts to the Church or go on a pilgrimage. In 1443, Margaret Paston promised to go on a pilgrimage for her husband during a serious illness, to Walsingham and St Leonards. His mother's response was to offer a wax statue, the same weight as her son, as a gift to 'Our Lady of Walsingham', and to send four servants to Norwich to pray with the friars there.

The influence of religion and superstition in medicine was great. Many people reported miracles of God as explanations for their recovery, but a combination of Christian and pagan ideas sometimes co-existed. Prayers to 'mother earth' to be said while picking herbs, for example, have been found in medieval manuscripts. Astrologers studied the stars and the birth details of patients and made recommendations as to a lucky day for bleeding or taking medicine. Some of the remedies used by all types of medical practitioner were based on superstition and strange logic. One cure for toothache, for example, was to heat the painful tooth with the flame from a candle; it was thought that the illness would then be driven out by the heat, causing the pain to cease.

Medieval medical experts

The physician

The most important type of medical expert in the Middle Ages was the physician. Physicians were originally all members of the Church. They had studied medicine and could use the most modern and expensive remedies of the day.

Less wealthy townsfolk and villagers visited a barber surgeon (see page 229) instead of a physician, but were generally treated at home by their wife, mother or neighbour. Knowledge of the real causes of disease was limited, and expensive treatments could just as well kill a patient as cure them; often the herbal remedies tried and tested in the countryside were more reliable.

I am grown so 'slender' that I may not be girt in any girdle I have but of one. Elizabeth Peverel [a midwife] has lain sick fifteen or sixteen weeks of the sciatica, but she sent my mother word that she would come hither when God sent time, though she would be wheeled in a barrow.

Margaret Paston writes to her husband about arrangements for the forthcoming birth of their first child, December 1441.

SOURCE D

An illustration of medieval women treating a sick man, from a fifteenth-century manuscript.

SOURCE E

Mistress Margery,

I recommend myself to you and send me as quickly as possible, by the most reliable messenger that you can get, a large plaster [poultice] for the King's attorney, James Hobart. For although his disease is only an ache in the knees, he is the man who brought you and me together. And I would rather that your plaster stopped his pain than have 40 shillings!

But when you send me the plaster you must write to me telling me how it should be put on and taken off the knee. And how long it should stay on the knee. And how long the plaster will be of any use and whether or not he must wrap any cloth around the plaster to keep it warm. And God be with you.

John Paston III's letter to his wife Margery, c. 1490.

The work of physicians

Physicians would offer treatments based on their explanation of the illness. However, as many diseases were not known or described in any detail, most treatment was guesswork. The disease 'influenza' was used to describe various types of infection; it was originally thought to be the 'influence' of the air or atmosphere.

Physicians sometimes took urine samples and examined the colour of urine to make a diagnosis. Urine charts showing different colours and different diagnoses were created. Physicians sometimes recommended that the patient drank urine as a remedy! Another common treatment was to take blood or to purge a patient through bleeding. Cuts were made in people's arms and, later, leeches were used to suck out excess blood. There were many complex herbal remedies available, some using items with natural healing powers such as lavender, vinegar and oils. However, there were also some bizarre remedies in use, such as powdered worms.

A physician treats his patient through blood letting – cutting a vein in his patient's arm. From the Luttrell Psalter, *a fourteenth-century manuscript.*

Barber surgeons – the 'hands-on' approach

Barber surgeons were responsible for treating less wealthy patients. Their strength lay in their practical skills, as their name suggests. They extracted teeth and even did amputations, in addition to cutting hair. Their trademark was their red-and-white-striped pole outside their shop. From these poles they hung the blood stained towels to dry after a busy day's surgery. This method of advertising would be unlikely to work today!

Slow progress

Some improvements in medical practice did take place during the medieval period. These included new drugs, more hospitals and new surgical techniques, some of which were gained from contact with Arabic doctors, through trade or during the Crusades. However, as we have seen, dissection was discouraged by the Church and actually banned in 1300 by the Pope. This limited progress in understanding the working of the human body. It was eventually allowed by the later Middle Ages, but physicians relied on an assistant to carry out the dissection and used it to understand the work of the Ancient Roman doctor, Galen, rather than to see how the body worked for themselves. Unfortunately, although Galen had compiled a comprehensive survey of the anatomy of the human body, he had largely dissected pigs and had therefore made some errors. These errors were not realised if the physician did not closely study the corpse.

Question time

1   Used together what do sources C, D and E tell us about much medical care in the Middle Ages?

2   Why is the physician using the treatment in Source F?

3   Cary out additional research into the medieval explanations of disease. Find out enough detail about the four humours to be able to draw a diagram with labels that explains how they worked.

4   In pairs, prepare a worksheet for another group of students studying the topic of medieval medicine. Research to find primary sources and additional information to include in your worksheet, and present information in diagram and cartoon format as well as text. Include some questions and activities for the students to work on but make sure that they can be answered from the material you provide!

Law and order, crime and punishment

Problems of law and order

The main point to realise about law and order in the medieval period is that there was no police force. There was no organisation responsible for maintaining law and order. You have already read about actions that towns took to help to prevent problems occurring. Less than one-fifth of all crimes were violent crimes against people. Most criminals were thieves who stole relatively small amounts of money or low value possessions; or they might be people charged with letting their animals stray over someone else's land. The justice system also had to deal with regulating trade and the settling of disputes over land or business. However, some violent struggles did take place. The Paston family, for example, was attacked by the Duke of Suffolk's men in a land dispute that was eventually, after a long struggle, settled in the court.

Catching the criminals

Constables

Constables were paid little in towns and villages, and had to work part time to supplement their income. They could make arrests, break up fights and prevent fires. They also held the key to the stocks, where criminals were publicly punished. The stocks were a wooden frame with holes into which the offender's feet or hands were locked (see Source A); passers-by would often throw rotten food and other waste at the criminal.

Watchmen

Most towns also had a watch: a night watchman who checked that the curfew was being maintained. The night watch was intended to prevent crime as well as catch any suspects. Watchmen were volunteers or workers who were obliged to do a duty. Some watches were organised on a rota system with different trades taking it in turns. Often watchmen made their duty time an opportunity to get together and drink and did not take the work seriously.

Hue and cry

In order to catch criminals most towns and villages relied on the system of 'hue and cry'. This system placed the responsibility on all townsfolk to intervene to stop any crime. Spectators had to raise the hue and cry – make a clamour of protest – and stop work or their daily business to chase the suspects and catch them. Villagers ignoring their social responsibility to intervene in crime could be fined.

Crime prevention

Curfews

To maintain law and order curfews were introduced. These stated that people could not leave home after a certain time each night. Curfew breakers were spotted by the night watchman and taken to court.

Contemporary portrait of a person in the stocks, from a French manuscript c. 1296.

Tithing

In order to encourage public responsibility for maintaining law and order, authority was given to groups of people through the Saxon system of tithing. Males of 12 years and over were put into groups of ten to twelve men. Each member of the group had to monitor the behaviour of the others and report on it at sessions of the mayor's court. The knowledge that your friends and work mates were watching you was intended to prevent individuals breaking the law. You were also fined if a member of your group broke the law.

Public punishment and harsh penalties

If caught for lesser deeds, criminals would be taken to the mayor's or manor court. They could be locked up temporarily but punishments tended to be issued very quickly – there were no real prisons in which to hold criminals and imprisonment itself was only a punishment for serious political prisoners. Convicts were placed in the stocks or the pillory, or they were whipped at the whipping post. Local lords might just fine a first-time thief, for example, someone caught stealing wood from the lord's land, but a repeat offender could be hanged. For serious crimes or serial offenders, mutilation and execution were common and were carried out in public as a warning to any potential criminals. Hands were often chopped off as a punishment for poaching or theft.

In general, medieval courts used to make the punishment fit the crime. For lesser cases, criminals sometimes had to wear a banner or walk around the town carrying a symbol of their crime: a large loaf of bread or a faulty piece of craftsmanship, for example. Such punishments were a form of entertainment for the public and the criminal's humiliation was intended to act as a prevention of further crime.

Implementing justice – the court system

There were several different types of court which became more organised during the Middle Ages. The most powerful court was obviously that of the king. This would deal with only the most serious offences, including treason or rebellion. For example, King Richard II and the Mayor of London ordered the execution of the leading members of the Peasants' Revolt in 1381 (see page 103).

Judges appointed by the king travelled around the country to hold courts in each area. There were also shire or county courts which were led by leading landowners, who held the position of Justices of the Peace. They oversaw the trials of slightly less serious crimes or disputes. These trials were led by the sheriff of the area who, as the king's representative, had to investigate crimes and collect any evidence to be heard by a jury. Where no evidence was available the jury made decisions based on knowledge of the character of the accused.

Hundred courts were more local and presided over by important local lords. The most local of all courts, often held weekly, was the manor court, where the lord or his bailiff would preside. In towns the mayor and council were in charge and had to maintain law and order; there were also mayors' courts. In addition to this hierarchy there were Church courts (see page 136).

Trials took approximately 15 minutes to reach a verdict. The juries in medieval courts were not chosen randomly or anonymously as they are today; medieval criminals were tried by juries who often consisted of their neighbours or fellow tradesmen. Jurors had to swear an oath on whether they thought the accused was innocent or guilty, but juries were often influenced or even bribed before the trial. There were no lawyers to represent the accused – the accused had to give his or her own evidence; witnesses spoke for and against the accused. Once this was done, juries quickly came to a decision. Until the thirteenth century, if the jury could not reach a verdict, then the decision was left to God. This was called trial by ordeal and the accused would have to carry out a series of religious tests to prove whether they were innocent or guilty.

Digging deeper

Trial by ordeal

The religious tests used to determine whether a man or woman was guilty of a crime in the early medieval period included:

- Trial by hot iron (mainly for women) and trial by hot water (mainly for men). In both these ordeals the accused would have to burn their hand badly by lifting an object that was either red-hot or by putting it in boiling water. If the wound healed cleanly after a few days then they were found to be innocent.

- Trial by cold water (usually for men). The accused was lowered into water with a rope tied around his waist. Water was believed to be pure and therefore would reveal the innocence or guilt of a person. If the accused sank (and sometimes drowned) then it was seen that the water had let him enter; the accused was then deemed to be pure and innocent.

- Trial by eating consecrated (blessed) bread. This trial was for priests. If an accused priest choked whilst eating some sacred bread then he was found guilty. The Church believed that any priest who lied would be severely punished by God.

- Trail by combat. This trial was introduced by the Normans. The victor in a duel or fight was seen to have had God's approval; the loser was deemed to be guilty and was hanged.

Trial by ordeal was really a religious ceremony and, apart from trial by cold water, was carried out inside a church. The accused fasted for three days before the trial and then a mass was said. Trial by ordeal was not used after the early thirteenth century because the Church disapproved of the methods and issued a ban.

Isabella Porter is attached to reply to Matilda Alured on a charge of keeping a sow which killed and ate 14 young ducks belonging to the said Matilda.

John Davey, on the feast of St Mary Magdalen, arrested Joan Bacoun, took her to Robert Sayer's house in the suburb, locked the door and imprisoned her, stripped her of her clothes and with drawn sword assaulted her. Whereupon the wife of Robert Sayer raised the hue and cry.

Henry Derex is accused of being found with a long knife after the ringing of the last bell, against the custom of the town.

John Knight and Rose his wife, being lepers, roam in the market place, selling and buying geese and capons. They are accustomed to embrace and kiss children whereby they may, as many think, take the leprosy. Their removal is demanded.

Henry Fylbrigge, William Paccard, Thomas Causton and the servant of Thomas Whitmersh are charged with being common gamblers and dice players who shut themselves up in their houses until the early morning, then stripping off their clothes they go home naked, to the scandal of the people.

Details of offences from the Colchester court rolls, 1310. This shire or borough court was dealing with offences against the peace and petty crimes. The court also wanted to preserve the reputation of Colchester.

A system under pressure?

The law and order system in medieval England was based on Anglo-Saxon methods, but it began to show weaknesses as people became more mobile. As peasants were released from their manors it became increasingly hard for sheriffs, bailiffs or constables to track down criminals or try them using evidence. The effectiveness of the system also varied with individual monarchs. Henry V was a strong leader who made sure that the courts worked efficiently; he sent judges around the country more regularly and he sometimes took action himself, intervening in serious local disputes. Henry VI, in contrast, did nothing to tackle crime. For example, when the Paston family was being attacked again by a neighbouring family (see page 223) Henry ordered the sheriff to choose a jury whose sympathies lay against the Pastons. During the medieval period as a whole, however, more judges were appointed and the court system became more complex, though weaknesses in the system remained. It was, however, cheap to run and, despite the weaknesses, stayed almost untouched for several hundred years.

Question time

1   In groups, study the court rolls of Colchester (Source B).

   a   What sort of crimes have been taken to these hundred courts? Are most of the crimes against people, property or the peace – or in another category?

   b   What does the extracts tell us about the role of women in medieval society?

2   In groups, try to establish the weaknesses in the medieval law and order system. Focus on:

   a   catching criminals

   b   their trial

   c   the methods of punishments.

Write up your findings in a report but explain the strengths of the law and order system too.

1   Work in threes to explain as much as you can remember about life in medieval England using the word box below. One person chooses one word and talks about it, then explains how it links to another word in the box, and so on. Keep talking until you run out of links and then let the second person try to cover more words than you did – if possible using more specific knowledge. The quality of the connection and explanation is really more important than how many links you can make. The third person in the group has to judge the quality of the explanation – based on what information is used, how many key words are tackled, and how complicated the ideas are that are explained, and so on.

guilds	disease	freemen
feudal system		entertainment
regulations	villein	Church
freedom	boon work	markets
three field system		population
taxes	journeyman	children
guildmaster	public health	women

When you have finished you can compile your own word boxes for three other people to work on. Take it in turns to be the judge – and choose difficult words as a challenge.

2   Was it better to be a medieval townsperson than a peasant? Work in groups to argue for or against town life in the Middle Ages. One group should represent rural living and argue for its advantages and the dangers of town living; the other group should argue against village life and for the town. You could argue over several different points but you will need to organise them logically and find examples as evidence. Some issues to consider are: entertainment, work, health and hygiene, medical care, the environment and freedom.

3   One historian gave this interpretation of work in the Middle Ages:

'It was a hand-made world throughout, a world without power, a world in which all things were made one by one, a slow world, dependent upon human muscular power and the muscular power of animals, a slow world.'

Using your knowledge of life and work in this period, write an essay to explain how far you agree with this interpretation. You will need to plan your answer and include different paragraphs per point or theme covered. Use plenty of examples to support your ideas.

4   In groups prepare either a museum display or a script for the tour guide of a medieval castle, village or town. Focus on the differences between the experiences of rich and poor people in the Middle Ages, and inform your audience about the many different aspects of medieval life. You will need to carry out additional research before you start to plan your work.

Further reading

Kevin Crossley-Holland, *The Seeing Stone* (Orion Children's, 2000)

Cynthia Harnett, *Ring out Bow Bells* (London, 1953)

Tony McAleavy, *Life in A Medieval Castle* (English Heritage, 1998)

Martyn Whittock (Ed), *The Pastons in Medieval England* (Heinemann, 1993)

Barbara Willard, *The Miller's Boy* (Macdonald Children's, 1989)

11 Boils, bodies and shockwaves

SOURCE A

An illustration of a mass burial in Tournai in the Netherlands, 1349.

SOURCE B

A fourteenth-century illustration showing Death as the King of All, from a fifteenth-century Italian manuscript.

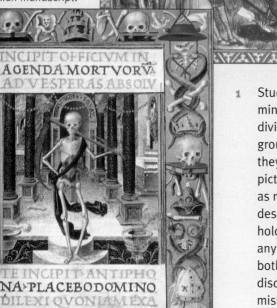

1   Study Sources A and B for a couple of minutes. Then cover up the pictures. Now divide into groups of three. Two of the group members should each describe what they can remember about one of the pictures without looking back at it. Include as much information as you can in your description. The third group member can hold the sources and make a quick note of any aspects that the others miss. When both have finished their descriptions, discuss which aspects of the source were missed and what aspects were most easily remembered.

2 In the same groups, make two lists of all the questions that you would like answered about Sources A and B. Start by asking questions about small details in the picture and then try to ask wider questions that spring to mind. Collect your questions as a class inside a big circle – with the small observation questions in the middle, working out to the wider questions on the outskirts of the circle.

3 Read the information box below.

a Having read this information, return to your circle of questions. Tick off any which have now been answered.

b Add any more questions to the diagram that you can now think of. We often need to know a little about a topic before we can make sense of it and think of all the investigating which can be done.

c Discuss which questions you might have answered only in part, or which you might have some suggestions for. You are just starting your investigation, so feel free to use words like 'perhaps', 'possibly', 'could' and 'might' in your discussions.

Answering questions about the Black Death

Sources A and B both relate to the Black Death, a deadly disease that swept through Europe in the fourteenth century. In the Middle Ages there were many infectious disease which often killed people. Leprosy, for example, was a disfiguring skin disease; however, few cases existed and those who did catch it were easily isolated in special buildings. Deaths from contagious diseases like tuberculosis, measles and whooping cough were also common, and crowded living conditions sometimes meant that diseases reached epidemic proportions, affecting many hundreds and sometimes thousands of people. But by far the worst epidemic of all was that of the Black Death; millions of people were infected across Europe and few people who caught the disease survived.

The Black Death killed nearly one half of the population of England, which was about 3.5 million before 1348. The Black Death hit England and Ireland in 1348 and Scotland and Wales in 1349. It returned again in 1361–2, 1368–9 and in 1375. The outbreak of 1348–9 killed most people; London's population is thought to have dropped from 70,000 to 40,000 in two years. There were smaller outbreaks all through the medieval period, until the Great Fire of London in 1666. Although we have no exact records it is estimated that 1.5 million people died in England as a result of the plague. In Europe 20 million people died in just four years, during the main spread of the disease between the years of 1347 and 1351.

The Black Death

Why was the Black Death so important?

Contemporary writers called the plague the Great Dying or Great Pestilence. It became known as the Black Death as a result of the black pus-filled boils, called buboes, which emerged in the victim's armpits and groin. The Black Death is important in history not only because of the number of people (and animals and birds) it killed. It gives us great insight into medieval beliefs and understanding and is also important for the changes that it brought to society. Any society losing such vast numbers of its population needs to adjust to that loss, and English society had to do just that. The Black Death changed people's attitudes and freedoms, as you will see.

What caused the Black Death?

People at the time had no certain idea about the causes of the Black Death. The most common explanation for disease, as well as many other events in the Middle Ages, was a divine one. God was seen as being in control of people's lives. However, as the scale of the Black Death became apparent, people began to wonder about alternative explanations. They were desperate to work out the causes of the disease and to take effective action against it – especially after all the praying didn't seem to be working.

Other explanations for the disease were:

- Astrology: the movement of the planets and the stars.

- Strangers in town were blamed and used as scapegoats.

- Jewish people were often accused of poisoning local wells and deliberately spreading the plague.

- Bad or corrupt air, made worse by dirty streets and living conditions.

- A stare from an infected person was thought to spread the disease.

- Three interesting theories were over-eating, sexual relations with an older woman and disobedient children.

What was it like to catch the disease?

Though medieval doctors had no scientific explanation as to why the disease was spread, they described it effectively – in great detail! Guy de Chauliac, physician to the Pope at Avignon, described what he thought were two different forms of the Black Death. These were the bubonic plague, which brought fever and large pus-filled buboes or boils, and the pneumonic plague, which attacked the lungs and was more deadly. According to Chauliac, when the buboes burst they stank! There was also a third strain of the Black Death which Guy de Chauliac did not notice – septicaemic plague, where blood poisoning set in so quickly that the victim did not live long enough to show any of the other symptoms.

Painting of monks with the boils of the Black Death, from a manuscript c. 1370.

SOURCE B

We see death coming into our midst like black smoke, a plague which cuts off the young, and has no mercy for the fair of face. Woe is me of the shilling in the armpit; it is seething, terrible, wherever it may come, a white lump that gives pain and causes a loud cry, a burden carried under the arms, a painful angry knob. It is of the form of an apple, like the head of an onion, a small boil that spares no one. Great is its seething, like a burning cinder.

A contemporary Welsh poet, Ieuan Gethin, describes the finding of a buboe as the terrible 'shilling in the armpit'.

SOURCE C

... in men and women alike it first showed itself by the emergence of certain tumours in the groin or in the armpits, some of which grew as large as an apple, others an egg ... the deadly tumours began to multiply and spread in all directions over the body ... After this, it changed; black spots appearing on the body ... these spots were a sure sign of approaching death ... almost all died within three days.

... it was not just by speaking to or being near a sick person that one could die, but any that touched the clothes of the sick or anything that had been used by them seemed thereby to catch the disease ... The rags of a poor man who died of the disease were thrown into the street. Two hogs came hither and took the rags between their teeth and tossed them to and fro ... whereupon almost immediately, they gave a few turns and fell down dead.

A passage about the Black Death, adapted from the Decameron, *a story written in the 1300s.*

Digging deeper

Modern scientific explanations of the Black Death

The germ that caused the Black Death was only discovered in the nineteenth century. The bacillus (disease-producing bacteria) was known by the Latin name *Pasturella pestis*. It was found to live in the bloodstream of the black rat, as well as on the fleas living on the rat. It was thought that the fleas transferring to human beings from rats spread the bubonic plague (accompanied by boils or buboes). This is not the only way in which the plague is thought to have spread. The second form of the plague which Chauliac identified – the pneumonic plague (see page 237) – was spread by germs from person to person. This airborne form of the disease was highly contagious, and spread very quickly. The recent cases of anthrax in the USA remind us of how deadly such airborne diseases are, and how much fear is involved during an outbreak.

The spread of the plague

N

Key
- Areas affected by plague 1347
- Areas newly affected June 1348
- Areas newly affected Dec. 1348
- Areas newly affected June 1349
- Areas newly affected Dec. 1349
- Areas unaffected by Jan. 1350

Melcombe • London
Cologne
Paris
Vienna
Bordeaux
Venice
Genoa
Marseilles
Leghorn
Seville
Naples
Constantinople

The spread of the plague, 1347–50.

From country to country

The Black Death came from Asia. The fact that it then spread such a great distance and so quickly tells us that the trade and communications network was more advanced than we might otherwise expect. Rats on ships from the Crimea must have spread the fleas to rats on European ships, and in turn to rats in coastal towns, wagons and barges in the south of England. The black rat was probably found in most houses and carts in the country. Many medieval houses were home to animals as well as families, and public hygiene was limited, so rats and therefore their own parasitic fleas were common.

The plague spread from the Crimea to Sicily, then to northern Italy and on to Marseilles in France. From France it headed north to Normandy and then to southern England. Its arrival in England is attributed to a sailor from Gascony in France, who landed at a small port in Dorset called Melcombe Regis in June 1348. The spread of the Black Death was worsened by a mild winter in 1348–9, which failed to kill off the deadly germs, and then a hot summer in 1349, which allowed the disease to spread more quickly. However, these are modern explanations of the spread of the Black Death – the medieval doctor had no such explanations.

From person to person

The disease itself could be passed from person to person in two ways, and led to different symptoms:

- Bubonic plague was spread via the bloodstream, from bites from fleas. This form of the plague resulted in the characteristic swellings – or buboes (see Source B). Not everybody who contracted bubonic plague died; many people survived the infection.

- Pneumonic plague was spread via respiration – breathing in the germs. This was a more deadly strain of the disease that was highly contagious and almost always fatal.

Was the plague incurable?

You will have probably worked out the answer to this question. Scientists today are able to vaccinate against most infectious diseases and give a scientific treatment so long as the diseases are diagnosed quickly. Medieval doctors did not understand the scientific causes of disease so they were unable to cure it. Doctors could ease the symptoms, for example by bursting the buboes and relieving the pain. Doctors also bled patients to restore the balance of the humours (see page 227), but otherwise there was little that could be done for their patients. Victims had to wait in fear and pain to see if they would be lucky – or not.

Taking action

There were so many possible explanations about the causes of the Black Death that people carried out any actions which they thought might possibly make a difference.

- Victims were bled and given laxatives to remove blood or bad humours from the body.

- Dried toads were placed on the buboes to draw out the poison.

- Butchery regulations were set to keep streets clean from blood and animal intestines, and thus the insects and animals they attracted.

- The clothes of the victims were burnt. This was a dangerous task since the disease could be spread by contact with victims' clothes. Those who volunteered for this task therefore took to wearing protective clothing – long snouts to cover their faces, and gloves.

- Towns were closed to people leaving or visiting. Quarantine restrictions badly affected trade.

- Streets were cleared of muck heaps and rotting waste of every description.

- The number of mourners allowed at a funeral was limited. Times for funerals were restricted to keep relatives who might have been infected off the streets in the middle of the day.

- In their fear, some towns wrongly blamed the spread of the plague on its Jewish inhabitants – they became scapegoats (see page 150). Jews were tortured and forced to confess to poisoning wells and deliberately infecting people with the Black Death. They were punished, and some were killed.

Question time

1 Research to find a full description of the symptoms of different types of plague and produce a booklet like one which could have been produced by Guy de Chauliac, describing common features and chances of survival. Make sure you include lots of detail to help a medieval doctor in his job, but be careful not to include anything that you have learnt about the plague which comes from modern scientific knowledge.

2 With which type of plague are the monks in Source A infected, and how might they have caught it?

3 With reference to the map on page 239, research to find out about other specific places that the plague spread to, when it affected each country, region or town, and what the effects were.

4 Which, if any, of the medieval solutions to the Black Death do you think might have helped to cut down the spread of the disease?

Digging deeper

Penitents and flagellation

One reaction to the Black Death was considered by many onlookers to be rather hysterical. Processions took place in northern Europe, where groups of people performed a public penance in the hope that God would spare them from the plague. They were called penitents, and they beat themselves with whips of hard, knotted leather with little iron spikes. Such beating is called flagellation, so the penitents were called flagellants.

Groups of 50 to 500 men, often monks, travelled from town to town to demonstrate their dedication. They carried out their act of penitence in the centre of a town, often in a market square or in front of an important building. The penitents would throw themselves onto the ground in the shape of a cross, then stand up and beat their upper bodies until bruised or bloody. According to the medieval chronicler, Friossart, women sometimes followed the penitents with cloths to catch their blood, believing that it had miraculous powers and, if smeared upon themselves, would protect them from death.

The flagellant processions lasted for 33 and a half days before the group would disband and return home. This was to symbolise the 33 and a half years that Christ was alive on earth. Such processions travelled through Hungary,

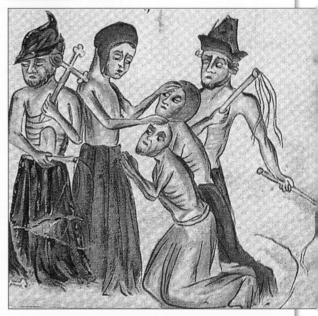

Contemporary illustration of a medieval flagellant procession.

Flanders, France and Germany during the years of the Black Death. One group visited England and beat themselves outside St Paul's Cathedral in London, but they received little support. They were condemned by the Church, banned from France by the king, and ordered to be suppressed by the Pope.

How did towns and villages cope with the epidemic?

Usually only the rich had formal funerals; there were common graves, or pits, for the poor. However, when there was no one to perform a funeral, then the rich had to be buried in this way too. During the plague epidemic, priests in Somerset were so scared of being infected by the disease that they refused to give last rites to the dying. This meant that the victims not only died a painful death, they also would not go to heaven with a blessing from God.

Sometimes the huge numbers of corpses meant that they were left rotting in the streets or fields. You can probably imagine the additional problems that this caused. In Provence in France, some greedy men, called gavoti, were keen to make money from the increased rates of pay offered to grave diggers. These opportunists suffered, however, because many ended up infected with the disease themselves.

Towns were particularly affected. For example, over 50 per cent of the population of Bristol and Winchester died.

Question time

1 Describe several reasons why the Black Death spread so quickly through medieval towns.

2 Do you think that the rich were less likely to catch the Black Death than the poor?

Digging deeper

Contemporary voices

Not many, but some, of the actions taken to try to combat the Black Death made some impact. Writers advised that people should take more care with cleanliness, especially if they were in contact with the sick (see Source E). Other writers wrote of the terrible impact the plague had had (Sources F and H), or despaired about their future (Source G).

SOURCE E

Relations and doctors who visit plague victims on entering their houses should open the windows so that the air is renewed, and wash their hands with vinegar and rose water and also their faces, especially around the mouth and nostrils. It is also a good idea before entering the room to place in your mouth several cloves and eat two slices of bread soaked in the best wine and then drink the rest of the wine. Then when leaving the room you should douse yourself and your pulses with vinegar and rose water and touch your nose frequently with a sponge soaked in vinegar. Take care not to stay too close to the patient.

Contemporary advice on how to avoid the plague, written by Tommaso del Garbo.

SOURCE F

A great plague raged in 1349 and this graveyard was specially consecrated. There are more than 50,000 bodies of the dead here. God have mercy on their souls. Amen.

An inscription from 1349 found in Spittlecroft churchyard, London.

SOURCE G

Man and wife with their children travelled the same road, the road of death. To stop these notable events from perishing with time and fading from memory, I have set them down in writing while waiting among the dead for the coming of death. And to stop the writing perishing with the writer, I leave the parchment for the work to be continued in case in future any human survivor should remain.

John of Clyn, an Irish friar, writing in 1349.

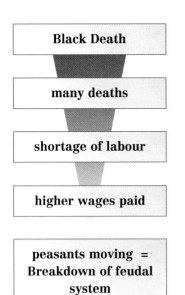

These words were scratched in Latin on a church wall in Ashwell, Hertfordshire. They say: '1349, the pestilence; 1350, pitiless, wild, violent; 1350, the dregs of the people live to tell the tale'.

Question time

1 Why would the author of Source E believe that his advice would help to prevent catching the Black Death?

2 What do Sources E–H tell us about contemporary attitudes towards the Black Death?

How much was England affected by the Black Death?

Work, wages and freedom

If the same proportion of people who were killed by the Black Death were affected today, about 20 million people would die in its clutches. Because so many people, particularly peasants, died of the disease this led to a shortage of labour. Lords, who relied on their peasants to farm their land and as a source of income, became desperate. They were forced to pay more to each peasant worker in order to keep him or her on their land. Wages rose so much that Edward III had to issue new coins, called groats and half-groats (a groat was worth 4 pence), as larger denominations (values and sizes) of currency were needed. However, because they could earn higher wages and were in greater demand, some peasants left their own lords in search of higher pay elsewhere.

It was not only men whose lives changed during the Black Death. Prior to 1349 women were paid far less and could not get the better jobs within a village or town. The labour shortage meant that working opportunities increased for women, as did their wages. The flow diagram summarises the changes to English society and economy as a result of the Black Death.

Black Death

↓

many deaths

↓

shortage of labour

↓

higher wages paid

↓

peasants moving = Breakdown of feudal system

The government tried to stop this new development by issuing an ordinance in 1349. Then, in 1351, it sent the Statute of Labourers to every sheriff and county in the kingdom.

The Statute of Labourers 1351

Due to the number of people killed by the pestilence, and seeing that the landowners have limited workers to help, the King ordains the following:

1. *Every able person under the age of 36 who is not a craftsman must work for his lord for the same wages as before the plague.*

2. *Any worker or servant leaving his lord's services without cause or licence should be imprisoned.*

3. *A man must not pay his servant more than the above wages, on pain of a fine of twice the labourer's wage.*

4. *A lord of town or manor must not pay his servant more than the above wages, on pain of a fine of thrice the labourer's wage.*

5. *Any craftsman charging more for his goods or service than pre-plague levels should be imprisoned.*

6. *Traders and merchants overcharging for their goods will pay a fine of three times the amount.*

7. *Traders and merchants overcharging for their goods will pay a fine of three times the amount.*

8. *Anyone giving alms to the poor or gifts to beggars will be imprisoned. This is to ensure that they carry out rightful employment.*

Summary of the Statute of Labourers

a. The statute set maximum pay rates (at 1346–7 levels), so that peasants could no longer bargain for the best possible pay.

b. It confirmed the rights of manorial lords to claim free labour from the serfs.

c. It made arrangement for the return to manors of runaway serfs.

In reality the Statute of Labourers was not effectively enforced and some people chose to ignore its orders. However, it was successful in preventing wages from getting out of hand and villages from becoming even more deserted, and in these ways it stabilised society.

Glossary

Pestilence	plague
Ordains	orders, instructs
Licence	permission
Thrice	three times

Question time

1. In pairs, explain each of the stages on the flow diagram on page 244.

2. Write a paragraph to explain how the Black Death helped break down the feudal system.

3. What types of people would have been affected by the Statute of Labourers?

4. What were the punishments ordered for:

   a. labourers and craftsmen who broke the Statute

   b. disobedient lords, mayors and men with servants?

   What conclusions do these answers give you about society after the Black Death?

5. Point 7 was not intended to protect the lords or ensure that rates of pay were capped – so why do you think that it was passed?

Shockwaves in land, agriculture and the Church

Changes in farming

Some lords responded to the labour crisis and the Statute of Labourers arising from the Black Death by changing the way in which they managed their estates. Sheep farming was far less labour intensive and therefore became more popular. Grazing animals on abandoned land brought some extra income to landlords and tenants. In some parts of the country landowners also began to split their land into smaller, hedged-off sections to be cultivated privately, rather than have open fields. This process, called enclosure, was extended in later centuries. Many landowners were forced to develop more efficient methods of farming because their labour supply had run dry.

SOURCE A

Aerial view of land farmed by the 'open field' system of agriculture.

SOURCE B

Aerial view of land farmed by the 'patchwork quilt' method of enclosure.

Changes in land ownership

Owing to the massive population drop resulting from the Black Death there was much more land available. Some land was totally abandoned after the Black Death, and some villages were deserted. A particularly high proportion of villages was lost in Northumberland. Most villages certainly shrank in size. Some landowners and tenants left their land temporarily, to return after the epidemic had passed. Some landowners turned their land into parkland because they had fewer peasants to work for them; unworked land was also taken over by heirs or distant family members.

Landowners also leased out increasingly large plots of land which they could not manage themselves – often they could not afford the extra wages that their villeins now demanded. The local manorial records, called account rolls, of villages in medieval Suffolk show that in the 70 years following the Black Death cases of landowners leasing out land more than tripled. This meant that, in the long term, tenant farmers took the opportunity to increase their own land holding. Some men traded labour for rent to their landlords and so farmed larger areas of land for themselves. This trading process is called commutation. The farming families who gradually gained land in the fourteenth century often became important smaller farmers in later centuries. In the long term, this meant that more wealth spread to the working peasants, and they were able to spend more money on luxuries such as clothes and stone building.

Changes in Church communities

It was not only landowners and workers who were affected by the Black Death – the Church was also hit. Although some monasteries actually turned away the sick to prevent monks and nuns being infected, many continued to treat victims in their infirmaries and therefore caught the disease themselves. Priests who did not belong to a monastery – secular priests – were also at risk. Parishes often lost their priest and therefore the use of their parish church; in Suffolk, two-thirds of the Church offices became vacant after 1349. Communities that grew up around churches were sometimes lost.

Percentage of priests who died from the Black Death.

Exeter	50
Winchester	49
Norwich	49
Ely	48
Lincoln	44
York	39

SOURCE C

The death of workers and livestock in the plague had a disastrous effect upon farming. However, the drastic fall in population meant that there was enough food to feed those who survived.

In the same year there was a great loss of sheep everywhere in the realm, so that in one place more than 5000 sheep died in a single pasture; and they rotted so much that neither beast nor bird would approach them. And there was a great cheapness of all things for fear of death, for very few took any account of riches or of possessions of any kind. A man could have a horse which was formerly worth forty shillings for half a mark [6s 8d], a big fat ox for four shillings, a cow for 12d, a sheep for 3d, a lamb for 2d, a large pig for 5d, and a stone of wool for 9d.

At this time there was so great a scarcity of priests everywhere that many churches were left destitute, lacking divine offices, masses, matins, vespers, and sacraments. Within a short while, however, a great multitude of men, whose wives had died in the plague, flocked to take orders, many of whom were illiterate, and almost laymen, except they could read a little but without understanding.

The impact of the Black Death in the years 1348–9 described by the chronicler Henry Knighton.

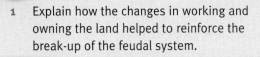

Question time

1   Explain how the changes in working and owning the land helped to reinforce the break-up of the feudal system.

2   Who lost and who gained from the changes in land and agriculture after the Black Death?

3   Source C can be divided up into smaller extracts based on two main themes:

   a   effects of the Black Death on the Church

   b   effects of the Black Death on the countryside.

   Make a list of two other things about the Black Death that this source tells us.

Political implications of the Black Death

> **SOURCE D**
>
> The Scots, hearing of the cruel pestilence in England, imagined that it had come about at the hand of an avenging God, and they adopted it as an oath, according to the common report, under the form, when they wished to swear, 'by the foul death of England'. And thus believing that a terrible vengeance of God had overtaken the English, they gathered in Selkirk forest with the intention of invading the kingdom of England. There the horrible death overtook them, and their ranks were thinned by sudden and terrible mortality, so that in a short time about 5000 had perished. And as the rest, some strong, some feeble, were preparing to return to their own country, they were surprised by pursuing Englishmen, who killed a very great number of them …
>
> *Henry Knighton describes the Scots' attempt to invade England in the early years of the Black Death, 1348–9.*

Source D illustrates one problem that was made worse by the Black Death – that of invading enemies. The chaos in England meant that the Scots took advantage of the panic and attempted an invasion. However, the deadly disease itself stopped the political effects of the epidemic from being far worse because many of the invaders died. Wars against France stopped during this period too. A history textbook written in the 1930s summed up the situation: 'While it lasted no one could think about wars, or about anything, except keeping well.'

Changing attitudes

Think back to the news coverage seen in Autumn 2001 on the anthrax cases in the USA. How much more terrified would people have been if doctors had no effective cures for this deadly disease? Now consider the effects of such an epidemic on the mentality or attitude of medieval people, who did not know how to cure disease or stop it spreading. There are facts about the ways in which people reacted to the Black Death that might help us to find out something about what people of the time thought and how they felt:

- There was religious hysteria, for example the flagellant processions in Europe (see page 242).

- Some people were used as scapegoats, for example anti-Semitic attacks increased in England during this period (see page 150).

- The medieval writer, Boccacio (see page 179), wrote about people who stopped showing any restraint in their lives, and lived for the day even if it meant committing sins of the flesh.

- Chroniclers such as Henry Knighton wrote about thieves and criminals who flocked to big cities, and the looting that took place there. Towns suffered more than villages with a lack of law and order.

Obsessed with death

The extent and speed of the plague epidemic caused a morbid obsession with death. People had absolutely no certainty in their lives – apart from the power of Death. Death was personified in art, being represented as a human, usually a skeleton, that caused havoc (see Source B on page 235). Some people became more obsessed with the religious teachings about Judgement Day, when all souls would be judged by God.

New questions about medicine and disease

The Black Death also influenced attitudes towards disease itself. In the short term doctors and teachers became scarce as populations were wiped out by the plague. However, after the Black Death passed, attitudes towards medicine began to change. People no longer had such strong faith that God was the cause of every disease; the Black Death had seemed to affect people indiscriminately. Physicians and scholars began to investigate medicine more carefully. More medical schools were opened in Europe and most monarchs received personal health advice from an expert doctor.

Activity time

1   Look back to Sources A and B on page 235 to see how it illustrates any of the following reactions to the Black Death: fear, wonder, lack of restraint, panic, depression, questioning.

2   Research other examples of people's attitudes towards the Black Death. Can you find any other sources which show Death as a person?

3   Collect evidence about the effects of the Black Death throughout England. In groups design a large diagram with different sections representing different aspects of life that were affected by the epidemic. Decide on your own headings and collect examples of the plague's effects under each one. On your diagram see if you can decide which effects were:

a   permanent

b   long-term

c   temporary

d   short-term.

Add a symbol and key to show this where you can.

Digging deeper

How far was the Black Death a turning point in English society?

The simple answer to this complex question is 'not as much as you would expect', or at least, society did not suddenly change after the initial outbreak of the plague in 1348–9. Historians make two main points about the effects of the Black Death:

- Many of the changes in society had started before the first outbreak.

- A combination of gradual change and recurrent plague epidemics led to long-term changes in land ownership and the economy.

In the 20 years following the Black Death, landowners' incomes fell only by 10 per cent. This would suggest that lords did manage to maintain their workforce and number of tenants. In populated areas lords could easily replace tenants and thereby maintain their income from rent. In areas that were badly affected by the plague, the lack of workers meant that some villages were deserted, but this rarely happened as a direct result of the Black Death – other factors were usually involved.

It was the effects of several more bouts of plague, which returned for several smaller, localised and often urban epidemics, that reduced the population permanently. The population fell quite dramatically and only began to rise again in the fifteenth century. The long-term effects on the population were drastic. It is estimated that it did not reach the pre-plague level until as late as the seventeenth century. Historians also point out that in many parts of the country the population was falling even before 1349, as a result of famine, rising prices and social unrest. You can see from these interpretations that the long-term effects of the Black Death on England is a complex topic to investigate.

Activity time

1   Create a flow diagram to show the relationship between an already falling population, different outbreaks of plague and the overall population decrease.

2   On a large piece of paper draw a set of weighing scales. Now weigh up the varied effects of the Black Death, listing all the negative effects on one side, and all the positive effects on the other. You could include subheadings on each side for different groups in society, for example, the Church, landowners and peasants.

3   When you have completed your list draw the scales at an angle to show how much you think that the positive outweighed the negative, or vice versa. Discuss the problems and difficulties in making this decision in pairs and then with the rest of your class.

4   Return to Sources A and B on page 235. In groups explain what is going on in each source using as much knowledge as you can. Using the text you have read in this chapter, explain what message the medieval artist was trying to give.

5   Search on the Internet and in your library to find a range of other primary sources about the Black Death. Share your sources in groups then decide:

   a   which individual sources tell you the most about the Black Death

   b   which two sources you think best sum up the Black Death – they do not have to be the sources which tell us the most. Write a short paragraph explaining why these sources are your chosen ones.

11 Assessment section

1 Your task is to write a medieval story about the Black Death. It should include plenty of historical detail, some additional research, a carefully planned plot and some central characters to whom people might relate. Use a planning grid on a big piece of paper, based on the one below, to work out the main features of your story.

Main plots	Main characters and their features / personality / background	Possible scenes and cliff hangers
Sub plots	Smaller characters and their details	Key words, details and facts to include

Here are some hints for getting a top grade for your story – use them as a checklist:

- No anachronisms – try not to include ideas, details, or words and sayings that obviously come from a different period.

- Include different attitudes and points of view from different characters in your story – not everyone nowadays agrees with each other and neither would they have done so then.

- Include small details from daily life, which will make your story both more realistic and more interesting. It may help to look back at the previous chapter to include facts and descriptions of homes, food, medicine and other aspects of medieval life, for example, the feudal system. It might also help to look back through all the primary sources and use some of the ideas that they contain. You will get marks for interesting details that you have researched.

- Try to include scenes in a town as well as a village.

- Try to include different aspects of life during the Black Death in your story. For example, you could mention different explanations of the disease in one scene; gruesome descriptions of the disease's symptoms in another; and the plague's effects on a range of different people and places.

- Think carefully about your opening scene – it needs to be exciting and interesting enough to make the reader want to read more!

- You might want to add an epilogue (concluding section), or an extra scene, which is set many years after the Black Death, looking back at its effects on the story's characters and English society in general.

- Your plots do not all have to be about the Black Death: include some action, some love, some arguments, some business – all the ingredients that you see in your favourite soap opera!

Further reading

J. Burnap, *Dragonscale Summer* (Blackie, 1980)

Susanna Gregory, *A Plague on both your Houses* (Warner, 1996)

Penelope Lively, *Astercote* (Puffin, 1987)

12 The changing scene of medieval England

The term the 'Middle Ages' suggests that this period in European history is less important than those that came directly before and after it; it is sandwiched between the mighty Roman Empire and the dynamic Renaissance. The Middle Ages were also known as the 'Dark Ages' which further reinforces this interpretation. In this final chapter, you will decide whether it is fair to suggest that the medieval period was one of total darkness and lack of achievement. You will also gain an overview of the main features of this period and look for patterns in the past.

Activity time

Get ready to create a map of the Middle Ages

As you read this chapter, you will need to discuss the issues raised and search back through your earlier work to create a large map of the events and changes of this period. This could be based on a timeline, century by century, but you will need to leave plenty of room for different sections and themes. You should also be on the lookout for chain reactions or connections between different events and changes – and add them to your medieval map with arrows and labels. By making links between entries on your timeline you will see the extent to which history is a series of interconnections. You will also see that the history of a supposedly backward period in the past is certainly not simple.

Power and the people

The medieval period brought about significant changes in the political control of monarchs but also in the basic freedoms of the people. By the end of the Middle Ages:

- Monarchs began to realise that ruling by force meant they ran the risk of being beaten by an enemy with a stronger army. Civil wars and revolts against monarchs like Henry I and Edward II demonstrate this.

- Monarchs began to use the law and the support of powerful people in a parliament to secure their rule.

- Parliament became more powerful, gaining freedom of speech and the right to control the monarch's finances. This prevented monarchs gaining total or absolute control.

- A relationship emerged between monarch and Parliament. Parliament drafted legislation and the monarch then approved it and agreed not to alter agreed laws or statutes.

- Under Henry II and Edward I, England increased its power over Wales, Scotland and Ireland. Relations with these countries remained tense.

- English lords had gained and lost land in France.

- People were no longer tied to the strict hierarchy of the feudal system. New groups like merchants and townsmen gained power.

- Peasants could leave their manors and be paid for the work that they did.

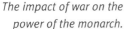

Question time

1 Look back to find specific examples of revolts by the people, or monarchs being challenged with force by their enemies. Add dates and key details to your medieval map.

2 Would any of these changes be likely to cause problems for future kings? Discuss your ideas with a partner.

The causes of political change

Many factors created these changes in the power and politics of the country. One example is the impact of war on the power of the monarch.

The impact of war on the power of the monarch.

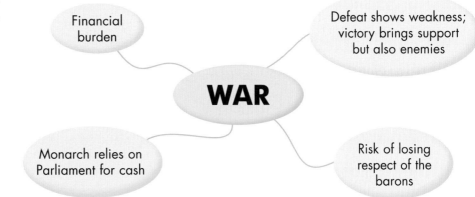

Other causes of political change were:

- population decrease

- increased trade and the power of merchants

- some monarchs were hampered by the mistakes of their fathers and grandfathers.

Question time

1. Discuss the diagram above and find medieval examples to illustrate as many points as you can.

2. How did the decrease in population in the fourteenth century lead to the removal of many feudal ties?

3. If trade was becoming more important to England, how would this affect the political importance of those involved in trade? Can you link the growth of towns to the increasing influence of Parliament? If so, add a link to your medieval map.

4. Edward I is one example of a king whose actions were strongly influenced by his father and grandfather. Research back in your notes or this book to find out how John's problems with Wales, France and the barons, followed by Henry II's failure in France, led to Edward's attempts to strengthen his position as king.

Medieval living

Life in 1485 was very different from that in 1100. Not only had the population changed but people's freedom and their quality of life had changed also. Another major development was the growth of towns.

Changing population

By the mid-thirteenth century the population of England had almost tripled. As a result the land was over-used and the gap between rich and poor increased as landlords profited from the rise in the number of available workers. In the 100 years after the Black Death the population of England decreased massively. From information in Chapter 11 you will know how this massive fall in population changed the lives of people in England. Population change is connected with all the other changes in medieval society.

The end of serfdom

Before the Black Death the freedom of peasants was actually declining. As population rose, available land decreased and lords realised that they needed to ensure a loyal and static workforce. The rise in corn prices meant that a lord could make a profit as long as his lands were well tended. He therefore needed to keep his peasants within his manor. By the mid-fourteenth century the population had tripled, only to fall drastically after the Black Death and several years of bad harvest and famine. The Black Death and Peasants' Revolt are two events considered to be turning points in the freedom of peasants, which also led to some change in their standard of living. These events are a good example of the connections between the economy and other aspects of society that you can label on your medieval map.

Where did people live?

The population increase in the early Middle Ages helped to produce many new towns which you will have read about earlier. These new towns helped to increase trade at home and abroad and also improved the wealth of the country. More markets and fairs enabled many people to have access to a greater variety of food and clothes. The growth of towns slowed by the fifteenth century as the population was falling. In addition to the emergence of new towns, the amount of land being farmed rose rapidly – more of the countryside was actually in use until the mid-thirteenth century and the Black Death. For the whole of the medieval period, most of the population still lived in villages. Villages grew during the early Middle Ages and many changed when people moved into the centre of a village settlement from outlying hamlets to be closer to plots of land and the common. In the 50 years after the Black Death, as the population declined, many villages were deserted. In these ways, the landscape of the country as a whole changed during the medieval period.

The quality of medieval life

Prosperity and a greater variety of food helped everyone to lead a more comfortable life. Taxes did rise in every century, and there were periods of serious famine, but on the whole people were better off than they had been before. Ironically, the Black Death helped to improve people's living standards (see page 244) – at least for the survivors! The wealth of the country also improved as a result of successful management of the land. Corn, dairy produce and livestock farming were successful and the wool trade became an early industry. The standard of living also increased owing to improved trade, nationally and internationally. The Middle Ages brought an increase in trade, as the population and the number of markets increased. Better shipping helped English merchants take the lead in the import of wine and the wool trade. The increase in consumer spending meant that luxuries such as fine, new houses were affordable. Goods from all over Europe were imported and gave greater variety and comfort to those who could afford them. Pottery from France, tapestries from Flanders and paintings from Italy were enjoyed by the rich. Trade not only brought wealth and a better standard of living to England, but a new merchant class of people was slowly emerging

However ...

Although people could afford more, life expectancy was still very low. On average most people lived to about 40 years, though this may have been increased by ten years for a wealthy person. Accidents, death during childbirth, infant mortality and epidemics spread by rats and filthy water were responsible for most deaths. As you have seen, medical care made little difference to these figures (see page 240). Apart from the unpleasant smells caused by sewage and rubbish in the streets, there was no real reason for mayors and councils to clean up the streets of medieval towns. Real progress in public health and medicine was a long way off.

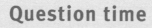

Question time

1. Make a list of all the aspects of life that would be affected if the population of a country rapidly rose or declined.

2. Research to find the state of the population in each century of the Middle Ages.

   a. Say whether the population is rising or falling and whether the changes are quick or slow.

   b. What are the difficulties with the answers to part a?

3. Why might a wealthy merchant choose to spend money on foreign goods rather than buy pots or cloth made locally?

4. Can you think of modern-day equivalents to French pottery and Flanders tapestries, i.e. sought after imported goods?

Technological change

You have seen so far that there were changes during the medieval period but these do not really contradict the suggestion that there was little actual progress made. Unlike later periods, such as the Industrial Revolution of the eighteenth century, the medieval period is not known for its great technological advances. The table below demonstrates some of the technological changes that took place in different aspects of life:

Textiles	• Spinning wheel
	• Improved weaving and fulling techniques
Transport	• Faster and better designed carts
	• Larger ships
	• Stronger bridges made from wood, and then stone
Inventions and machines	• Cranes
	• Gunpowder and some guns were used in Europe
	• Full suits of armour replaced Norman chain mail
	• The compass (magnetic needle)
	• Optics – used for spectacles
	• A working clock
Agriculture	• Better designed harnesses for horses rather than oxen
	• Windmills built on low land
	• Heavy wheeled plough for horses

Question time

1 Think of at least three different ways in which the use of gunpowder changed history after the Middle Ages. (Think about possible changes in medicine, warfare, defence and politics.)

2 Reorganise the technological developments in the table on page 256, and on a chart or diagram show their impact on life in the Middle Ages. Three suggested headings for your diagram are:

a improved communications

b improved production

c the future of science.

Can you add further headings?

3 Which two of these technological changes do you think are the most important and why? Discuss your ideas in groups to try to gain a consensus (a majority view).

4 At the bottom of your diagram write a summary box with at least three statements to say how people's lives changed as a result of slowly improving technology.

The influence of the Church on ideas and investigation

The power of the Church increased during the Middle Ages to influence all aspects of life, from healing to marriage and taxes. The Church also controlled learning and those ideas accepted in society and was a major contributor to the lack of progress in science and medicine. Investigation was considered to be unnecessary or even heretical because it was felt that God alone could explain the workings of the world. The power of religion was certainly a constant force during the medieval period. Religious wars against the Islamic Empire actually brought progress to the West by bringing people into close contact with the more advanced East and its science, medicine and culture. Religious wars also brought improvements in the technology of warfare. You will remember the benefits brought to Christendom during the Crusades (see Chapter 9).

By the end of the Middle Ages the Church was losing its tight grip on ideas and investigation. Right at the end of the medieval period we can see the beginnings of change in the way that people thought and studied. In Christendom, these changes emerged from Italy, where artists and medical men began to observe the natural world closely and investigate to find answers to their many questions. Seeds of change were being sown at the end of the Middle Ages.

The English language

The start of the medieval period brought Norman French into use, along with Latin, in the court and official papers in England. It took 300 years to incorporate French into the existing Anglo-Saxon language used by ordinary people. Some vocabulary was added, some adapted, as had happened before with earlier invasions. In many cases the English language we use today has several different words for the same object or action – this stems from the variety of languages that have combined to create modern English. Throughout the medieval period the language spoken in the fields and towns remained Anglo-Saxon. By the end of the period, the new adapted formal English was used as well as Latin as the language of court and law and chroniclers. One invention that helped spread the use of the English language was the printing press. Once books began to be printed in English in the late fifteenth century it was accepted as a language for most people.

Question time

1. Search back through your notes to find out about other developments during the Middle Ages. You could focus on changes in law and order. Plot any changes on your medieval map and discuss if the legal system could be said to have modernised during this period.

2. The English language changes continually. Can you think of any words that have been added to our everyday language in the past few years?

3. Why would the increasing use of English as the main language increase the idea of England as a united 'nation'?

Looking for patterns of change through time

Consider these three tough questions. The explanation for the third question has been started for you to discuss and finish.

What *hadn't* changed during the medieval period?

The most obvious lack of change was in the structure of society and the distribution of wealth. Land-owning families still had most of the wealth, and influenced society, the economy and politics. In the first half of the medieval period, it was almost impossible to rise in status in a significant way unless you became a part of the clergy. Even when merchants became wealthy they still did not hold the land and power that accompanies it. The wealth of the majority of the population still depended on the land and the weather for survival. Bad harvests easily caused famine, as did flooding. Mortality rates did not reduce because knowledge of disease and treatments continued to be based on old knowledge, wives' tales and superstition.

How fast was the pace of change?

The pace of change was slower in some areas than others. In Ireland and the isolated highland areas of Scotland and England, towns did not grow as they did elsewhere. Most people still lived in tiny hamlets or solitary small towns. As a result of the space available in Ireland, Scotland and Wales many English people migrated in the twelfth century to establish their businesses or farm in a less populated and competitive area.

Were there any significant turning points?

It is possible to identify several events in medieval history which have been significant in causing change. The first of these is the Norman conquest because the Normans not only reorganised society but also influenced ...

Another turning point is the Black Death ...

Question time

1   Why was there so little progress in medicine and public health? What caused the few improvements that did occur? Show your understanding of this period by explaining how several factors influenced medicine – you may need to search back through your notes or this book for help. For each factor explain how it helped or hindered progress in medicine during the Middle Ages:

   a   increased power of the Church until the mid-fifteenth century

   b   declining power of the Church at the end of the era

   c   improved trade across and beyond Europe

   d   the Crusades

   e   the use of gunpowder

   f   the popularity of monasteries

   g   wars with France and civil wars.

2   The Black Death affected England economically, politically and socially. Draw a revision flow diagram to show the impact of the Black Death (see Chapter 11) on work, wages, trade and traditional ideas.

Assessment section

1 How far do you agree with each of these statements?

 a It was better living in a town in the Middle Ages than in a village.

 b Monarchs had lost power and made little difference to people's lives by the end of the medieval period.

 c It is not fair to call the medieval period the 'Dark Ages'.

 Discuss your answers in groups. Use your medieval map and the earlier chapters in this book to search for the answers.

2 Produce a storyboard for an epic film or novel as a proposal to a film company or publishers. Sell them a great story set in medieval England, Wales, Ireland or Scotland.

 Your storyboard will need to span at least 300 years of the Middle Ages and several generations. You may choose to base your story around a few families and one part of your proposal could be a family tree with labels to show the occupations, events and story lines which affect them.

 Flick though your notes on the Middle Ages and use this book for ideas of events which your characters could be caught up in. Your storyboard needs to split up into at least three main sections – these could be based on specific events in time. Include highs and lows for each family, some cliffhangers and a suitable ending to leave the editor wanting you to produce a sequel for the sixteenth and seventeenth centuries!

3 Compile a list of websites for next year's students to use during their study of the Middle Ages. Split into groups to try to find sites that help with one or two particular topics, although many sites you come across will be useful for more than one area. You can categorise these under a heading of 'General' but it would still be useful to say which sites are best for which topics. Create a chart for each site to enable the class to build a database of sites for the future. Aim to find at least ten different sites each. You can include the following information:

 ● site address

 ● medieval topics

 ● understanding rating – easy/medium/challenging/very hard

 ● best for topic/s

 ● what's good about this site

 ● what's not good about this site.

 When searching the Internet for information, remember to look critically at and evaluate carefully the websites you find. Use key words to help limit your search so that you find the sites which are most relevant to you.

4 In groups, discuss these questions to sum up your experience of the medieval world.

 ● What aspect of medieval life you have most liked to be involved in and why?

 ● What aspect of medieval life are you most relieved to have avoided and why?

 ● What has most surprised you about the Middle Ages?

 ● What has been hardest to discover about life in the Middle Ages, and why?

 ● What medieval experience seems most similar to what happens in the twenty-first century?

 ● What medieval experience is most different to what happens in the twenty-first century?

Index